THE FAMOUS
MISS BURNEY

Diaries and Letters of
Fanny Burney

THE FAMOUS MISS BURNEY

The Diaries and Letters of Fanny Burney

Edited by Barbara G. Schrank
and David J. Supino

The John Day Company
NEW YORK

Library of Congress Cataloging in Publication Data

Arblay, Frances Burney d', 1752–1840.
   The famous Miss Burney.

   Bibliography: p.
   1. Arblay, Frances Burney d', 1752–1840—Diaries.
2. Arblay, Frances Burney d', 1752–1840—Correspondence. I. Schrank, Barbara G. II. Supino, David
J. III. Title.
PR3316.A4Z496 1976   823'.6   75-25622
ISBN 0-381-98285-8 (hardcover)
     0-308-10231-2 (Minerva paperback)

10 9 8 7 6 5 4 3 2 1

CONTENTS

CHRONOLOGY

1749 Marriage of Charles Burney and Esther Sleepe, in London
1751 The Burneys move to King's Lynn
1752 JUNE 13 Frances (Fanny) Burney is born in King's Lynn
1760 The Burney family moves to London; Burney becomes a sought-after music teacher
1762 SEPTEMBER 27 Death of Esther Sleepe Burney
1767 OCTOBER Burney marries Mrs. Elizabeth Allen
1768 MARCH Fanny begins her diary
1769 Burney receives a Doctor of Music degree from Oxford
1775 Publication of the first volume of Dr. Burney's *The General History of Music*
1778 JANUARY Publication of *Evelina, or, The History of a Young Lady's Entrance Into the World*
     AUGUST Fanny's first visit to Streatham
1779 Fanny writes a play, *The Witlings,* never produced
     JULY 14 The storming of the Bastille, beginning of the French Revolution
1782 JUNE Publication of *Cecilia, or, Memoirs of an Heiress*
1783 APRIL Death of Samuel Crisp ("Daddy Crisp")
1784 JULY Mrs. Thrale marries Gabriel Piozzi
     Breakup of the Streatham Circle
     DECEMBER Death of Dr. Samuel Johnson
1786 JULY Fanny enters the Court of George III as Second Keeper of the Robes
1788 APRIL Death of Mrs. Mary Delany

1791 JULY Fanny released from service at court
1793 JANUARY Fanny first meets General Alexander d'Arblay
      JULY Fanny marries General d'Arblay
      Publication of *Brief Reflections relative to the Emigrant French Clergy*
1794 DECEMBER Birth of Fanny's only child, Alexander d'Arblay
1795 MARCH Staging of Fanny's play *Edwy and Elgiva*
1796 JUNE Publication of *Camilla: or, a Picture of Youth*
      OCTOBER Death of Elizabeth Allen Burney
1797 The d'Arblays move into Camilla Cottage
1800 JANUARY 6 Death of Susan Burney Phillips
1801 OCTOBER Peace of Amiens between England and France
1802 Fanny and Alexander join General d'Arblay in Paris
1803 War resumed between France and England
1811 Fanny operated on for breast cancer
1812 Fanny returns to England with Alexander; General d'Arblay remains in France
1813 Alexander d'Arblay enters Cambridge University
1814 MARCH Publication of *The Wanderer; or, Female Difficulties*
      APRIL Death of Dr. Burney
      Fanny rejoins General d'Arblay in Paris
1815 Fanny and General d'Arblay return to England, settle in Bath
1818 MAY 3 Death of General d'Arblay
      Fanny moves to London
1819 Alexander d'Arblay ordained a priest in the Church of England
1832 Publication of *Memoirs of Dr. Burney*
1837 JANUARY 19 Death of Alexander d'Arblay
1840 JANUARY 6 Death of Fanny Burney, in London

PREFACE

No complete edition of Fanny Burney's diary has been published in over half a century. While selections from her diary have appeared since that time, most are out of print and hard to find: the one British edition still in print was edited almost twenty-five years ago. In addition, past editors have focused less on Fanny as a woman and a writer than on her diary as a source of social history and for the light it sheds on her famous contemporaries, particularly Dr. Samuel Johnson. Our interest in Fanny herself, coupled with these shortcomings, led to this present book, not only to make available this fascinating and too-little-known work, but also to present more fully the self-portrait of Fanny that emerges from a reading of the diary in its entirety. We believe it is a portrait long overdue, as women reexamine the past as part of their own struggle toward self-realization.

Fanny's diary was actually published as two separate works, almost fifty years apart, and, unfortunately, no one definitive edition exists. The two basic sources, which we used in making our selections, are the two-volume *The Early Diary of Fanny Burney,* edited by Annie Raine Ellis (London, 1907), covering the period 1768–78, and the six-volume *Diary & Letters of Madame d'Arblay,* edited by her niece Charlotte Barrett, with preface and notes by Austin Dobson (London, 1904–5), covering the period 1778–1840. Aside from the clearly indicated deletions, the only change we have made in the diary entries was correcting obvious spelling errors. The transition passages, indicated in italics, were written by the original editors. We have substituted our own notes to clarify the text for the modern reader. No attempt has been made to be exhaustive.

With over 1,500,000 words to contend with at the outset, we became increasingly grateful for our many friends who encouraged us over the months by their genuine interest in the diary. We especially want to thank Jacqueline Goldenberg, Gerard Van der Leun, Professor W. Stanley Lindberg, and Sheila Weller, who in addition gave their time and sound critical judgment to the introduction and offered many valuable suggestions. Above all, our appreciation and deep gratitude go to our agent Elaine Markson and our editor Linda O'Brien, who early recognized the merit of Fanny's diary and worked closely and cheerfully with us throughout the long project.

Our own reluctance in editing the diary to about one-tenth its length came from realizing how many worthwhile episodes necessarily had to be sacrificed. The choices often produced a decided pang. But we console ourselves that ultimately we will have succeeded if we make Fanny Burney better known, as she justly deserves, and if we interest some readers in turning to the original diary for a fuller appreciation of this exceptional woman.

THE FAMOUS
MISS BURNEY

Diaries and Letters of
Fanny Burney

INTRODUCTION

In a time of great resurgence of interest in women and their roles in history, a number of remarkable British women are still virtually unknown to the American reading public. One of the most prominent of these women is Frances Burney, who, with the publication of her first novel *Evelina* in 1778, took an eminent place in the literary hierarchy of the late eighteenth century. Today she is the acknowledged forerunner of a line of distinguished women novelists. It is to her, said the critic Lord Macaulay, that we owe Jane Austen.

In her lifetime Fanny Burney published four novels, became a celebrated personality and an active participant in the literary and social circles of London, served five years in the court of George III, and witnessed the aftermath of the French Revolution and the reign of Napoleon Bonaparte. Her illustrious friends and acquaintances included Dr. Samuel Johnson; the actor David Garrick; the painter Joshua Reynolds; the dramatist Richard Sheridan; the statesman Edmund Burke; and the "Bluestocking" women Mrs. Elizabeth Montagu, Mrs. Mary Delany, and Mrs. Hester Thrale.

Although her fame was as a novelist during her own lifetime, it is her diary, published posthumously, that assures Fanny Burney an enduring place in literature. Begun in 1768, when she was fifteen, the diary is a record of her own experiences over a span of seventy years and a vivid portrait of her literary and social milieu. Equally important today, the diary graphically illustrates the life of a woman writer in the male-dominated European society of two hundred years ago.

The qualities that would bring Fanny Burney such distinction were far from evident in her childhood. The young Fanny was described as a shy, quiet, even backward child. "She was wholly unnoticed in the nursery for any talents, or quickness of study," recalled her father. In fact, when she didn't know her letters by the age of eight, she was nicknamed "the little dunce" by her older brother James. Physically she was equally nonprepossessing, being small in stature, dark complexioned, and extremely near-sighted.

Diffident Fanny stood in marked contrast to her parents. Her father, Charles Burney, was a man of great charm and intellect, who in later years became a well-known doctor of music. Born in Shrewsbury in 1726, he moved to London in 1744 as a young musician apprenticed to the composer Arne. There he was exposed to the theater, met the composer Handel, and acquired a wide circle of prominent friends, including the actor David Garrick. In 1748, he was hired as the musical companion of a rich gentleman, Fulke Greville, an experience which further increased his sophistication and social graces. At the same time, he met the lovely, high-spirited Esther Sleepe, whom he married the following year. In quick succession the Burneys had three children, two of whom survived, Esther, or Hetty, and James.

A man of tremendous energies, Mr. Burney earned his living as a music teacher and as organist of a church. In his spare time he composed music. Perhaps due to his exhausting schedule, in 1751 he developed symptoms of consumption and was advised to get a change of air. So it was that he obtained the post of church organist in the provincial seacoast town of King's Lynn in Norfolk, a hundred miles from London. There Fanny was born June 13, 1752.

The Burneys lived eight years in Lynn, during which time Mrs. Burney gave birth to four more children, of whom only Susanna (or Susan) and Charles survived. Mr. Burney was soon absorbed again in his former pace with his duties as organist and teacher. Life was quiet in the small town, and Charles and Esther Burney spent many evenings tête-à-tête, reading from histories, voyages, books of poetry, and such weighty works as the famed Encyclopédie. Their home also became the nucleus of a small group which met weekly for literary discussions.

It is from the Lynn years that we get the best picture of Fanny's mother, Esther Sleepe Burney. A "Lady of great strength of mind, possessing a taste for literature, with an engaging manner, & much beauty" was how a close relative described her. She shared her love of learning with her children and tutored her eldest daughter in the classics. Although Fanny could not yet read, she listened to her sister's lessons and learned by heart long passages from Pope, the first sign of her remarkable ability to remember and accurately memorize all she heard. Her mother, noting the accomplishment, said that she "had no fear for Fanny."

In 1760, Burney's health restored, the family moved back to London. Mr. Burney resumed his former friendships and soon became the most sought-after music teacher among the prominent families in the capital. For many years he was typically on his musical rounds from eight in the morning to past eleven at night, then often retired to his study where he composed music and wrote.

Mrs. Burney, however, now became ill and, after giving birth to her ninth child, Charlotte, she died in September 1762. Fanny was only ten, and her grief was intense.

Yet even with the loss of her mother, Fanny enjoyed a happy, unstructured adolescence. A major reason was her love for her father, which amounted to almost a passion. "How forcibly do I feel to whom I owe all the earthly happiness I enjoy!—it is to my father!" she later wrote in her diary. "To this dearest, most amiable, this best beloved—most worthy of men!"

In the early 1760s Fanny had long days and months to herself. Her eldest brother, James, had been apprenticed to sea; her younger brother, Charles, was at boarding school; her youngest sister, Charlotte, was still in the nursery; and, for two years, her sisters Esther and Susan were studying in Paris. Her widowed father, generous with affection but limited by time, ran his house with a loose hand, and Fanny freely pursued her own interests.

These interests now became reading and writing. Although she was illiterate until the age of eight, by age ten she was reading histories, novels, and courtesy books. She also taught herself French and quickly became a "scribbler." In the years 1762–67 she wrote "Elegies, Odes, Plays, Songs, Stories, Farces—nay Tragedies and Epic Poems." A significant piece of early writing was a novel entitled *The Adventures of Caroline Evelyn.*

It was the courtesy-book literature that helped shape Fanny's already serious nature and would later appear as a major theme in both her writing and her personal life. An eighteenth-century genre written expressly to instruct young women in proper female conduct, the courtesy books stressed such "moral" qualities as delicacy, prudence, and forbearance. One such book Fanny mentioned was *Sermons to Young Women*. Published in 1765, it had gone through five editions before 1768. Typical chapters in this book are "Modesty of Apparel," "Female Reserve," and "Female Virtue with Domestic and Elegant Accomplishments."

The courtesy books undoubtedly reinforced Fanny's extreme modesty, a quality even her close friends were apt to mistake for affectation. She feared being known as a "scribbler," and long after she became famous a mere hint of her authorship to a stranger was enough to make her blush and, occasionally, run out of the room. She was also called a prude, a fact she readily admitted. She clung to a delicacy of manners in all things, finding it painful even to enter a drawing room without being formally announced.

Unlike her sisters, Fanny never received any formal education; and her father, absorbed in his music, writing, and extensive social life, gave her little guidance. In a very real sense, her small world at home became her classroom.

Although Mr. Burney's profession would normally have relegated him to middle-class society, his wit, intellect, charm, and conversational powers gained him entry to the social ranks of his aristocratic patrons. Before long he was a welcome visitor in their homes. Gregarious by nature, his own home became in turn a gathering place for many noted intellectuals and artists. In this unique household, young Fanny learned well. She was exposed to the company and conversations of politicians, actors, writers, opera singers, explorers, and philosophers. Bashful and grave, Fanny remained unobtrusive with these visitors. But she observed everything she saw and heard, a quality that along with her ability for memorization, became another hallmark of her writing.

As her father recalled her early adolescence: "She had a great deal of invention and humor in her childish sports. . . . But in company, or before strangers, she was silent, backward, and timid, even to sheepishness: and, from her shyness, had such profound gravity and composure of features, that those of my friends who came often to my house . . . never called Fanny by any other name

. . . than The Old Lady." A family friend also dubbed her "The silent observant Miss Burney."

It was with her family and close friends that Fanny revealed her humor and gaiety, another important side to her personality. With them, she was mischievous, fun-loving, and highly imaginative. She often was taken to the Drury Lane Theatre and, after seeing the actors on stage, enchanted her small audiences at home with her gift for mimicry. She not only impersonated the actors but often made up entire speeches to go with their roles. At times she was even exuberant. A diary entry of 1778, for instance, shows twenty-six-year-old Fanny dancing a wild jig around a mulberry tree after hearing that Dr. Samuel Johnson had praised her novel *Evelina*.

In October 1767, when Fanny was fifteen, her father married Mrs. Elizabeth Allen, a longtime friend of the Burneys from their years in Lynn. The marriage signaled an end to Fanny's serene home life. Allegedly, the new Mrs. Burney was soon admonishing Fanny on the evils attendant on young woman writers, with the result that Fanny threw all her early works into a bonfire. In fairness, the second Mrs. Burney was not alone in her opinion. Society in general held the attitude that writing was best left to men.

But Fanny was by nature a "scribbler," and a few months later found her writing again, this time a diary addressed to "Dear Nobody." The first entry is dated March 1768. Thus began the diary Fanny was to keep consistently, if at times intermittently, for the rest of her life. After a few years Fanny began writing her diary for her sister Susan and later for a few close friends, as well.

Due to opposition from the Allen family, Burney and Mrs. Allen kept their marriage secret at first, and lived in separate houses. In 1770, however, when the two families were united under one roof, the real dissension began. Although devoted to her husband, the second Mrs. Burney soon grew obsessively jealous of the closeness shared by the Burney family. Her behavior became correspondingly rude, demanding, and spiteful. Most of Fanny's disparaging remarks about her stepmother were deleted from the published diary, yet occasional muted references attest to rampant discord when Mr. Burney was out of the house.

But Fanny, almost eighteen by this time, had other people to turn to. She adored her charming, gifted father and, in their comings and goings, shared a high-spirited camaraderie with her sisters Hetty and Susan, cousins, and neighborhood friends. If anything, the late 1760s was a giddy period for the young girls coming of age, and the diary of those years reads like a social calendar, its pages crowded with accounts of masquerades, beaux, balls, theater going, home musicales, and trips to the countryside.

It was her sister Susan, two and a half years younger, who over the years was Fanny's closest confidant. The two were inseparable from childhood and shared such a similar sensibility that a family friend remarked: "There seems but one mind between you." In 1784, two years after Susan's marriage, Fanny wrote her: "I have not been really in spirits, nor had one natural laugh, since I lost you; . . . I know not, in truth, whether I most miss you when happy or when sad. That I wish for you most when happy is certain; but that nothing upon earth can do so much good, when sad, as your society, is certain too."

Because of her sweet and gracious nature, Susan was the favorite of all the family. She, too, was known for her writing ability and her lively letters, but, unlike Fanny, she never wrote fiction. She was also the most delicate of the Burney children and, from childhood, suffered long periods of illness brought on by weak lungs. She died at age of forty-four, on January 6, 1800. Until her own death forty years later, a grieved Fanny set aside every January 6 as a day of commemoration of her sister and her best friend. In an uncanny coincidence, Fanny herself would die on a January 6.

Next to Susan, Fanny's other cherished confidant was the kind and gracious Samuel Crisp, a family friend twenty years older than her father. Fanny adored him from their first meeting in 1764 and, as time went by, he became her "Daddy Crisp"; she became his "Fannikin," the "dearest thing on earth." He would become one of the most important influences in her life, and he was to provide better counsel than her own father, particularly in regard to her writing.

Born in 1704, Samuel Crisp was described "by birth and education a gentleman . . . in mind, manners and habit yet more truly so." Tall and handsome, he had a noble Roman nose and bright, hazel, penetrating eyes. He had spent his early years as a man-about-town in London's artistic circles, fraternizing with such notables as David Garrick, Mrs. Elizabeth Montagu, and the Duchess of Portland. He himself was a painter, musician, and patron of the arts. In 1754 he had a play produced, *Virginia,* which ran for eleven nights in the famed Drury Lane Theatre.

In the late 1750s Crisp left London and moved to Chessington Hall, a boardinghouse in the remote Surrey countryside. One reason given for his move to the wild and lonely area was his chagrin at what he considered the failure of his play. More important reasons were probably a dwindling supply of money and a bad case of the gout. For some years, Crisp visited London every spring, where he was eagerly awaited by the Burneys. With them he shared his love of music, literature, and good conversation. In turn, over the years, and even after his death in 1783, his home became a haven for the Burneys from London's demanding social life.

Fanny first visited Chessington in 1767, and in the years ahead she spent long periods of time there. It was at Chessington, in fact, that she wrote large portions of her first two novels, *Evelina* and *Cecilia.* In 1786, long after Fanny had become a famous novelist, she recalled: "Dear, ever dear Chessington, whereat passed the scenes of the greatest ease, gaiety, and native mirth that have fallen to my lot."

In the early 1770s Fanny and Daddy Crisp began an animated correspondence. Fanny's letters provided him with lively accounts of social life in the capital, while his letters to her, full of wit and instruction, showed him as an astute critic of her writing. On occasion he chided her: "You are devilish long-winded, Fan, pray mend that fault—". More often he applauded and encouraged her natural, spontaneous style: "Dash away, whatever comes uppermost; and believe me you'll succeed better, than by leaning on your elbow, and studying what to say."

In the early 1770s Fanny began writing fiction again. Her new work was *Evelina,* a continuation of *Caroline Evelyn,* the earlier novel she had thrown into the bonfire. At first Fanny scribbled merely for her own amusement and that of her sisters Susan and Charlotte. Only at a later date did she consider sending her novel to a publisher. Her actual writing went slowly. Her father, who had received his Doctor of Music degree from Oxford in 1769, was now writing his voluminous *General History of Music,* and Fanny was kept busy transcribing his manuscript. Because of the prevailing disparagement of women writers, Fanny also had to write in secret, stealing what spare moments she could in unoccupied corners of the house. More often than not, the candle in her bed-room burned late into the night. Even after she finished the writing, her work was not done. She next had to transcribe her novel in a feigned handwriting so that it wouldn't be recognized by typesetters who had seen her father's manuscript.

It was not until December 1776 that Fanny finished the first two volumes of her three-volume work. Taking her brother Charles into her confidence, Fanny gave him her unsigned novel to carry to the publisher, Mr. Lowndes. To Fanny's delight, Lowndes accepted her novel, conditional on receiving the final volume. But to her dismay, it meant the prospect of more "fagging," as she now called her work, into the late hours of the night.

Fanny now dutifully informed her father she had submitted a manuscript for publication. Characteristically, Dr. Burney took the important news casually, almost offhandedly. He didn't ask to see her work or even express curiosity about its title. By the fall of 1777, a weary Fanny had finished the third volume and sent it to Lowndes. She received £20 for her book.

Evelina, or, a Young Lady's Entrance Into The World, published anonymously in January 1778, was quickly acclaimed. *The Monthly Review* for April 1778 reported: "This novel has given us so much pleasure in the perusal, that we do not hesitate to pronounce it one of the most sprightly, entertaining and agreeable productions of this kind which has of late fallen under our notice." Within six months of its publication, the novel was being read by the literary elite and the middle class alike. By the end of 1779, the book had gone through four editions.

The plot of *Evelina* is conventional, even crude, and, true to its title, follows a young, virtuous, unworldly girl through a series of potential mishaps to ultimate salvation in a suitable marriage. Its strength comes from its lively, witty, unaffected writing; its farcical depiction of manners and mannerisms; and its delineation of characters spanning the whole spectrum of society.

Alternately moving, suspenseful, and hilarious, it had all the eighteenth-century requisites for success: pathos, sentimentality, and virtue rewarded. But Fanny had added new ingredients to eighteenth-century fiction. She introduced the study of domestic manners and, as critic Chauncey Brewster Tinker remarked in 1911, produced "the first great analysis in English literature of the mind of a young woman, produced by a young woman."

In retrospect, Fanny had achieved a breakthrough in the history of the novel.

Fanny's own great adventure as a novelist was to begin. But in June 1786, at Chessington recuperating from an illness, Fanny was still unaware of her triumph. The first news to reach her was that her father was reading *Evelina*. She sobbed when she heard of his reaction: "Upon my word, I think it is the best novel I know, excepting Fielding's and, in some respects, better than his." Soon other reports arrived in letters from Susan. The witty savants Mrs. Thrale and Mrs. Cholmondeley were telling all their famous friends about *Evelina,* and before long Dr. Samuel Johnson was praising it, too. By this time Dr. Burney had proudly announced that the author was none other than his daughter Fanny.

Only Daddy Crisp remained in the dark. Fanny had been reading *Evelina* to him, but playfully pretending she had no idea of the author's identity. Finally, he had to be told. "You little hussy, you," he said with feigned indignation. But he, too, swelled with fatherly pride. "It's wonderful," he said, "wonderful!"

Afraid of the consequences of her authorship, Fanny's own reaction fluctuated between fear and joy. She wrote Susan from Chessington: "I am now at the summit of a high hill; my prospects on one side are bright, glowing, and invitingly beautiful; but when I turn around, I perceive, on the other side, sundry caverns, gulphs, pits and precipices that, to look at, make my head giddy and my heart sick."

Inevitably, the acclaim accorded *Evelina* led to Fanny Burney's entrance into the great literary world. Fanny noted the momentous occasion in her diary entry of August 1778: "I have now to write an account of the most consequential day I have spent since my birth: namely, my Streatham visit."

Streatham, the country home of society hostess Mrs. Hester Thrale, was the symbol of London society at its most brilliant. The so-called Streatham Circle included Dr. Johnson and his friends; the Bluestockings; and many of the literary, artistic, and political elite. Dr. Johnson himself had lived there part of each year since the late 1760s, and referred to it as home.

Mrs. Thrale, the wife of a wealthy brewer, is yet another fascinating and controversial woman of the late eighteenth century. Of a distinguished background, she was widely read, talented, good-natured, with a wit and charm that attracted all who knew her. In later years, Mrs. Thrale gained her own literary fame through the publication of her memoirs, diaries, and letters.

Soon Fanny was spending months at a time with Mrs. Thrale, and Streatham, in effect, became her home away from home from 1778 to 1782. Treated like a member of the family, she became Mrs. Thrale's friend and confidant. There she became the darling of Dr. Johnson, received the praises of Sir Joshua Reynolds, and met Mrs. Elizabeth Montagu, Queen of the Bluestockings. The most touching passages of the Streatham journal deal with the deepening friendship between the young Fanny and the formidable Dr. Johnson, forty years her senior. Revered as the literary giant of his day, he also inspired fear through his abrupt, even rude manner and biting tongue. But, with Fanny, he revealed a different side of his nature. In these pages we see a kind, relaxed, even jolly and sportive man. He was enchanted with the contrast between Fanny's meek outward appearance and the satire she displayed in her writing. "Oh, she's a toad," cried Dr. Johnson, laughing,"—a sly young rogue!" Before long, no matter where he was in the house, he wanted Fanny by his side. "Don't you leave me," he said more than once. Fanny remained his "dear young Burney," until his death in 1784.

Fanny was also besieged with an outpouring of social invitations. Her popularity proved a mixed blessing. While the exposure to society gave her new opportunities to observe and learn, its very demands limited her time for writing. More importantly, Fanny would never be totally comfortable in the limelight.

Even more than her fear of being known as an author, Fanny had a dread, amounting almost to a phobia, of having her name appear in print with the attendant possibility of personal criticism. Mrs. Thrale chided her, calling it an "over delicacy," but Fanny never lost those feelings. All her life she felt: "Let them criticize, slash, without mercy my book, and let them neglect me; but may God avert my becoming a public theme of ridicule."

Yet Fanny also enjoyed her new status. From 1778 to 1786, as described in her diary, her social world ranged from London's most glittering drawing rooms to the glamorous watering spas of Brighton and Bath. Other introductions in those years brought her accolades from the dramatist Richard Sheridan, the statesman Edmund Burke, the author Horace Walpole, and the esteemed dowagers, the Duchess of Portland and Mrs. Mary Delany. Dozens of other well-known names appear in the diary pages of this period, for all of fashionable London wanted to meet the author of *Evelina*.

Always in the background, but clearly crucial to her continued development as a writer, was Daddy Crisp. Understanding the vagaries of fate, he exhorted Fanny to keep writing. "You are now young, lively, gay. You please, and the world smiles upon you. . . . Years and wrinkles in their due season (perhaps attended by want of health and spirits) will succeed. You will then no longer be the same Fanny of 1778, feasted, caressed, admired, with all the soothing circumstances of your present situation. . . . Let me only earnestly urge you to act vigorously . . . 'now while it is yet day, and before the night cometh, when no man can work.' "

Mrs. Thrale, Richard Sheridan, and many of Fanny's other famous friends were also urging her to write. Their suggestion, based on the comic scenes and dialogue in *Evelina,* was that she turn to comedy. Thus encouraged, in 1779 Fanny secretly wrote a play called *The Witlings*. Both her father and Daddy Crisp condemned it outright, however, and, after halfhearted attempts to revise it, Fanny laid it aside.

Now, sobered still more by the fear of failure, Fanny found the act of writing even more painful. Yet her two fathers continued to pressure her, and she wrote fitfully throughout the next three years. Her eagerly awaited second novel, *Cecilia*, published in June 1782, was an immediate success. While critics then and now rank it as a lesser achievement than *Evelina,* it sold so rapidly that booksellers couldn't keep it in stock. Fanny became "the famous Miss Burney."

Fanny, age thirty, was now talked about and stared at wherever she went. Various contemporaries described her at this time as being extremely slight, with a youthful and almost girlish appearance. Although she was not beautiful, her great charm of expression gave her an attractive air.

Still Daddy Crisp pushed on. "Work hard—stick to it. This is the harvest-time of your life; your sun shines hot; lose not a moment, then, but make your hay directly. . . ." His words proved prophetic, for, at the zenith of her fame, Fanny's fortunes were to change.

In 1781, with Mr. Thrale's death, the glorious Streatham era was drawing to an end. The next year Mrs. Thrale began a ro-

mance with an Italian music master named Piozzi. Against the
wishes of her children, Dr. Johnson, and Fanny, she married him
in 1784, an event so scandalous that it effectively removed her
from society. In December of that year, Dr. Johnson died. The
loss of her two close friends, coupled with the death of Daddy
Crisp the year before, brought Fanny to a new juncture.

The event that would change her life was her introduction to
King George III and Queen Charlotte in December 1785, at the
home of their mutual friend, Mrs. Delany. The queen was impressed with Fanny, and when a vacancy occurred in court a few
months later, she offered Fanny a permanent position as Second
Keeper of the Robes. Title aside, the job was essentially that of a
menial, at the beck and call of the queen and her wardrobe. Fanny
had grave misgivings. Horrified at the idea of constant attendance
and permanency, she knew she would be giving up the life she
loved best with family and friends. "What can make *me* amends
for all I shall forfeit?" she wrote a friend. Still, she reluctantly
accepted.

To understand this drastic decision is to appreciate Fanny's
position in the year 1786. Thirty-four years old, the last unmar-
ried child of six, without a dowry, having earned a mere £230
in eight years from her novels, she was living at home with her
father and an abrasive stepmother. At the same time she was in
love with the Reverend George Owen Cambridge, a young man
who had been courting her for several years. It had reached the
point where not only Fanny, but her friends as well, anticipated
a proposal. As she agonized over whether to accept the queen's
offer, she waited in vain for Cambridge to propose.

These factors no doubt all played a part in Fanny's decision to
enter court, but, ultimately, it was the wish to please her father
that proved decisive. Despite the tender solicitude he showed his
children, Dr. Burney had never provided them with the wise
counsel of a parent. The father who hadn't taken *Evelina* seriously enough to discuss the possible consequences of its publication with his daughter was the man who didn't stop to consider
the effect that the hardships of court life might have on his
sensitive daughter. Rather, he was overjoyed at the offer.

Dr. Burney's feelings came from his own social aspirations. In
this instance, he was a lover of royalty, believing that court was
only a short step from heaven, if not closer in terms of potential

favors for his family. Dr. Burney was not alone in his feelings. In the eighteenth century, court service held out the promise of honor, prestige, and security. Most of Fanny's friends rejoiced for her, too. The critic Lord Macaulay, however, writing in 1842, was appalled at Fanny's decision. "Domestic happiness, friendship, independence, leisure, letters, all these things were hers; and she flung them all away," he said. Macaulay reserved his greatest contempt for Dr. Burney for his failure to be a judicious parent. Although Macaulay and other critics recognized the inequity of Fanny's position, what they failed to understand was her motivation. Fanny explained it simply in her diary: "The matter ought to be settled by (my) father." Thus, in June 1786, Fanny entered what she called a marriage, one she had tried to escape. Others had prevailed and the knot was tied.

Fanny served five years at court. Her diary journals of that period, highlighted by George III's madness, provide a fascinating glimpse into court life, but for Fanny it meant almost exclusive association with the dull, narrow, and petty people surrounding the king and queen. Her particular nemesis was her superior, Mrs. Schwellenberg, a nasty, ill-tempered despot. Fanny's one comfort was her daily visits to Mrs. Delany, but her elderly friend died in April 1788.

For Fanny, these were dreary years indeed. In 1790, her physical and psychological health severely undermined, she asked her father for permission to resign. He agreed, but another long year was to pass before Fanny, with the queen's consent, was free. She received a pension of £100 a year. At this point, in a sense, the public Miss Burney ceased to exist. But for Fanny, her happiest personal years lay ahead in her marriage to General d'Arblay.

The catalyst for Fanny's marriage was the French Revolution of 1789, which led large numbers of French noblemen to flee their country and emigrate to England. In 1791, a colony of Frenchmen settled in the neighborhood of Mickleham, close to the home of Fanny's sister Susan and to Norbury Park, home of Fanny and Susan's close friends the Lockes. It was there, on a visit to Susan in January 1793, that Fanny met General Alexander d'Arblay, the man who would become her husband.

Susan had earlier described General d'Arblay to Fanny in a letter: "He seems to me a true militaire, franc et loyal—open as the day—warmly affectionate to his friends—intelligent, ready and amusing in conversation, with a great share of gaité de coeur, and, at the same time, of naïveté and bonne foi." Upon meeting him, Fanny agreed, saying he was "one of the most delightful characters she'd ever met." A year younger than Fanny, General d'Arblay had come from a well-to-do background but had lost his property in the aftermath of the revolution. Before leaving France, he had been an adjutant to Lafayette.

In England, General d'Arblay was socially handicapped not only by his poverty but because he was a Roman Catholic and a constitutionalist. Yet the courtship proceeded rapidly. Soon Fanny and the general were tutoring one another in their respective languages and sharing their fondness for literature. Despite the fact that her father disapproved of d'Arblay, Fanny married him on July 28, 1793. As Fanny explained to a friend: "Domestic comfort and social affection have invariably been the sole as well as ultimate objects of my choice."

It was to prove a happy, if financially troubled, marriage, and Dr. Burney was soon reconciled with his daughter. The d'Arblays' only child, Alexander, was born in 1794. Thirty years after her marriage, Fanny wrote: "Never, never was union more blessed and felicitous; though, after the first eight years of unmingled happiness, it was assailed by many calamities, chiefly of separation or illness, yet still mentally unbroken."

With money the d'Arblays' ever-present concern, Fanny, in 1795, agreed to the staging of *Edwy and Elgiva,* a tragedy she had written in court. It closed after one night. In 1796, fourteen years after *Cecilia,* Fanny published her third novel, *Camilla.* More successful, at least commercially, it earned Fanny £2000, a sum which enabled the d'Arblays to build their own small house, Camilla Cottage, on the Lockes' property, Norbury Park. There with her husband and child, close to her sister Susan and the Lockes, Fanny knew her greatest contentment.

Although she would live forty years more, the end of the century marked an ending for Fanny as well. Her beloved sister Susan died in 1800 and, as a distraught Fanny described it, "it was the end of my perfect happiness on earth." The tangible symbol of Susan's death was the loss of Fanny's intimate journal letters written for her sister alone. In the 1800s, Fanny's diary became formalized, often containing entries written many years after the event.

At the same time, Fanny's marriage was to undergo a long

series of hardships, the first of which was leaving Camilla Cottage—forever, as it turned out. Ironically, it was the Peace of Amiens between France and England in 1801 that disrupted Fanny's home life, for it made possible General d'Arblay's return to his homeland. He left for France in October of that year to inquire about his property and a possible military pension. Fanny and their son joined him in 1802, intending to spend a year.

But war broke out, the coasts were blockaded, and Fanny's one-year stay turned into ten years of exile from her country and family. With great effort she managed to return to England with her son in 1812, where she nursed her ailing father until his death in 1814. In that year she published her fourth and last novel, *The Wanderer*, a financial success but a critical failure. She then rejoined her husband in France, fleeing to Belgium during the Hundred Days of Napoleon. In 1815, they returned to England, where Fanny remained for the rest of her life.

General d'Arblay died on May 3, 1818. He was sixty-five. From that time Fanny passed her years in relative isolation, editing her voluminous papers and those of her father. Despite failing eyesight and health, she published her last work, *Memoirs of Dr. Burney*, in 1832.

One of the last pictures of Fanny is given us by Sir Walter Scott, who met her in 1826, when she was seventy-four: "Introduced . . . to Mad. d'Arblay, the celebrated authoress of *Evelina* and *Cecilia*—an elderly lady with no remains of personal beauty, but with a simple and gentle manner, a pleasing expression of countenance, and apparently quick feelings. . . ."

Fanny's continuing worry was her impractical son, now a minister, whom she wanted to see settled in a marriage. Her wish ended in tragedy. Alexander, for whom she held such great hope mingled with concern, died a bachelor in 1837 at the age of forty-two. Fanny's own death came peacefully on January 6, 1840.

It is Fanny's diary, excerpts of which make up the present work, that best captures the flavor of her era. Her father aptly commented: "Fanny carries bird-lime in her brains—for everything that lights there sticks." And what stuck, minutely recorded in thousands of manuscript pages, were the keen observations of seventy eventful years.

The first journal, dated March 1768, was found wrapped in soft, old-fashioned blue paper. In it, the fifteen-year-old Fanny stated her reasons for keeping a journal. She wanted an account of her thoughts and actions when, late in life, as she put it, "time is more nimble than memory." But because Fanny became a celebrated novelist and, more importantly, because she was a storyteller of the highest order, her diary transcends the pedestrian quality of most personal diaries. It is, instead, a dramatic rendering of one of the most brilliant periods in the literary history of England.

The diary itself was actually published as two separate works, *The Early Diary of Fanny Burney* (1768–1778) and the *Diary and Letters of Madame d'Arblay* (1778–1840). It was originally addressed to "Dear Nobody," but after a few years Fanny began writing her diary in the form of long, animated journals to her sister Susan and later to Daddy Crisp and a few other friends. The diaries, as we know them today, are composed of personal entries, journal accounts, and personal letters.

Unfortunately, the editions of the diary published to date are far from complete. In the years before her death, Fanny suppressed, effaced, and revised material she believed would be harmful to her family and friends. Fanny's niece Charlotte Barrett, who was bequeathed the diary, likewise deleted large portions. Finally, concerned over its length, the original publisher of the *Diary and Letters,* Henry Colburn, drastically curtailed and further discarded large sections. Still, the published versions of the diaries are voluminous and leave much to appreciate.

The diary, particularly to 1800, is Fanny's writing at its best. The style is simple, unaffected, spontaneous, and lively. Its outstanding quality is its drama. Its content is its people.

Dr. Johnson called Fanny a "character-monger" and, as always, his wording was precise. Fanny had a positive genius for acute and accurate observation, and she was a master at delineating people and manners with a few strokes of her pen. Perhaps because she was notoriously nearsighted, her diary is somewhat lacking in physical description, but her infallible sense of the ridiculous, her talent for capturing speech patterns and singular personality traits, and her remarkable ability to recall long conversations verbatim make her individuals memorable characters all.

There is Dr. Johnson, perpetually twitching in all his extremities; irrepressible Mrs. Thrale, playing hostess and boudoir confident at Streatham; Joshua Reynolds, as courtly and serene as the portraits he painted; Mrs. Elizabeth Montagu, imperiously arbitrating literary reputations; eloquent Edmund Burke, awing spectators at the trial of Warren Hastings in Westminister Hall; King George, ranting at the height of his madness; Mrs. Schwellenberg, alternating between murdering the English language and poisoning her tea-table companions with her venom. Like a revolving kaleidoscope, the diary presents sketch after sketch of the famed and the not-so-famed, the foolish, the pompous, the sensible.

This high drama, which lends the diary the aura of a novel, prompted Fanny to defend herself to Daddy Crisp: "I never mix truth and fiction: all that I relate in journalising is strictly, nay plainly, fact . . . the world, and especially the Great World, is so filled with absurdity of various sorts, now bursting forth in impertinence, now in pomposity, now giggling in silliness, and now yawning in dulness that there is no occasion for invention to draw what is striking in every possible species of the ridiculous." Therein lies its enduring quality: The diary is a consistently fascinating story of real people, their warts and their virtues as palpable today as they were two hundred years ago.

The critic William Hazlitt, writing in 1815, dismissed Fanny as a "mere common observer of manners." True, he did not have the benefit of her diary and was referring to her novels, but he nevertheless ranked her far too low. In her diary, as well as in *Evelina,* Fanny contributed far more than a study in manners. Next to Boswell, she left perhaps the most valuable and readable social document of upper-middle-class life in late eighteenth-century England. The critic Austin Dobson, writing in 1903, stated that the diary deserves to rank with the great diaries of literature. No critic since has disputed his literary judgment.

Today Fanny's diary deserves to rank equally high for its contribution to feminist literature. As Mrs. Annie Raine Ellis, the editor of the *Early Diary,* commented, the diary is believed to be the only published, perhaps the only existing, record of the life of an English girl written by herself, in the eighteenth century. As such, it is a rare and valuable document in the neglected history of women.

Fanny was not an introspective person, and, despite the wealth of detail in her diary, her observations unfortunately did not extend to any in-depth analysis either of herself or of society. For the most part she recorded events and conversations whole, with little reflection or afterthought. Yet by its very nature a diary reveals much about the life of its author. Fanny's diary is no exception.

From a modern viewpoint, Fanny was neither a feminist nor even an enlightened woman. Her thinking was no different, of course, than that of the vast majority of her contemporaries, but, given her ability to observe society and her position as an eminent author, one nevertheless wishes Fanny had spoken up for her sex. Although she was a contemporary of Mary Wollstonecroft, whose *A Vindication of the Rights of Woman* was published in 1792, the two women might have been writing in different centuries. Fanny's novels and diary do mirror the restricted roles open to women in the eighteenth century, but for the most part Fanny never goes beyond the mirror to examine those roles, let alone advocate greater rights and freedoms for women.

Fanny's novels, in fact, were morality tales, stressing that a woman's virtuous behavior would lead to happiness, that is, marriage. Fanny explained why she didn't write about politics in her novels: "Once I had had an idea of bringing in such as suited me, but that, upon second thought, I returned to my more native opinion they were not a feminine subject for discussion. . . ."

In her diary, where one turns for her private comments, Fanny's feelings about herself as a woman come out almost as a postscript. Nor, in a larger context, does she question the many rigid moral and social codes which governed the women of her day. Indeed, the diary reveals her a captive of those very codes. Instructed to avoid women of "ill repute," or women who had liaisons with men, Fanny shunned the company of any woman whose reputation was the least bit questionable. In one instance, she denied herself the proffered friendship of Madame de Staël, certainly one of the most fascinating women and intellectuals of the day.

Fanny's attitudes on other subjects were equally narrow. On the topic of money, still an issue for women today, Fanny said: "There is something, after all, in money, by itself money, that I can never take possession of without a secret feeling of something like a degredation." And, sadly, of education for women, she wrote: "It has no recommendation of sufficient value to compensate its evil excitement of envy and satire."

Perhaps only her views on marriage are destined to captivate the modern reader. In a letter written to a friend shortly after her marriage at age forty, she said: "I remember . . . when I was thirteen, being asked when I intended to marry! and surprising my playmates by solemnly replying, 'When I think I shall be happier than I am in being single.' . . . I have only this peculiar, —that what many contently assert or adopt in theory, I have had the courage to be guided by in practice."

The contemporary impression of Fanny that emerges from the diary is the portrait of a woman with all the flaws and strengths associated with her sex. Because so little is known of the lives of women in the eighteenth century, it is somewhat difficult to judge to what extent Fanny was representative of her era. Clearly, by the mere virtue of her being a writer, she was far from typical of the eighteenth-century woman. She wrote novels at a time when women writers were frowned upon, even censured. In love, too, she showed an unconventional behavior by her marriage to a poverty-stricken French Catholic émigré.

Yet, in a subtle way, much of Fanny's unconventional behavior was made possible not by an obvious independence but by an artful skill in dealing with people. When she resolved to resign from court, a rare event in any case, she not only obtained the queen's consent but also remained on friendly terms with the queen until her death. And while Fanny's marriage was unconventional, Fanny, unlike her impetuous friend Mrs. Thrale, had others pave the way for hers to be accepted. The result was that while Mrs. Thrale was ostracized by society Fanny was able to reconcile her family and friends and even Queen Charlotte to the French, Roman Catholic, constitutionalist d'Arblay. Mrs. Thrale, shrewd in her observations of others, recognized this trait in her portrait of Fanny: "Her skill in Life and Manners . . . superior to that of any Man or Woman in this Age or Nation . . . with knowledge of the world and ingenuity of expediency, delicacy of conduct . . ."

Fanny occasionally seemed naive, or at best unwilling to see fault in those she liked, regardless of the evidence. Confronted with various improprieties of Madame de Genlis, Fanny, in her defense, appears at her most credulous: "There was a dignity with her sweetness, and a frankness with her modesty, that assured, that convinced one, beyond all powers of report, of her real worth and innocence."

In a similar vein, Fanny was prone to confuse manners with

motives, particularly in the men she admired. This accounts for her ardent defense of Warren Hastings, who stood trial for impeachment in 1788. She does not appear to have known any of the facts in the case, but she had met Hastings socially before she entered court, and his gentle manners convinced her of his innocence. Her family friend and eminent member of Parliament William Windham tried to enlighten her: " 'Tis amazing how little unison there may be between manners and characters, and how softly gentle a man may appear without, whose nature within is all ferocity and cruelty." He went on: "This is a part of mankind of which you cannot judge, of which, indeed, you can scarce form an idea."

In a situation closer to her heart, this lack of perception caused Fanny great pain and confusion. The man was Mr. Fairly, the queen's vice-chamberlain. While he was reading sentimental poetry to Fanny in enjoyable tête-à-têtes, almost everybody else in court was aware of his plans to marry another woman. Though early apprised of this, Fanny refused to believe it and remained skeptical even after his engagement was announced.

Offsetting her naiveté and artful manipulation was a formidable strength, both physical and mental. Small in stature and delicate in health, Fanny had a continual series of illnesses, many brought on by emotional upsets. Her basic constitution was strong, however, and, as is often the case, she outlived her brothers and all but one sister.

Her emotional strength proved the most impressive. In 1811, at the age of fifty-nine, she was told she had breast cancer. In exile in Paris with her husband and son, removed from the support of family and friends, she consented to an operation in a time when neither anesthetics nor operating tables were in use. Having sent her son to her husband with a misleading message on the day of the operation to keep them away and spare them the trauma, she waited alone for the surgeons to arrive. She remained conscious during the entire twenty-minute operation, while seven black-robed doctors stood over her, scraping and cutting. Miraculously, she survived both the surgery and the postoperative period, gaining the name *l'Ange* for her conduct.

The same title could have been applied by her family and friends. Fanny's diary is filled with concern for all those close to her, and she constantly brought sound reasoning and support to them in regard to their problems and misfortunes. As the years went by, she was consulted more and more on family matters, becoming in effect the head of the household. Devoted and loyal, she had a genius for friendship and, as her prodigious correspondence shows, maintained scores of friendships for the greater part of her life. Even Queen Charlotte, her vision limited to the concerns of royalty, acknowledged that Fanny was "true as gold."

The diary poses yet other questions about Fanny as a woman, particularly as a woman writer. The most difficult, perhaps, given her unique talent, is why she was never again to come near the promise she had shown in *Evelina*. This novel, still in print today, is considered a minor classic of eighteenth-century literature. The critic Austin Dobson defined its importance: "*Evelina* makes a definite deviation in the progress of national fiction, for leaving Fielding's breezing and bustling highway, leaving the analytic hothouse of Richardson, it carries the novel of manners into domestic life, and prepares the way for Miss Edgeworth and the exquisite parlour pieces of Miss Austen."

A major factor in Fanny's decline as a novelist was what Macaulay termed a perversion of her style. In essence, the unaffected writing of her early years became progressively more stilted and convoluted, and the content more didactic. The progression can be traced from her second novel, *Cecilia*, through her fourth novel, *The Wanderer*, which was practically unreadable even in its day. Various critics have attributed this perversion of style to the influence of Johnson, the formality at court, and Fanny's ten-year exile in France, which removed her from her native tongue.

While these no doubt all played a part, a simpler explanation lies in Fanny herself. She had always possessed a delicate balance between gravity and gaiety and, as she matured, the gravity took over, bringing the courtesy-book moralist to the fore. Untempered by the gaiety of her youth, her need to instruct eventually outweighed her ability to entertain. By the time she wrote *Camilla* in 1796, her stated purpose was to produce, not a novel, but "a work of characters and morals put into action."

But perhaps the most crucial reason for Fanny's decline was that after *Evelina* she lost her sense of pleasure in writing. What had previously been a joy became drudgery. It can even be conjectured that if her father and Daddy Crisp had not pushed her, she would not have written her second novel, *Cecilia*. In the four years between *Cecilia* and court, Fanny wrote no fiction at all. Finally, although she did write four blank-verse tragedies at court, she did so more in a desperate attempt to occupy her mind rather than out of a compelling urge to create. Once out of court Fanny wrote, as she explained, because she needed the money. Gone forever seemed to be the need to "scribble" because she couldn't help herself.

Fanny herself appeared bewildered and frustrated. From Chessington, where she had written much of *Evelina* and *Cecilia* many years before, she wrote wistfully to her father in 1793: "As to les Muses—they are the most skittish ladies living—one, with Bowls & Daggars, pursues—another with a Mask escapes—However, I wind round and round their Recesses, where of old I found them—or where, rather, they found *me*—& perhaps we may yet encounter in some green Retreat." Fanny never did find the answer to her loss of creativity, or, if she did, she didn't mention it in her diary.

Sadly, what Fanny believed to be a loss of creativity was more likely a loss of spirit. One fact stands out above all others: Once *Evelina* entered the public domain, Fanny would never again "scribble" purely for her own amusement. Nor, given her fear of failure, could she ever again feel the unalloyed happiness she had once derived from the act of writing. Fanny's true genius as a satirist was crucially linked with her unobtrusive role as the silent, observant Miss Burney. Once she was recognized as the famous novelist, she became not only society's darling, but its prisoner, losing the freedom to write what she wanted without fear of personal criticism. Deprived of her anonymity, she lost the chance to create the brilliant work of which she may have been capable. Perhaps without realizing it, Fanny herself restricted her potential. As early as 1779, the year after *Evelina* was published, Fanny wrote in her diary: "I would a thousand times rather forfeit my character as a writer than risk ridicule or censure as a female."

So it is that Fanny's diary, written for the eyes of a few, remains her finest work. Its own story, that of a timid woman who managed to achieve unprecedented creative heights, is as absorbing as any novel. By her own accomplishments, Fanny paved the way for other women to more easily take their rightful place in the world of letters. Her diary is the record of that difficult and worthy achievement.

Barbara G. Schrank

YOUTH

[1768-1778]

[1768]

To a Certain Miss Nobody

Poland Street, London, March 27

To have some account of my thoughts, manners, acquaintance and actions, when the hour arrives in which time is more nimble than memory, is the reason which induces me to keep a Journal. A Journal in which I must confess my *every* thought, must open my whole heart! But a thing of this kind ought to be addressed to somebody—I must imagine myself to be talking—talking to the most intimate of friends—to one in whom I should take delight in confiding, and remorse in concealment:—but who must this friend be? to make choice of one in whom I can but *half* rely, would be to frustrate entirely the intention of my plan. The only one I could wholly, totally confide in, lives in the same house with me, and not only never *has*, but never *will*, leave me one secret to tell her.[1] To *whom*, then, *must* I dedicate my wonderful, surprising and interesting Adventures?—to *whom* dare I reveal my private opinion of my nearest relations? my secret thoughts of my dearest friends? my own hopes, fears, reflections, and dislikes? ——Nobody!

To Nobody, then, will I write my Journal! since to Nobody can I be wholly unreserved—to Nobody can I reveal every thought, every wish of my heart, with the most unlimited confidence, the most unremitting sincerity to the end of my life! For what chance, what accident can end my connections with Nobody? No secret *can* I conceal from Nobody, and to Nobody can I be *ever* unreserved. Disagreement cannot stop our affection, Time itself has no power to end our friendship. The love, the esteem I entertain for Nobody, Nobody's self has not power to destroy. From Nobody I have nothing to fear, the secrets sacred to friendship

Nobody will not reveal when the affair is doubtful, Nobody will not look towards the side least favourable. . . .

Saturday [Lynn Regis][2]

. . . I am going to tell you something concerning myself, which, (if I have not chanced to mention it before) will, I believe, a little surprise you—it is, that I scarce wish for anything so truly, really, and greatly, as to be *in love*—upon my word I am serious —and very *gravely* and *sedately*, assure you it is a *real* and *true* wish. I cannot help thinking it is a great happiness to have a strong and particular attachment to some one person, independent of duty, interest, relationship or pleasure; but I carry not my wish so far as for a *mutual tendresse*. No, I should be contented to love *Sola*—and let *Duets* be reserved for those who have a proper sense of their superiourity. For my own part, I vow and declare that the mere pleasure of having a great affection for some one person to which I was neither guided by fear, hope of profit, gratitude, respect, or any motive but mere *fancy*, would sufficiently satisfy me, and I should not at all wish a return. Bless me—how I run on! foolish and ill-judged! how despicable a picture have I drawn of an object of Love! mere giddiness, not inclination, I am sure, penn'd it—Love without respect or gratitude!—that could only be felt for a person wholly undeserving—but indeed I write so much at random, that it is much more a chance if I know what I am saying than if I do not. . . .

July 17

Such a set of tittle tattle, prittle prattle visitants! Oh dear! I am so sick of the ceremony and fuss of these fall lall people! So much dressing—chit chat—complimentary nonsense—In short—a Country Town is my detestation—all the conversation is scandal, all the attention, dress, and *almost* all the heart, folly, envy, and censoriousness. A City or a village are the only places which I think, can be comfortable, for a Country Town, I think has all the bad qualities, without one of the good ones, of both.

We live here, generally speaking, in a very regular way—we breakfast always at 10, and rise as much before as we please—we dine precisely at 2, drink tea about 6—and sup exactly at 9. I make a kind of rule, never to indulge myself in my two *most* favourite pursuits, reading and writing, in the morning—no, like a very good girl I give that up wholly, accidental occasions and preventions excepted, to needle work, by which means my reading and writing in the afternoon is a pleasure I cannot be blamed for by my mother, as it does not take up the time I ought to spend otherwise. . . .

Alas, alas! my poor Journal! how dull, unentertaining, uninteresting thou art!—oh what would I give for some Adventure worthy reciting—for something which would surprise—astonish you! . . . I have lately read the Prince of Abissinia[3]—I am almost equally charm'd and shocked at it—the style, the sentiments are inimitable—but the subject is dreadful—and handled as it is by Dr. Johnson, might make *any* young, perhaps old, person tremble. O, how dreadful, how terrible is it to be told by a man of his genius and knowledge, in so affectingly probable a manner, that true, real, happiness is ever unattainable in this world! . . . One thing during the course of the successless enquiry struck me, which gave me much comfort, which is, that those who wander in the world avowedly and purposely in search of happiness, who view every scene of present joy with an eye to what may succeed, certainly are more liable to disappointment, misfortune and unhappiness, than those who give up their fate to chance and take the goods and evils of fortune as they come, without making happiness their study or misery their foresight.

Cabin, Saturday, July

And so I suppose you are staring at the torn paper and unconnected sentence—I don't much wonder—I'll tell you what happen'd. Last Monday I was in the little parlour, which room my papa generally dresses in—and writing a letter to my grandmama. You must know I always have the last sheet of my Journal in my pocket, and when I have wrote it half full I join it to the rest, and take another sheet—and so on. Now I happen'd unluckily to take the last sheet out of my pocket with my letter—and laid it on the piano forte, and there, negligent fool!—I left it. . . . Well, as ill fortune would have it, papa went into the room—took my poor Journal—read, and pocketted it. Mama came up to me and told

me of it. O Dear! I was in a sad distress—I could not for the life of
me ask for it—and so *dawdled* and fretted the time away till Tuesday evening. Then, gathering courage "Pray papa," I said, "have
you got—any *papers* of mine?"

"Papers of yours?" said he—"how should *I* come by papers of
yours?"

"I'm sure—I don't know—but"—

"Why do you leave your papers about the house?" asked he,
gravely.

I could not say another word—he went on playing on the piano
forte. Well, to be sure, thought I, these same dear Journals are
most shocking plaguing things—I've a good mind to resolve never
to write a word more. However, I stayed still in the room, working, and looking wistfully at him for about an hour and half. At
last, he rose to dress—Again I look'd wistfully at him—He laughed
—"What, Fanny," said he, kindly, "are you in sad distress?" I
half laugh'd. "Well,—I'll give it you, now I see you are in such
distress—but take care, my dear, of leaving your writings about
the house again—suppose any body else had found it—I declare I
was going to read it loud—Here, take it—but if ever I find any
more of your Journals, I vow I'll stick them up in the market
place." And then he kiss'd me *so* kindly—never was parent so
properly, so *well*-judgedly affectionate! I was so frightened that I
have not had the heart to write since, till now, I should not but
that—in short, but that I cannot help it! As to the *paper,* I destroy'd it the moment I got it. . . .

Wednesday—August

We had a large party to the Assembly on Monday, which was
so-so-so—I danced but one country dance—the room was so hot,
'twas really fatiguing. Don't you laugh to hear a girl of fifteen
complain of the *fatigue* of dancing? Can't be helped! if you will
laugh, you must, I think.—My partner was a pretty youth enough
—and *quite* a youth—younger than myself—poor dear creature, I
really pitied him, for he seem'd to *long* for another caper—in vain
—I was inexorable—not that he quite *knelt* for my hand—if he had
I might have been *moved*—for I have an uncommonly soft heart
—I am interrupted, or else I am in an excellent humour to scribble nonsense.

10 o'clock [September]

. . . I am now reading the Illiad—I cannot help taking notice of one thing in the 3rd Book which has provoked me for the honour of the sex. Venus tempts Hellen with every delusion in favour of her darling, in vain—riches—power—honour—love—all in vain— the enraged Deity threatens to deprive her of her own beauty, and render her to the level of the most common of her sex. Blushing and trembling, Hellen immediately yields her hand. Thus has Homer proved his opinion of our poor sex—that the love of beauty is our most prevailing passion. It really grieves me to think that there certainly must be some reason for this insignificant opinion the greatest men have of women—at least I fear there must. But I don't in fact believe it.

[1769]

Monday, February 13

The ever charming, engaging, beloved Mr. Crisp spent the whole day with us yesterday.[4] I love him more than ever—every time I see him I cannot help saying so—never can there have been a more *truly* amiable man—he appears to take a *parental* interest in our affairs, and I do believe loves us all with a really fatherly affection. The frankness—the sincerity with which he corrects and reproves us, is more grateful to me, than the most flattering professions could be, because it is far, far more seriously and really kind and friendly. His very smile is all benevolence as well as playfulness. He protests he will take no denial from papa for Hetty[5] and me to go to Chessington[6] this summer, and told papa to remember that he had *bespoke* us. . . .

Saturday

If my dear Susette was here I should want nothing. We are still only us three together.[7] I seldom quit home considering my age and opportunities. But why should I when I am so happy in it? following my own vagaries, which my papa never controls I never can want employment, nor sigh for amusement. We have a library which is an everlasting resource when attack'd by the spleen—I have always a sufficiency of work to spend, if I pleased, my whole time at it—musick is a feast which can never grow insipid—and, in short, I have all the reason that ever mortal had to be contented with my lot—and I *am* contented with, I *am* grateful for it! If few people are more happy, few are more sensible *of* their happiness. But what of that?—is there any merit in paying the small tribute of gratitude, where blessings such as I have received *compel* it from me? How strongly, how forcibly do I feel to whom I owe all the earthly happiness I enjoy!—it is to my father! to this dearest, most amiable, this best beloved—most worthy of men!—it is his goodness to me which makes all appear so gay, it is his affection which makes *my* sun shine. . . .

—How truly does this Journal contain my real and undisguised thoughts!—I always write in it according to the humour I am in, and if any stranger was accidentally reading it, how capricious—inconsistent and whimsical I must appear! One moment flighty and half mad,—the next sad and melancholy. No matter! it's truth and simplicity are it's sole recommendation, and I doubt not but I shall hereafter receive great pleasure from *reviewing* and almost *renewing* my youth, and my former sentiments, unless, indeed, the latter part of my life is doomed to be as miserable as the beginning is the reverse, and then indeed, every line here will rend my heart! . . .

[1770]

January 10

. . . I have a most delightful subject to commence the present year with—such a one, as I fear I may never chance to meet with again.—Yet why should I look into futurity with a gloomy eye?—But let me wave all this nonsense, and tell you, my dear, faithful, ever attentive Nobody—that I was last Monday at a masquerade! . . .

This Masquerade—how does that word grace my Journal!
was, however, a very private one, and at the house of Mr. Laluze,
a French dancing master. . . .

Hetty had for three months thought of nothing but the masquerade—no more had I. She had long fixed upon her dress; my
stupid head only set about one on Friday evening. I could think of
no character I liked much, and could obtain; as to Nuns, Quak-
ers, etc. (which I was much advised to) I cannot help thinking
there is a gravity and extreme reserve required to support them
well, which would have made me necessarily so dull and stupid,
that I could not have met with much entertainment, and being
unable to fix on a *character*, I resolved at length to go in a meer
fancy dress. . . . It is really true that all Monday we passed in
preparationing for the evening. . . .

. . . Hetty went as a Savoyard, with a *hurdy gurdy* fastened round
her waist. Nothing could look more simple, innocent, or pretty.
My dress was, a close pink Persian *vest*, . . . covered with gauze, in
loose pleats, and with flowers &c. &c. . . . a little garland or wreath
of flowers on the left side of my head. . . .

The Room was large, and very well lighted, but, when we
first went in, not half filled, so that every eye was turned on each
new comer. I felt extremely awkward and abashed, notwithstanding my mask. . . . Hetty went in playing on her *hurdy gurdy*,
and the company flocked about her with much pleasure. . . . The
first Mask who accosted me was an old Witch, tall, shrivelled,
leaning on a broom stick, and, in short, a fear inspiring figure,
apparently, by his walk, a man. . . . "Thou thinkest, then, that that
little bit of black silk is a mask?" cried he. I was absolutely confounded for I thought directly that he meant to laugh at my
mask, but on recollection I believe he was going on with some
compliment, but I was so unable to rally, that with a silly half
laugh, I turned on my heel, and walked away as far off as I could.
. . . I observed a Nun, dressed in black, who was speaking with
great earnestness, and who I soon discovered by her voice to be a
Miss Milne, a pretty Scotch nymph I have met at Mrs. Strange's.[8]
I stopt to listen to her. She turn'd about and took my hand,
and led me into a corner of the room—"Beautiful creature," cried
she, in a plaintive voice, "with what pain do I see you here, beset
by this crowd of folly and deceit! O could I prevail on you to
quit this wicked world, and all it's vices, and to follow my footsteps!"

"But how am I to account," said I, "for the reason that one who so much despises the World, should choose to mix with the gayest part of it? What do you do here?"

"I come but," said she, "to see and to save such innocent, beautiful, young creatures as you from the snares of the wicked. Listen to me! I was once such as you are, I mixed with the world; I was caressed by it, I loved it—I was deceived! Surrounded by an artful set of flattering, designing men, I fell but too easily into the net they spread for me. I am now convinced of the vanity of life, and in this peaceful, tranquil state shall I pass the remainder of my days."

"It is so impossible," said I, "to listen to you without being benefitted by your conversation, that I shall to the utmost of my power *imitate you*, and always choose to despise the world, and hold it in contempt—at a *Masquerade!*"—

"Alas," said she, "I am here merely to contemplate on the strange follies and vices of mankind—this scene affords me only a subject of joy to think I have quitted it."

We were here interrupted, and parted. After that I had several short conversations with different Masks. I will tell you the principal dresses as well as I can recollect them. They were a Punch who was indeed very completely dressed, and who very well supported his character; the Witch whom I mentioned before was a very capital figure, and told many fortunes with great humour; a Shepherd, of all characters the last, were I a man, I should have wished to have assumed; a Harliquin, who hopped and skipped about very lightly and gayly; a Huntsman, who indeed seemed suited for nothing but the company of dogs; a Gardener; a Persian; two or three Turks, and two Friars; an admirable Merlin, who spoke of spells, magick and charms with all the *mock heroick* and bombast manner which his character could require. There were also two most jolly looking Sailors, and many Dominos, besides some dresses which I have forgot. Among the females, two sweet little Nuns in white pleased me most, there was a very complete Shepherdess, with the gayest crook, the smartest little hat, and most trifling conversation one might desire; nevertheless full as clever as her choice of so hackneyed and insipid a dress led one to expect. You may imagine that she was immediately and unavoidably paired with the amiable Shepherd I mentioned before. There were two or three young pastoral nymphs to keep her in countenance: and I can recollect no other dresses, save an Indian Queen; and Dominos. . . .

Hetty just then bid me observe a very droll old Dutchman, who soon after joined us. He accosted us in high Dutch—not that I would quarrel with any one who told me it was *low* Dutch! Heaven knows, it might be Arabick for aught I could tell! He was very completely dressed, and had on an exceeding droll old man's mask, and was smoking a pipe. He presented me with a quid of tobaco, I accepted it very cordially. The Nun was not disposed to be pleased. She attacked poor Mynheer with much haughtiness —"Thou savage! hence to thy native land of brutes and barbarians; smoak thy pipe there, but pollute not us with thy dull and coarse attempts at wit and pleasantry!" . . . The Dutchman, however, heeded her not, he amused himself with talking Dutch and making signs of devotion to me, while the Nun railed and I laughed. . . .

. . . Refreshments were then brought and everybody was engaged with a partner; Merlin, a delightful Mask, secured Hetty, and the Dutchman my ladyship. Every body was then unmasked, and when I presently turned hastily round, I saw a young man so very like Mr. Young that at the first glance I thought it was him, but what was my surprise at seeing the Dutchman! I had no idea that he was under fifty, when behold he scarce looked three and twenty. I believe my surprise was very manifest, for Mynheer could not forbear laughing. On his part he paid me many compliments, repeatedly and with much civility congratulating himself on his choice. "I have been smoking them all round," cried he, for he had always a tobaco pipe in his hand—"till at last a happy whiff blew away your mask, and fixed me so fortunately." . . .

Nothing could be more droll than the first dance we had after unmasking; the pleasure which appeared in some countenances, and the disappointment pictured in others made the most singular contrast imaginable, and to see the old turned young, and the young old—in short, every face appeared different from what we expected. The old Witch in particular we found was a young officer. The Punch who had made himself as broad as long, was a very young and handsome man; but what most surprised me, was the Shepherd whose own face was so stupid that we could *scarcely* tell whether he had taken off his mask or *not*. . . .

About this time we received the following note from the Masquerade Dutchman.

"The Dutchman presents his compliments to the Miss Burneys, and takes the liberty to enclose three tickets for the Chelsea Assembly hoping the Miss Burneys will have the goodness to find a chaperon. The Dutchman will do himself the honour to wait upon the Miss Burneys this evening, with the Doctor's permission, to know whether he may exist again or not."

I never coloured so in my life, for papa was in the room, and Hetty read the note out aloud, and then, laughing, flung it to me to answer, saying she knew she had nothing to do with it; and wishing me joy of my first serious conquest. I was so very much surprised I could not speak. Papa said it was coming to the point very quick indeed, and he must either be a very bold man, or a young man who knew nothing of the world. But he said I must return the tickets, but might let him come to tea, as he deserved civility, by naming him (papa), and then we might see more how to judge him. I was quite frightened at this—but very glad papa and Hetty both left me to answer the note for myself, for as they thought him serious I determined to be so too. . . .

I wrote the following answer, and sent it off without shewing it to papa, to put an end to the whole at once.

"Miss Burneys present their compliments to the Dutchman, and as they cannot go to the Chelsea Assembly, they beg leave to return the three tickets with many thanks.

"They are very sorry it will not be in their power to have the pleasure of seeing him this evening, having been some time preengaged. February 19th. Wed: Morn⁵."

This note will, I doubt not, be the last I shall have to answer from this gentleman—indeed it is the *first* also that I have *answered:* nevertheless I fancy he will condescend to exist still. . . .⁹

Poland Street

I have not written for an age—the reason is, my thoughts have been all drawn away from myself and given up to my dear Hetty—

and to her I have been writing without end;—so that all my time besides was due to my dearest Suzette with whom I have been reading French: having taught myself that charming language for the sake of its bewitching authors—for I shall never want to speak it.

With this dear Suzette and my sweet little Charlotte,[10] it is well I can be so happy: for Hetty, my dear Hetty, has given herself away from us. She has married at last her faithful Charles.[11] God send her happy! He is one of the worthiest young men living.—I am come up to town to spend a little time with them. They are now in our house till they can find a dwelling to their taste. . . .

Queen Square, November 16

I have now changed my abode, and quitted dear Poland Street for ever. How well satisfied shall I be if after having lived as long in Queen Square, I can look back to equally happy days![12]

We have a charming house here. It is situated at the upper end of the square, and has a delightful prospect of Hamstead and Hygate, we have more than room for our family, large as it is, and all the rooms are well fitted up, convenient, and handsome. . . .

I left Mr. Burney and my sister with regret; I passed five happy weeks with them. . . .

[1771]

May 8

My father's book, on *The present state of Music,* made its appearance in the world the 3rd of this month, and we flatter ourselves it will be favourably received.[13] Last Sunday was the first day for some time past, that my father has favoured us with his company in a sociable stile, having been so exceedingly occupied by writing in those few hours he spends at home, that he really seemed lost to his family; and the comfort of his society and conversation are now almost as new as grateful to us. He prints his book for himself. He has sent a multitude of them to his particular friends as presents; among others, to the famous Dr. Hawkesworth,[14] to that charming poet Mr. Mason,[15] to Mr. Garrick,[16] and Mr. Crisp, who, all four, were consulted about it when a manuscript, and interested themselves much with it. . . .

July 3

I am just returned from Chessington, to which dear place Miss Allen[17] took me. . . . I had not been for almost five years. The country is extremely pleasant at Chessington. The house is situated on very high ground, and has only cottages about it for some miles. A sketch of our party: Mrs. Hamilton is the mistress of the house, which was her brother's, who, having lived too much at his ease, left her in such circumstances as obliged her to take boarders for her maintainance. She is a very good little old woman, hospitable and even-tempered. Mademoiselle Rosat,—who boards with her; she is about . . . forty, tall and elegant in person and dress, very sensible, extremely well-bred, and when in spirits, droll and humorous. But she has been very unhappy, and her misfortunes have left indelible traces on her mind; which subjects her to extreme low spirits. Yet I think her a great acquisition to Chessington. Miss Cooke,[18]—who I believe is forty, too; but has so much good-nature and love of mirth in her, that she still appears a girl. . . . My sister Burney—than whom I know few prettier, more lively, or more agreeable. Miss Barsanti,[19] who is a great favourite of my sister's, and was by her and Miss Allen invited to Chessington. She is extremely clever and entertaining, possesses amazing power of mimickry, and an uncommon share of humour. Miss Allen, and myself, end the females. Mr. Crisp, whose health is happily restored,—I think I need not give his character. Mr. Featherstone,—brother of Sir Matthew, . . . a middle-aged gentleman, who, having broken his leg, walks upon crutches. He is equally ugly and cross. Mr. Charles Burney brings up the rear.[20] I would to Heaven my father did! . . .

[1772]

January 26

Mr. Garrick is this moment gone. Unfortunately my father was out, and mama not come downstairs; yet to my great satisfaction he came in. Dick[21] ran to him, as the door was opened,—we were all seated at breakfast. "What, my bright-eyed beauty!" cried he; and then flinging himself back in a theatrical posture, "and here ye all are—one—two—three—four—beauties all." He then came in and with a great deal of humour played with Dick. How many pities that he has no children; for he is extremely, nay passionately fond of them. "Well, but, Madam, so your father is out. Why I can never see him. He calls upon me—I call upon him, but we never meet. Can he come to dine with me to-day? can he?" I could not possibly tell. "Well don't let him send or make any fuss—if he can come he shall find beef and pudding: but I must have him on Tuesday. Some of his friends are to be with me: and I *must* have him then." I could not venture to promise. . . .

May 30

Maria, Susan, and myself had the happiness to see Garrick, last night, in Richard the Third. We had always longed to see him in all his great characters, though least in this which is so shocking, though not the least, of the praise of his acting. . . . Garrick was sublimely horrible! Good Heavens—how he made me shudder whenever he appeared! It is inconceivable how terribly great he is in this character! I will never see him so disfigured again; he seemed so truly the monster he performed, that I felt myself glow with indignation every time I saw him. The applause he met with, exceeds all belief of the absent. I thought at the end they would have torn the house down: our seats shook under us. . . .

[1773]

We had yesterday the most heavenly evening! Millico, the divine Millico was here, and with him Sig^r. Sacchini, and Sig^r. Celestini, that sweet violinist, whom I have often mentioned.[22] We had no further party, which I greatly rejoiced at, as we were at full liberty to devote every instant to these. Sig^r. Sacchini is a very elegant man and extremely handsome. . . . Millico is of a large or rather . . . an immense figure, and not handsome *at all, at all;* but his countenance is strongly expressive of sweetness of disposition, and his conversation is exceedingly sensible. He was very much surprised at the size of our family. My father has so young a look, that all strangers are astonished to find him such a *Patriarch.* . . . They enquired with great curiosity who we all were and if the Signorina, Hetty, . . . were all my father's. . . . declared he had taken us for his sisters! His next enquiry was "If we did not play?" My father came up to us, and told us—and went back with answer that *one* (Hetty) would play on condition that *he* should sing. . . . [Millico's] conversation was partly Italian and partly French, and Sacchini's almost all Italian; but they neither of them speak three words of English. . . .

Hetty being called upon to open the concert, . . . began a rondeau in the overture to Sacchini's new opera, which has been performed but twice; but she had been to three rehearsals, and has gotten almost half the opera by ear. Sacchini almost started; he looked at first in the utmost perplexity, as if doubting his own ears, as the music of *Il Cid* has never been published. Millico clapt his hands, and laughed—"Ah! brava! brava!" Sacchini then bowed, and my father explained the manner of her having got this rondeau; at which he seemed much pleased. When she had finished her lesson, . . . my father applied to Millico . . . who readily complied, and with the utmost good-nature sang his most favourite air in the new opera, only accompanied by Sacchini on the harpsichord. I have no words to express the delight which his singing gave me, more far away than I have ever received, even at the Opera; for his voice is so sweet, that it wants no instruments to cover it. He was not, however, satisfied with himself; he complained again of his cold; but seeing us all charmed,—with a sweetness that enchanted me in so great a performer, he said, "Eh bien, encore une fois; la voix commence à venir"; and sang it again. . . .

. . . I again repeat, the evening was *heavenly!* If any thing on *earth* can be so, 'tis surely perfection of vocal music. . . . Nothing is more charming than to see great talents without affectation. My father says, that there are hardly in all Italy three such modest men as Millico, Sacchini, and Celestini. They did whatever was asked of them with the most unaffected good-humour. They are wholly free from vanity, yet seemed as much to enjoy giving pleasure, as we did receiving it. . . .

Sunday, May 3

. . . We have had from the Cape of Good Hope the welcome news of my brother's promotion. Lieutenant Shanks, a young man who was on board the *Adventure,* one of the three sloops under Captain Cook, was so ill, that he was obliged to leave the ship and return to England, "in whose place," says the Captain's letter to Lord Sandwich, "I have appointed Mr. Burney, whom I have found very deserving." This is most comfortable intelligence and rejoices us unspeakably; he will be a lieutenant of three years' standing by his return. He has written to us in very good spirits, and assures us that the Cape of Good Hope is a very agreeable place! Lord Sandwich has interested himself very much about this affair, and behaved to my father, to whom he seems really attached, in the most friendly manner. I wish he may preserve his place of first Lord of the Admiralty to the time of James's return.[23]

Mr. and Mrs. Rishton[24] are turned absolute hermits for this summer, they have left Bath, and are gone to Tingmouth in Devonshire where they have taken a *cottage* rather than a house. The country she says is beautiful. They are however only to remain there till Stanhoe House which they have taken for 7 years is ready for them—I hear very often from Mrs. Rishton, whose friendship, affection, and confidence, will, I believe, end only with our lives.

My father's German tour has been published this week;[25] in it are inserted proposals for publishing by subscription his History of Music. If he has not 500 subscribers by next Christmas, he declares he will not publish it at all. . . .

[July]

. . . Tingmouth is situated the most beautifully of any town I ever saw, or perhaps in England, ever can see.[26] Mr. Rishton's house is . . . on *the Den,* which is the *Mall* here. It is a small, neat, thatched and white-washed cottage, neither more nor less. We are not a hundred yards from the sea, in which Mrs. Rishton bathes every morning. There is no end to the variety of delightful walks and rides which this sweet spot affords.

The morning after I came they insisted on my accompanying them to the Races, and I had a very civil invitation from Mrs. Phipps, in whose chaise and company Mrs. Rishton and myself went. Mr. Rishton drove Mr. Phipps in his *whiskey*. The Phipps' are newly married, and in great favour with Mr. Rishton and Maria.

We got a very good place in the stand, where there was a very great deal of company, and the races, being quite new to me, really afforded me a great deal of entertainment. . . .

Mr. Rishton is still more in love with retirement than his wife, if that is possible; there are but two families he approves keeping up acquaintance with: though I find there is at present a great deal of company at Tingmouth, as this is the *season* for sea-bathing, and as the rural beauties of the place become every year more known, in so much that the price of all provisions, &c., is actually doubled within these three years. The two families honoured with Mr. Rishton's preference are those of the Phipps and the Hurrels, which latter consists of Mr. Hurrel, a clergyman of 1500 per ann. his wife and her sister, Miss Davy, who are daughters of Sir John Davy. . . .

I was also introduced the same morning to Miss Bowdler, a young woman, who according to Mr. Rishton, bears a rather singular character.[27] She is very sensible and clever, and possesses a great share of wit and poignancy, which spares, he says, neither friend or foe. She reckons herself superior, he also adds, to the opinion of the world and to all common forms and customs, and therefore lives exactly as she pleases, guarding herself from all real evil, but wholly regardless and indifferent of appearances.

She is about six and twenty; a rather pretty little figure, but not at all handsome, though her countenance is very spirited and expressive. She has father, mother, and sisters alive; but yet is come to Tingmouth alone; though at present indeed, she is with a Miss Lockwood, a rich old maid; but she will very soon be entirely *at liberty*. She and her family are old acquaintances of Mrs. Rishton, and of mama; she is therefore frequently here; but Mr. Rishton, who gave me most of this account of her, cannot endure even the sight of her, a woman, he says, who despises the customs and manners of the country she lives in, must, consequently, conduct herself with impropriety. For *my* part I own myself of the same sentiment, but, nevertheless, we have not any one of us the most distant shadow of doubt of Miss Bowdler's being equally innocent with those who have more worldly prudence, at the same time, that her conduct appears to me highly improper: for she finds that the company of gentlemen is more entertaining than that of ladies, and therefore, without any scruples or punctilio, indulges her fancy. She is perpetually at Mr. Crispen's, notwithstanding a very young man, Mr. Green, lives in the same house; not contented with a *call*, she very frequently sups with them; and though she does this in the fair face of day, and speaks of it as openly and commonly as I should of visiting my sister, yet I can by no means approve so great a contempt of public opinion. . . .

[August]

. . . We all went on Monday evening to the sea-shore, to see the *seine* drawn; this is a most curious work, all done by women. The have a very long net, so considerable as to cost them thirteen or sixteen pounds. This they first draw into a boat, which they go off the shore in, and row in a kind of semicircle, till they land at some distance. All the way they spread this net, one side of which is kept above water by corks. Then they land and divide forces; half of them return to the beginning of the net, and half remain at the end; and then with amazing strength both divisions at the same time pull the net in by the two ends. Whatever fish they catch, are always encircled in the middle of the net, which comes out of the water the last; and, as they draw towards each other, they all join in getting their prey.

When once they perceive that there is fish in their nets, they set up a loud shout, and make an almost unintelligible noise in expressing their joy and in disputing at the same time upon their shares, and on what fish escaped them. They are all robust and well-made, and have remarkably beautiful teeth, and some of them are really very fine women. Their dress is barbarous; they have stays half-laced, and something by way of handkerchiefs about their necks; they wear one coloured flannel, or stuff petticoat; no shoes or stockings, notwithstanding the hard pebbles and stones all along the beach; and their coat is pinned up in the shape of a pair of trousers, leaving them wholly naked to the knee. Mr. Western declares he could not have imagined such a race of females existed in a civilized country; and had he come hither by sea, he should have almost fancied he had been cast on a newly discovered coast. They caught this evening at one time nine large salmon, a john dory, and a gurnet. On Tuesday evening we went again, and saw them catch four dozen of mackerel at a haul. . . .

Friday, August

To-day, for the first time, I bathed. Ever since I went to Torbay[28] I have been tormented with a dreadful cold, till within this day or two, and Mr. Rishton very much advised me to sea bathing in order to *harden* me. The women here are so poor, and this place till lately was so obscure and retired, that they wheel the bathing machine into the sea themselves. . . . I was terribly frightened, and really thought I should never have recovered from the plunge. I had not breath enough to speak for a minute or two, the shock was beyond expression great; but, after I got back to the machine, I presently felt myself in a glow that was delightful—it is the finest feeling in the world, and will induce me to bathe as often as will be safe.

Queen Square, October

Mr. Garrick, to my great confusion, has again surprised the house, before we were up; but really my father keeps such late hours at night, that I have not resolution to rise before eight in the morning. My father himself was only on the stairs, when this early, industrious, active, charming man came. I dressed myself immediately; but found he was going, as I entered the study. He stopped short, and with his accustomed drollery, exclaimed, "Why now, why are *you* come down, now, to keep me? But this will never do! (looking at his watch) upon my word, young ladies, this will never do! You must never marry at this rate! —to keep such late hours.—No, I shall keep all the young men from you!" He invited my father in Lord Shelbourne's name to go with him to dine at his lordship's, as he has a fine statue lately come from Italy, which has a musical instrument, and which he wishes to shew my father.

My father asked him for his box for us at night, to see the Mask of Alfred, which is revived. But he insisted upon our going to the front-boxes. "You shall have my box," said he, "another time that you please; but you will see nothing of the new scenes up there. Now, you shall have my box to see me, or the *old new* play that is coming out, with all my heart."

"O! dont say that," cried I; "dont say to see *you;* you don't know what you promise." He laughed; but I determined not to let such an offer be made with *impunity*.

He took much notice, as usual, of Charlotte; he seems indeed to love all that belong to my father, of whom he is really very fond. Nay, as he went out, he said, with a very comical face to me, "I like you! I like you all! I like your looks! I like your manner!" And then, opening his arms with an air of heroics, he cried, "I am tempted to run away with you all, one after another." We all longed to say, *Pray, do!* . . .

Seeing in the papers on Thursday Abel Drugger by Mr. Garrick,[29] I prevailed with my dear father to write him a note, which he did very drolly, claiming his promise, but begging for only two places. He sent immediately this answer:

> My dear Dr.,
> I had rather have your family in my front boxes, than all the Lords and Commons.
>
> > Yours ever,
> > D. G.

I have now entered into a very particular correspondence with Mr. Crisp. I write really a Journal to him, and in answer he sends me most delightful long, and incomparably clever, letters, animadverting upon all the facts &c., which I acquaint him with, and dealing with the utmost sincerity in stating his opinion and giving his advice. I am infinitely charmed with this correspondence—*ant* I mean—which is not more agreeable than it may prove instructive.

FROM MR. CRISP

[*1773*]

MY DEAR FANNY,—In consequence of our agreement, I shall now begin with an instance of the most pure and genuine sincerity, when I declare to you that I was delighted with your letter throughout,—a proof of which (that perhaps you would have excus'd) is this immediate answer with a demand for *more*— The horseleech hath two daughters, saith the wise man, saying, "Give! Give!"—I find myself nearly related to them on this occasion. I profess there is not a single word or expression or thought in your whole letter, that I do not relish,—not that in our Correspondence I shall set up for a Critic or Schoolmaster or observer of composition—the deuce take them all! I hate them. If once you set about framing studied letters, that are to be correct, nicely grammatical, and run in smooth periods, I shall mind them no otherwise than as newspapers of intelligence. I make this preface, because you have needlessly enjoined me to deal sincerely, and to tell you of your faults; and so let this declaration serve to tell you once for all, that there is no fault in an epistolary correspondence like stiffness and study. Dash away whatever comes uppermost; the sudden sallies of imagination, clap'd down on paper, just as they arise, are worth folios, and have all the warmth and merit of that sort of nonsense that is eloquent in love. Never think of being correct when you write to me. . . .

As to that rogue your father, if I did not know him to be incorrigible, I should say something of that regular course of irregularity he persists in—two, three, four, five o'clock in the morning, sups at twelve!—is it impossible for him to get the better of his constitution? has he forgot the condition he was in the winter after his first return to England? perhaps he is like a seasoned old drinker, whose inside is so lined with a coat of tartar, that his brandy only goes in . . . like a worm in a still, without affecting the vessel it passes through. Certain it is, that he uses his thin carcass most abominably. . . .

I am greatly pleased with the growing reputation of his Tours; of which I never had the least doubt; and no less so, with those marks of favour and esteem for the Great and the Eminent, and only wish him to make that worldly use of them, which he ought; in which particular he has hitherto been so deficient. . . .

[1774]

February 20

What will become of the world, if my Annals are thus irregular? Almost two months have elapsed without my recording one anecdote! I am really shocked for posterity! But for my pen, all the adventures of this noble family might sink to oblivion! I am amazed when I consider the greatness of my importance, the dignity of my task, and the novelty of my pursuits! I should be the Eighth Wonder of the World, if the world had not already, and too prematurely, nominated so many persons to that honour!

Thursday mama took us with her to Miss Reid, the celebrated paintress, to meet Mrs. Brooke, the celebrated authoress of 'Lady Julia Mandeville.' Miss Reid is shrewd and clever, where she has any opportunity given her to make it known; but she is so very deaf, that it is a fatigue to attempt conversing with her. She is most exceeding ugly, and of a very melancholy, or rather discontented, humour. Mrs. Brooke is very short and fat, and squints but has the art of showing agreeable ugliness. She is very well bred, and expresses herself with much modesty upon all subjects; which in an *authoress,* a woman of *known* understanding, is extremely pleasing.

The rest of the party consisted of Miss Beatson, a niece of Miss Reid's, Mr. Strange, and Dr. Shebbeare.[30] . . .

Dr. Shebbeare, who was once put actually in the pillory for a libel, is well known for political and other writings. He absolutely ruined our evening; for he is the most morose, rude, gross, and ill-mannered man I was ever in company with. He aims perpetually at wit, though he constantly stops short at rudeness. He reminded me of Swift's lines:

> "Thinks raillery consists in railing,
> Will tell aloud your greatest failing."

For he did, to the utmost of his power, *cut up* every body on their most favourite subject; though what most excited his spleen was *Woman,* to whom he professes a fixed aversion; and next to her his greatest disgust is against the *Scotch;* and these two subjects he wore thread-bare; though indeed they were pretty much fatigued, before he attacked them; and all the *satire* which he levelled at them, consisted of trite and hackneyed abuse. The only novelty which they owed to him was from the extraordinary coarseness of language he made use of. But I shall recollect as much of the conversation as I can, and make the parties speak for themselves. I will begin with Mr. Strange's entrance, which was soon after ours. After his compliments were paid to the *fair sex* he turned to the *Growler.*—

"Well, Dr. Shebbeare, and how do you do?"

Dr. Shebbeare.—Do? why, as you see, pestered by a parcel of women.

Mrs. Brooke.—*Women* and the *Scotch* always fare ill with Dr. Shebbeare.

Dr. Shebbeare.—Because they are the two greatest evils upon earth. The *best* woman that ever I knew is not worth the *worst* man. And as to the Scotch—there is but *one* thing in which they are clever and can excell the English, and that is they can use both hands at once to scratch themselves—the English never think of using more than one.

Miss Reid.—Ay, Dr., you only abuse us because you are sorry that you are not our countryman.

Dr. Shebbeare.—What, *envy,* hey? Why it's true enough that they get every thing into their own hands; and when once they come they take care never to return, no, no!

Miss Reid.—You was saying, Mrs. Brooke, that you did not know till I told you that Dr. Burney had a wife; what do you think then of seeing these grown up daughters?

Mrs. Brooke.—Why, I don't know how, or why, but I own I was never more surprised than when I heard that Dr. Burney was married.

Dr. Shebbeare.—What, I suppose you did not take him for a fool?—All men who marry are so, but above all God help him who takes a widow!

Mr. Strange.—This is a strange man, Mrs. Burney, but nobody ever minds him.

Dr. Shebbeare.—I don't wonder that Dr. Burney went abroad! —all my amazement is at his ever coming home! unless, indeed, he left his understanding behind him, which I suppose was the case.

Mrs. Brooke.—I am sure that does not appear from his Tour. I never received more pleasure than from reading his account of what he saw and did abroad.

Dr. Shebbeare.—I hate authors! but I suppose one wit must hate another.

Mrs. Brooke.—Those few authors that *I* know give me great reason *not* to hate them;—quite the contrary—Dr. Johnson, Dr. Armstrong, and I won't say *what* I think of Dr. Burney; but for Dr. Armstrong I have a very particular regard. I have known him more than twenty years.

Dr. Shebbeare.—What, I suppose you like him for his intrigues?

Mrs. Brooke.—Indeed, I never heard he had any.

Dr. Shebbeare.—What, I suppose you had too many yourself to keep his in your memory?

Mrs. Brooke.—O, women, you know, Dr., never have intrigues. I wish Dr. Burney was here, I am sure he would be our champion.

Dr. Shebbeare.—What, do you suppose he'd speak against himself? I know but too well what it is to be married! I think I have been yoked for one and forty years, and I have wished my wife under ground any time since.

Mama.—And if she were you'd marry in a week!

Dr. Shebbeare.—I wish I was tried.

Mr. Strange.—Why this is a sad man, Mrs. Burney, I think we must toss him in a blanket.

Dr. Shebbeare.—Ay, with all my heart. But speak for yourself (to Mrs. Brooke), do you suppose your husband was not long since tired of you?

Mrs. Brooke.—O, as to that—that is not a fair question;—I don't ask you if you're tired of *your* wife.

Dr. Shebbeare.—And if you did, I'd tell you.

Miss Beatson.—Then *I* ask you, Dr. Shebbeare, are you tired of your wife?

Dr. Shebbeare.—I did not say I'd tell *you,* Bold Face.

Mama.—I wish that Mrs. Strange was here; she'd fight our battles admirably.

Mr. Strange.—Why do you never come to see her, Doctor?

Dr. Shebbeare.—Because she has so much tongue, that I expect she'll talk herself to death, and I don't choose to be accessary.

[April or May]

My father has bought a House in St. Martin's Street, Leicester Fields,—an odious street—but well situated, and nearly in the centre of the town; and the house is a large and good one. It was built by Sir Isaac Newton! . . . and, when he constructed it, it stood in Leicester *Fields,*—not *Square,* that he might have his observatory unannoyed by neighbouring houses, and his observatory is my favorite sitting place, when I can retire to read or write any of my private fancies or vagaries. I burnt all up to my 15th year—thinking I grew too old for scribbling nonsense, but as I am less young, I grow, I fear, less wise, for I cannot any longer resist what I find to be irresistible, the pleasure of popping down my thoughts from time to time upon paper. . . .

Sunday Night, June 26

. . . But now let me come to a matter of more importance and, at the same time, pleasure: My brother is returned in health, spirits, and credit. He has made what he calls a very fine voyage; but it must have been very dangerous. Indeed, he has had several personal dangers; and in these voyages of hazard and enterprize, so, I imagine, must every individual of the ship. Captain Cook was parted from in bad weather, accidentally, in the passage from the Society Isles to New Zealand, in the second and so fatal visit which they made to that barbarous country, where they lost ten men in the most inhuman manner. My brother, unfortunately for himself, was the witness and informer of that horrid massacre. Mr. Rowe, (the acting Lieutenant), a midshipman, and eight men were sent from the ship in a boat to shore, to get some greens. The whole ship's company had lived so long upon good terms with the New Zealanders, that there was no suspicion of treachery or ill usage. They were ordered to return at three o'clock; but upon their failure, Captain Furneaux sent a launch, with Jem to command it, in search of them. They went among the people, and bought fish; and Jem says he imagined they were gone further up the country, but never supposed how *very* long a way they were gone. At the third place, it is almost too terrible to mention, they found[31]——

[August]

The present *Lyon* of the times, according to the author of "The Placid Man's" term, is Omai, the native of Otaheite;[32] and next to him, the present object is Mr. Bruce, a gentleman who has been abroad twelve years, and spent four of them in Abyssinia and other places in Africa, where no Englishman before has gained admission.[33] His adventures are very marvellous. He is expected to publish them, and I hope he will. He is very intimate with the Stranges, and one evening called here with Miss Strange. His figure is almost gigantic! he is the tallest man I ever saw; and exceedingly well made, neither fat or lean in proportion to his amazing height. I cannot say I was charmed with him; for he seems rather arrogant, and to have so large a share of good opinion of himself, as to have nothing left for the rest of the world but contempt. His self-approbation is not that of a *fop;* on the contrary, he is a very manly character, and looks so dauntless and intrepid, so that I believe he could never in his life know what fear meant.

To Mr. Crisp

St. Martin's Street, Thursday Night [December 1]

My Dear Daddy— . . . And now my dearest Sir, to make you some amends for all the scolding and impertinence with which I have begun this letter, I will tell you that I have seen Omai, and if I am, as I intend to be, very minute in my account, will you shake hands and be friends?

"Yes, you little Devil you! so *to business,* and no more words." Very well, I obey. You must know then, in the first place, that glad as I was to see this great personage, I extremely regretted not having *you* of the party, as you had half promised you would be,—and as I am sure you would have been extremely well pleased, and that the Journey would have more than answered to you: but the notice was so extremely short it was impossible. Now to facts. . . .

Mr. Strange and Mr. Hayes,[34] at their own motion, came to dinner to meet our guest. We did not dine till four. But Omai came at two, and Mr. Banks and Dr. Solander[35] brought him, in order to make a short visit to my father. They were all just come from the House of Lords, where they had taken Omai to hear the King make his speech from the Throne.

For my part, I had been confined up stairs for three days—however, I was much better, and obtained leave to come down, though very much wrapt up, and *quite a figure,* but I did not chuse to appear till Mr. Banks and Dr. Solander were gone. I found Omai seated on the great chair, and my brother next to him, and talking Otaheite as fast as possible. You cannot suppose how fluently and easily Jem speaks it. Mama and Susy and Charlotte were opposite. As soon as there was a *cessation* of talk, Jem introduced me, and told him I was another sister. He rose, and made a very fine bow, and then seated himself again. But when Jem went on, and told him that I was not well, he again directly rose, and muttering something of the *fire,* in a very polite *manner,* without *speech* insisting upon my taking his seat,—and he *would* not be refused. He then drew his chair next to mine, and looking at me with an expression of pity said "very well to-*morrow-mor-row?*"—I imagine he meant *I hope* you will be very well in *two or three morrows*—and when I shook my head, he said *"no? O very bad!"* When Mr. Strange and Mr. Hayes were introduced to him, he paid his compliments with great politeness to them, which he has found a method of doing without *words.*

As he had been to Court, he was very fine. He had on a suit of Manchester velvet, lined with white satten, a *bag,* lace ruffles, and a very handsome sword which the King had given to him. He is tall and very well made, much darker than I expected to see him, but has a pleasing countenance.

He makes *remarkable* good bows—not for *him,* but for *anybody,* however long under a Dancing Master's care. Indeed he seems to shame Education, for his manners are so extremely graceful, and he is so polite, attentive, and easy, that you would have thought he came from some foreign Court. You will think that I speak in a *high* style; but I assure you there was but one opinion about him.

At dinner I had the pleasure of sitting next to him, as my cold kept me near the fire. The moment he was helped, he presented his plate to me, which, when I declined, he had not the *over-shot* politeness to offer *all round,* as I have seen some people do, but took it quietly again. He eat heartily and committed not the slightest blunder at table, neither did he do anything *awkwardly* or *ungainly.* He found by the turn of the conversation, and some wry faces, that a joint of beef was not roasted enough, and therefore when he was helped, he took great pains to assure mama that he liked it, and said two or three times—*"very dood,—* very *dood."* It is very odd, but true, that he can pronounce the *th,* as in *thank you,* and the *w,* as in *well,* and yet cannot say *g,* which he uses a *d* for. But I now recollect, that in the beginning of a word, as *George,* he *can* pronounce it. . . .

He told Jem that he had an engagement at six o'clock, to go with Dr. Solander to see no less than twelve ladies.—Jem translated this to us—he understands enough of English to find out when he is talked of, in general, and so he did now, and he laughed heartily, and began to count, with his fingers, in order to be understood—"1, 2, 3, 4, 5, 6, 7, 8, 9, 10—*twelve—woman!"* said he. . . .

Before six, the coach came. Our man came in and said "Mr. Omai's servant." He heard it at once, and answered *"very well."* He kept his seat about five minutes after, and then rose and got his hat and sword. My father happening to be talking to Mr. Strange, Omai stood still, neither chusing to interrupt him, nor to make his compliments to any body else first. When he was disengaged, Omai went up to him, and made an exceeding fine bow —the same to mama—then separately to every one in the company, and then went out with Jem to his coach.

He must certainly possess an uncommon share of observation and attention. I assure you every body was delighted with him. I only wished I could have spoke his language. Lord Sandwich has actually studied it so as to make himself understood in it. His *hands* are very much *tattooed,* but his face is not at all. He is *by no means* handsome, though I like his *countenance.* . . .

If I have been too *prolix,* you must excuse me, because it is wholly owing to the great curiosity I have heard you express for whatever concerns Omai. My father desires his love to you, and says that if you will but come to town, as soon as Omai returns from Hinchinbrooke, he will promise you that you shall still have a meeting with him. . . .

> Adieu, my dear Sir,
> I beg you to believe me,
> Your ever affectionate
> and obliged
> F. BURNEY

[1775]

[January (?)]

I am now going to give myself the delight of recounting an evening with the celebrated Signora Agujari; *detta la Bastardini,* from some misfortune that preceded her birth, but of which none so innocent as herself.[36] The visit had been some time arranged, and we expected her with extreme impatience. Dr. Matty who is a little, formal, affected man, but held in the highest class for learning, handed and presented Signora Agujari. She was accompanied by Signor Colla, an Italian musician, and the Revd. Mr. Penneck. She is of the middle stature, and has the misfortune to be lame; owing perhaps if there is any truth in the story to her being mauled when an infant by a pig, in consequence of which she is reported to have a silver side. Her face is handsome, and expressive of all her words. She has the character of being immensely proud. She was, however, all civility here, though her excessive *vanity* was perpetually self betrayed. Signor Colla, to whom she is reported to be married, is a lively,—I might almost say, *fiery* Italian.[37] She sings no songs but of his composition, and he is her constant attendant. . . .

The conversation was chiefly in French. As soon as public plans
were mentioned, Signora Agujari asked us if we had been to the
Pantheon?[38] and lifted up her hands and eyes, when she heard
we had not, doubtless concluding us to the highest degree barbarous and Gothic, not to have flown on the wings of—*half
Guineas*—to see and hear this Wonder of the World. We all were,
however, languishing to hear her, though as it was not perfectly
convenient to us to offer her fifty guineas for a song, we were
somewhat in fear of requesting one. My father *hinted* it to Dr.
Maty, Dr. Maty hinted it to Signor Colla; Signor Colla did not
take the hint of hinting it to the Bastardini. He said that she certainly would sing to *the Doctor Burney;* but that she had a slight
sore throat, and would wish to sing *to him* to the greatest advantage. He then launched into most profuse panygyric of my
father, of his fame abroad, and of the great happiness he had in
being introduced to a so *célèbre homme.*

We were all disappointed; but Signora Agujari promised to
make us another visit very soon, when she would bring two of her
most favourite airs with her. . . .

This singer is really a *slave* to her voice; she fears the least
breath of air. She is equally apprehensive of any heat. She
seems to have a perpetual anxiety lest she should take cold; and
I do believe that she neither eats, drinks, sleeps, nor talks, without
considering in what manner she may perform those vulgar duties
of life, so as to be most beneficial to her voice. However, there are
so few who are gifted with eminent talents, that it is better to
cultivate them, even laboriously, than to let them suffer injury
from carelessness or neglect. . . .

March 4

I had yesterday the honour of drinking tea in company with
His *Abyssinian Majesty* Mr. Bruce; for so Mrs. Strange calls Mr.
Bruce. My mother and I went to Mr. Strange's by appointment,
to meet Mr. and Mrs. Turner of Lynn, who are lately become
acquainted in that family, and who are in town for the winter;[39] and this Majestic Personage chanced to be there. He has
been acquainted intimately with Mrs. Strange all his life, and
is very much attached to her and her family. He seldom passes

a day without visiting her; but Miss Strange who has told me of many of his singularities, says that he is generally put into a *pet* when they have any company, as his excessive haughtiness prevents his being sociable with them, and makes him think them impertinant, if they take the liberty to speak to him. Indeed, she told me he has been really very ill-used from the curiosity, which previous to his provocation, he *did* satisfy, for many people gathered anecdotes and observations from him, and then printed them. This ... as he intends ... to publish his travels himself, was most abominably provoking. It is not enough to say, that this put him *upon his guard,* it has really made him shy of being asked how he does? or, what's o'clock? Haughty by nature, his extraordinary travels, and perhaps his long residence among savages have contributed to render him one of the most imperious of men; he is indeed by far the most so, that *I* ever saw. He is more than six foot high, is extremely well proportioned in shape, and has a handsome and expressive face. If his vanity is half as great as his pride, he would certainly become more courteous, if he knew how much smiles become him, for when he is pleased to soften the severity of his countenance, and to suffer his features to relax into smiling, he is quite another creature. ... Mr. Bruce, as my father did not accompany us, I doubt not wished himself alone with the Stranges; for he looked so important, that he awed almost into total silence Mr. and Mrs. Turner; who secretly wished the same for themselves. Mr. Turner, who is a very *jocular* man, could not bear to be deprived of his laugh, and yet had not courage sufficient to venture at joking before so terrible a man, who looks as if born to command the world! Besides, he had heard so much of his character before they met, that he was *prepared* to fear him; and Mrs. Turner is too little used to the company of strangers, to be at her ease when in it.

As to my little self, I sat next to Miss Strange, and was comfortable enough in conversing with her, till my mother finding herself little noticed by the Great Man, quitted her seat, and went and placed herself next to Mrs. Turner, saying, "I shall come and sit by you, and leave Mr. Bruce to the young lassies." I do heartily hate these sort of speeches, which *oblige* one to be remarked; nothing can be more provoking. Mr. Bruce, accordingly turning towards me, said, "Well, Miss Burney, I think you can do no less than take the seat your mamma has left." I did not half like it; but thought he would suppose *me* afraid of him, if I refused; so, I . . . changed chairs, but made signs to Miss Strange to move next to me, and immediately renewed our conversation, lest he should think himself obliged to take further notice of me.

A very strange Advertisement had been put in the papers the evening before, which said that Mr. Bruce was *dying* or *dead*. My father who knew he was well, wafered the paragraph upon a sheet of paper, and sent it to his lodgings. My mother asked him if he had seen it? "I thought," answered he, "it had come from *Brucey*," for Miss Strange, who was christened *Bruce*, he always calls *Brucey*. "Yes; I saw it and read my death with great composure." Then turning himself to me, he added, "was you not sorry, Miss Burney, to read of my death?"

These immense-sized men speak to little women, as if they were children. I answered, that, as my father had seen him the day before, I was not much *alarmed*. Mr. Turner, then gathering courage, said, "Well, Sir, I think, as times go, it is very well that when they killed you, they said no ill of you."

"I know of no reason they had to do otherwise," answered Mr. Bruce so haughtily, that Mr. Turner, failing in his first attempt, never afterwards spoke to him, or indeed hardly opened his mouth.

May 8

This month is called a *tender* one. It has proved so *to* me—but not *in* me. I have not breathed one sigh,—felt one sensation,—or uttered one folly the more for the softness of the season. However I have met with a youth whose heart, if he is to be credited, has been less guarded—indeed it has yielded itself so suddenly, that had it been in any other month—I should not have known how to have accounted for so easy a conquest.

The first day of this month I drank tea and spent the evening at Mr. Burney's, at the request of my sister, to meet a very stupid family, which she told me it would be charity to herself to give my time to. This family consisted of Mrs. O'Connor and her daughter, by a first marriage, Miss Dickenson, who, poor creature, has the misfortune to be deaf and dumb. They are very old acquaintances of my grandmother Burney, to oblige whom my sister invited them. My grandmother and two aunts therefore were of the party:—as was also Mr. Barlow, a young man who has lived and boarded with Mrs. O'Connor for about two years.[40]

Mr. Barlow is rather short, but handsome. He is a very well bred . . . good-tempered and sensible young man. . . . He bears an excellent character both for disposition and morals. He has read more than he has conversed, and seems to know but little of the world; his language therefore is stiff and uncommon, and seems laboured, if not affected—he has a great desire to please, but no elegance of manners; neither, though he may be very worthy, is he at all agreeable.

Unfortunately, however, he happened to be prodigiously civil to me, and though I have met with much more gallantry occasionally, yet I could not but observe a *seriousness* of attention much more expressive than complimenting.

As my sister knew not well how to *wile away the time*, I proposed, after supper, a round of cross questions. This was agreed to. Mr. Barlow, who sat next to me, took near half an hour to settle upon what he should ask me, and at last his question was —What I thought most necessary in Love? I answered—*Constancy*. I hope for his own sake he will not remember this answer long, though he readily subscribed to it at the time.

The coach came for me about eleven. I rose to go. He earnestly entreated me to stay one or two minutes. I did not, however, think such compliance at all requisite, and therefore only offered to set my grandmother down in my way. The party then broke up. Mrs. O'Connor began an urgent invitation to all present to return the visit the next week. Mr. Barlow, who followed me, repeated it very pressingly, to *me*, hoping I would make one. I promised that I would. . . .

Four days after this meeting, my mother and Mrs. Young[41] happened to be in the parlour when I received a letter which, from the strong resemblance of the handwriting in the direction to that of Mr. Crisp, I immediately opened and thought came from Chessington; but what was my surprise to see "Madam," at the beginning, and at the conclusion,—"Your sincere admirer and very humble ser^t Thos. Barlow."

I read it three or four times before I could credit my eyes. An acquaintance so short, and a procedure so hasty astonished me. It is a most tender epistle, and contains a passionate declaration of attachment, hinting at hopes of a *return*, and so forth. . . .

I took not a moment to deliberate.—I felt that my heart was totally insensible—and I felt that I could never consent to unite myself to a man who I did not *very* highly value.

However, as I do not consider myself as an independent member of society, and as I knew I could depend upon my father's kindness, I thought it incumbent upon me to act with his concurrence, I therefore, at night, before I sent an answer shewed him the letter. He asked me a great many questions. I assured him that forming a connection without attachment—(and that I was totally indifferent to the youth in question) was what I could never think of. My father was all indulgence and goodness. He at first proposed that I should write him word that our acquaintance had been too short to authorise so high an opinion as he expressed for me; but I objected to that as seeming to infer that a *longer* acquaintance might be acceptable: he therefore concluded upon the whole that I should send no answer at all.

I was not very easy at this determination, as it seemed to treat Mr. Barlow with a degree of contempt which his partiality to me by no means merited from myself; and I apprehended it to be possible for him to put, perhaps, *another* and more favourable interpretation upon my silence. I shewed Hetty the letter next day. She most vehemently took the young man's part; urged me to think differently, and above all advised me to certainly write an answer, and to be of their party, according to my promise, when they went to Mrs. O'Connor's.

I told her I would speak to my father again in regard to writing an answer, which I wished much to do, but could not now without his consent; but as to the party I could not make one as it would be a kind of tacit approbation and assent of his further attentions.

I went afterwards to call on my grandmother; my sister followed me, and directly told her and my aunts of the affair. They all of them became most zealous advocates for Mr. Barlow. They spoke most highly of the character they had heard of him, and my aunt Anne humourously bid me beware of her and Beckey's fate!

I assured them I was not intimidated, and that I had rather a thousand times die an old maid than be married, except from affection.

When I came home I wrote the following answer which I proposed sending, with my father's leave.

> Miss Burney presents her compliments to Mr. Barlow. She is much obliged for, though greatly surprised at the good opinion with which on so short an acquaintance he is pleased to honour her. She wishes Mr. Barlow all happiness, but must beg leave to recommend to him to transfer to some person better known to him a partiality which she so little merits.

My father, however, did not approve of my writing, I could not imagine why; but have since heard from my sister that he was unwilling I should give a No without some further knowledge of the young man.

Further knowledge will little avail in connections of this sort; the *heart* ought to be heard, and mine will never speak a word I am sure, for any one I do not truly enough honour to cheerfully, in all things serious, obey. How hard must be the duty of a wife practised without high esteem! And I am too spoilt by such men as my father and Mr. Crisp to content myself with a character merely inoffensive. I should expire of fatigue with him.

My sister was not contented with giving her own advice; she wrote about the affair to Mr. Crisp, representing in the strongest light the utility of my listening to Mr. Barlow. He has written me such a letter! God knows how I shall answer it. Every body is against me but my beloved father. . . . They all of them are kindly interested in my welfare; but they know not so well as myself what may make me happy or miserable. To unite myself for life to a man who is not *infinitely* dear to me is what I can never, never consent to, unless, indeed, I was strongly urged by my father. I thank God most gratefully he has not interfered. . . .

From Mr. Crisp

Chessington, May 8

So much of the future good or ill of your life seems now depending, Fanny, that I cannot dispense with myself from giving you (without being called upon) my whole sentiments on a subject, which I dare say you already guess at. Hetty (as she told you she would) has disclosed the affair to me. . . .

. . . Such a man, as this young Barlow if ever you are so lucky and so well-advis'd, as to be united to him, will improve upon you every hour. You will discover in him graces and charms which kindness will bring to light, that at present you have no idea of;—I mean, if his character is truly given by Hetty. That is the grand object of enquiry, as likewise his circumstances; this last, as the great sheet-anchor, upon which we are to depend in our voyage through life, ought most minutely to be scrutiniz'd. Is he of any profession, or only of an independent fortune? if either, or both, sufficient to promise a . . . comfortable income. You may live to the age of your grandmother, and not meet with so valuable an offer. . . . Look round you, Fan; look at your aunts! *Fanny Burney* won't always be what she is now! Mrs. Hamilton once had an offer of £3000 a-year, or near it; a parcel of young giggling girls laugh'd her out of it.[42] The man, forsooth, was not quite smart enough, though otherwise estimable. Oh, Fan, this is not a marrying age, without a handsome Fortune! . . . . Suppose you to lose your father,—take in all chances. Consider the situation of an unprotected, unprovided woman! Excuse my being so earnest with you. Assure yourself it proceeds from my regard, and from (let me say it though it savors of vanity) a deep knowledge of the world. Observe how far I go; I don't urge you, hand over head, to have this man at all events; but, for God's sake and your own sake, give him and yourself fair play. Don't decide so positively against it. If you do, you are ridiculous to a high degree. If you don't answer his letter, don't avoid seeing him. At all events, I charge you on my blessing to attend Hetty in her visit to the O'Connors, according to your promise, and which you can't get off without positive rudeness. This binds you to nothing; it leaves an opening for future consideration and enquiry, and is barely decent. . . . So, adieu! you have the best wishes of your affectionate Daddy,

S. C.

[*June*]

. . . [O]n Saturday morning, while we were at breakfast, I had a letter brought me in a hand which I immediately knew to be his. . . .

Notwithstanding I was at once sorry and provoked at perceiving how sanguine this youth chose to be I was not absolutely concerned at receiving this 2ⁿᵈ letter, because I regarded it as a fortunate opportunity of putting an unalterable conclusion to the whole affair. However, . . . I thought it my duty to speak to my father before I sent an answer, never doubting his immediate concurrence.

My mother, Sukey,[43] and I went to the Opera that evening; it was therefore too late when I returned to send a letter to Hoxton—but I went up stairs into the study, and told my father I had received another epistle from Mr. Barlow, which I could only attribute to my not answering, as I had wished, his first. I added that I proposed, with his leave, to write to Mr. Barlow the next morning.

My father looked grave, asked me for the letter, put it in his pocket unread, and wished me good night.

I was seized with a kind of *pannic*. I trembled at the idea of his espousing, however mildly, the cause of this young man. I passed a restless night, and in the morning dared not write without his permisson, which I was now half afraid to ask.

About 2 o'clock, while I was dawdling in the study, and waiting for an opportunity to speak, we heard a rap at the door and soon after John came in and said—"A gentleman is below, who asks for Miss Burney: Mr. Barlow." I think I was never more distressed in my life—to have taken pains to avoid a private conversation so highly disagreeable to me, and at last to be forced into it at so unfavourable a juncture, for I had now *two* letters from him, both unanswered, and consequently open to his conjectures. I exclaimed—"Lord! how provoking! what shall I do?"

My father looked uneasy and perplexed: he said something about not being hasty, which I did not desire him to explain. Terrified lest he should hint at the advantage of an early establishment—like Mr. Crisp—quick from the study—but slow enough afterwards—I went down stairs. I saw my mother pass from the front into the back parlour; which did not add to the *graciousness* of my reception of poor Mr. Barlow, who I found alone in the front parlour. I was not sorry that none of the family were there, as I now began to seriously dread any protraction of this affair.

He came up to me with an air of *tenderness* and satisfaction, began some anxious enquiries about my health; but I interrupted him with saying—"I fancy, Sir, you have not received a letter I—I——"

I stopt, for I could not say which I had *sent!*

"A letter?—No, Ma'am!"

"You will have it, then, to-morrow, Sir."

We were both silent for a minute or two, when he said—"In consequence I presume, Ma'am, of the one I——"

"Yes, Sir," cried I.

"And pray—Ma'am—Miss Burney!—may I—beg to ask the contents?—that is—the—the—." He could not go on.

"Sir—I—it was only—it was merely—in short, you will see it to-morrow."

"But if you would favour me with the contents now, I could perhaps answer it at once?"

"Sir, it requires no answer!"

A second silence ensued. I was really distressed myself to see *his* distress, which was very apparent. After some time he stammered out something of *hoping,* and *beseeching*—which, gathering more firmness, I answered—"I am much obliged to you, Sir, for the too good opinion you are pleased to have of me—but I should be very sorry you should lose any more time upon my account—as I have no thoughts of changing my situation and abode."

He seemed to be quite overset: having, therefore, so freely explained myself, I then asked him to sit down, and began to talk of the weather. When he had a little recovered himself, he drew a chair close to me and began making most ardent professions of respect and regard, and so forth. I interrupted him as soon as I could, and begged him to rest satisfied with my answer. . . .

He looked very much mortified, and said in a dejected voice—"If there is anything in me—in my connexions—or in my situation in life, which you wholly think unworthy of you—and beneath you—or if my character, or disposition meet with your disapprobation—I will immediately forgo all—I will not—I would not——"

"No, indeed, Sir," cried I, "I have neither seen or heard of anything of you that was to your disadvantage—and I have no doubts of your worthiness—"

He thanked me, and seemed reassured; but renewed his solicitations in the most urgent manner. He repeatedly begged my permission to acquaint my family of the state of his affairs, and to abide by their decision; but I would not let him say two words following upon that subject. I told him that my answer was a final one, and begged him to take it as such.

He remonstrated very earnestly. "This is the severest decision! . . . Surely you must allow that the *social state* is what we were all meant for?—that we were created for one another?—that to form such a resolution is contrary to the design of our being?"—

"All this may be true," said I, "I have nothing to say in contradiction to it—but you know there are many odd characters in the world—and I am one of them."

"O, no, no, no,—that can never be! but is it possible that you can have so bad an opinion of the Married State? It seems to me the *only* state for happiness!"

"Well, Sir, *you* are attracted to the married life—I am to the single—therefore *every man in his humour*—do *you* follow *your* opinion—and let *me* follow *mine*."

"But, surely—is not this *singular?*"

"I give you leave, Sir," cried I, laughing, "to think me singular—odd—queer—nay, even whimsical, if you please."

"But, my *dear* Miss Burney, only——"

"I entreat you, Sir, to take my answer—you really pain me by being so urgent."

"That would not I do for the world!—I only beg you to suffer me—perhaps in future——"

"No, indeed, I shall never change—I do assure you you will find me very obstinate!"

He began to lament his own destiny. I grew extremely tired of so often saying the same thing; but I could not absolutely turn him out of the house; and, indeed, he seemed so dejected and unhappy, that I made it my study to soften my refusal as much as I could without leaving room for future expectations. . . .

His entreaties grew now extremely . . . distressing to me. He besought me to take more time, and said it should be the study of his life to make me happy. "Allow me, my *dear* Miss Burney, only to hope that my future conduct——"

"I shall always think myself obliged, nay, honoured by your good opinion—and you are entitled to my best wishes for your health and happiness—but, indeed, the less we meet the better."

"What—what can I do?" cried he very sorrowfully.

"Why—go and *ponder* upon this affair for about half an hour. Then say—what an odd, queer, strange creature she is—and then —think of something else."

"O no, no!—you cannot suppose all that? I shall think of nothing else;—*your* refusal is more pleasing than any other lady's acceptance—"

He said this very simply, but too seriously for me to laugh at. . . .

He then took his leave:—returned back;—took leave;—and returned again. I now made a more formal reverence of the head, at the same time expressing my good wishes for his welfare, in a sort of way that implied I expected never to see him again. He would fain have taken a more *tender* leave of me,—but I repulsed him with great surprise and displeasure. I did not, however, as he was so terribly sorrowful refuse him my hand, which he had made sundry attempts to take in the course of conversation. When I withdrew it, as I did presently, I rang the bell to prevent his again returning from the door.

Though I was really sorry for the unfortunate and misplaced attachment which this young man professes for me, yet I could almost have *jumped* for joy when he was gone, to think that the affair was thus finally over.

Indeed I think it hardly possible for a woman to be in a more irksome situation than when rejecting a worthy man, who is all humility, respect, and submission, and who throws himself and his fortune at her feet. . . .

My father sent for Hetty up stairs and made a thousand enquiries concerning Mr. Barlow.

The next day, a day, the remembrance of which will be never erased from my memory,—my father first spoke to me *in favour* of Mr. Barlow, and desired me not to be *peremptory* in the answer I was going to write, though it was to appear written previously.

I scarce made any answer; I was terrified to death. I felt the utter impossibility of resisting not merely my father's *persuasion*, but even his *advice*. I felt too, that I had no argumentative objections to make to Mr. Barlow, his character—disposition—situation—I know nothing against; but, O! I felt he was no companion for my heart! I wept like an infant, when alone; eat nothing; seemed as if already married, and passed the whole day in more misery than, merely on my own account, I ever did before in my life, except when a child, upon the loss of my own beloved mother, and ever revered and most dear grandmother!

After supper I went into the study, while my dear father was alone, to wish him good night; which I did as cheerfully as I could, though pretty evidently in dreadful uneasiness. When I had got to the door, he called me back, and asked some questions concerning a new Court mourning gown . . . kindly saying he would assist Susey and me in our fitting-out, which he accordingly did, and affectionately embraced me, saying, "I wish I could do more for thee, Fanny!" "Oh, Sir;" cried I, "*I* wish for nothing! only let me live with you." "My life!" cried he, kissing me kindly, "Thou shalt live with me for ever, if thee wilt! Thou canst not think I meant to get rid of thee?"

"I could not Sir; I could not!" cried I; "I could not outlive such a thought!" and, as I kissed him—O! how gratefully and thankfully! with what a relief to my heart! I saw his eyes full of tears! a mark of his tenderness which I shall never forget! "God knows," continued he, "I wish not to part with my girls! only, don't be too hasty!"

Thus relieved, restored to future hopes, I went to bed, light, happy, and thankful, as if escaped from destruction. . . .

From that day to this my father, I thank Heaven, has never again mentioned Mr. Barlow.

November 21

My father had a little Concert in honour of Prince Orloff, of Russia,[44] at the request of Dr. King,[45] to whom he was patron during his chaplainship in Petersburg.

This Prince is, by some, supposed to be the very man, who seized the late Czar; but however that may have been, he was certainly the man, who was honoured with the Czarina's most unbounded favour, loaded with marks of distinction, and known as the chief influencer of her conduct, and favourite of her heart. He went lately on an Embassy to Constantinople, about the Peace with the Turks; and on his return found that the Empress had suffered some other to supplant him in her good graces; and this has induced him to travel, and occasioned his visit to England. Many Russians of distinction are in his suite, and they were all invited here. . . .

Enter His Highness Prince Orloff. This prince is of a prodigious stature, something resembling Mr. Bruce. He is handsome, tall, fat, upright, and *magnifique*. His dress was superb; besides a Blue Ribbon, he had a Star of Diamonds of the most dazzling lustre; a shoulder-knot of the same brilliancy, . . . and a picture of the Empress was hung upon his neck, which was set round with three rows of diamonds of the first magnitude and beauty. His air and address were gracious and condescending; and he seemed to have a very agreeable share of drollery in his composition. He was attended by a Russian nobleman, whose name I have forgot, and by General Baur, a Hessian. . . . His introduction to my father, in which Dr. King figured, passed in the dining-room; after which he came into the library. Lord Bruce immediately rose and made way for him. The Prince who knew him, called out, "Ah! Milord me fuye!" Mr. Brudenel who had also the honour of being known to him, made a profound reverence, and was removing from his seat, to offer it to *Son Altesse*, but the Prince would by no means be induced to accept it. He retreated;—insisted on Mr. Brudenel's keeping his place; or declared he would himself retire. . . .

I said in a low voice to Mr. Chamier, that I *hated* such monstrous tall men. Mr. Chamier, with a very arch look, said, "He has not been so unhappy, as to meet with such objections *every* where!" I knew he meant the Empress; but not *choosing* to understand him, I only added, according, indeed, to all my meaning, that they made *me*, and such as *me*, look so very insignificantly pigmy. . . .

Prince Orloff enquired of Dr. King very particularly who we all were. The Doctor (who told us afterwards) to save trouble, told His Highness, that all who were in black, were Dr. Burney's daughters. At which the Prince exclaimed, he should have thought it impossible, for that my father did not look above thirty years of age.

Mr. Harris in a whisper said to me that he wished some of *the ladies* would express a desire of seeing the Empress's picture; "for," continued he, "*I*, you know, as a *man*, cannot, though I much wish it, for my old eyes cannot see it at this distance."

I immediately applied to Dr. King, who whispered to M. de Demidoff, who hinted to the General, who boldly made the request to the Prince, in the name of *the ladies*.

The Prince instantly, and with the utmost good-humour, asked the General to untie the picture from his neck, and had it

handed about. He was very facetious upon the occasion, and declared that, if they wished *the ladies* might *strip him entirely!*
Mr. Pogenpohl's gallantry was far more polished. I was amazed,
at this near view, at the size of the diamonds, which are set round
the picture; one of them, I really believe, was as big as a nutmeg.

They stayed and chatted some time after the music was over,
and were extremely lively and agreeable. . . .

December 30

My brother James, to our great joy and satisfaction, is returned
home safe from America, which he has left in most terrible disorder. He is extremely well in health and spirits; and has undergone great hardships, which he has, however, gained both credit
and friends by. He has a brave soul, and disdains all self-ap-
plause and egotism; nevertheless he has so honourably increased
his friends and gained reputation, that it is not in the power of
his forbearance or modesty to conceal it. He is now in very good
time for his favourite voyage to the South Seas, which we believe
will take place in February.[46] . . .

[1777]

TO MR. CRISP

March 27 and 28

MY DEAR DADDY—. . . So now, to our Thursday morning party.
Mrs. and Miss Thrale,[47] Miss Owen,[48] and Mr. Seward[49]
came long before *Lexiphanes.*[50] Mrs. Thrale is a very pretty
woman still; she is extremely lively and chatty; has no supercil-
ious or pedantic airs, and is really gay and agreeable. Her daughter is about twelve years old, stiff and proud, I believe, or else shy
and reserved: I don't yet know which. Miss Owen, who is a relation, is good-humoured and *sensible enough;* she is a sort of butt,
and, as such, a general favourite; for those sort of characters are

prodigiously useful in drawing out the wit and pleasantry of others. Mr. Seward is a very polite, agreeable young man.

My sister Burney was invited to meet and play to them. The conversation was supported with a good deal of vivacity (N.B. my father being at home) for about half an hour, and then Hetty and *Sukey,* for the first time *in public,* played a duet; and in the midst of this performance Dr. Johnson was announced. He is, indeed, very ill-favoured; is tall and stout; but stoops terribly; he is almost bent double. His mouth is almost constantly opening and shutting, as if he was chewing. He has a strange method of frequently twirling his fingers, and twisting his hands. His body is in continual agitation, *see-sawing* up and down; his feet are never a moment quiet; and, in short, his whole person is in *perpetual motion.* His dress, too, considering the times, and that he had meant to put on his *best becomes,* being engaged to dine in a large company, was as much out of the common road as his figure; he had a large wig, snuff-colour coat, and gold buttons, but no ruffles to his shirt, doughty fists, and black worsted stockings. He is shockingly near-sighted, and did not, till she held out her hand to him, even know Mrs. Thrale. He *poked his nose* over the keys of the harpsichord, till the duet was finished, and then my father introduced Hetty to him as an old acquaintance, and he cordially kissed her! When she was a little girl, he had made her a present of *"The Idler."*[51]

His attention, however, was not to be diverted five minutes from the books, as we were in the library; he pored over them, shelf by shelf, almost touching the backs of them with his eyelashes, as he read their titles. At last, having fixed upon one, he began, without further ceremony, to read to himself, all the time standing at a distance from the company. We were all very much provoked, as we perfectly languished to hear him talk; but it seems he is the most silent creature, when not particularly drawn out, in the world. . . .

Chocolate being then brought, we adjourned to the dining-room. And here, Dr. Johnson being taken from the books, entered freely and most cleverly into conversation; though it is remarkable he never speaks at all, but when spoken to; nor does he ever *start,* though he so admirably *supports,* any subject.

The whole party was engaged to dine at Mrs. Montagu's.[52] Dr. Johnson said he had received the most flattering note he had ever read, or that any body else had ever read, by way of invitation. "Well! so have I too," cried Mrs. Thrale; "so if a note from Mrs. Montagu is to be boasted of; I beg mine may not be forgot."

"*Your* note," cried Dr. Johnson, "can bear no comparison with *mine;* I am *at the head of the Philosophers,* she says."

"And I," cried Mrs. Thrale, "*have all the Muses in my train!*"

"A fair battle," said my father. "Come, compliment for compliment, and see who will hold out longest."

"O! I am afraid for Mrs. Thrale," cried Mr. Seward; "for I know Mrs. Montagu exerts all her forces, when she attacks Dr. Johnson."

"O, yes!" said Mrs. Thrale, "she has often, I know, flattered *him,* till he has been ready to faint."

"Well, ladies," said my father, "you must get him between you to-day, and see which can lay on the paint thickest, Mrs. Thrale or Mrs. Montagu." . . .

After this, they talked of Mr. Garrick and his late exhibition before the King, to whom and to the Queen and Royal Family he read Lethe *in character, c'est à dire,* in different voices, and theatrically.[53] Mr. Seward gave us an account of a Fable, which Mr. Garrick had written, by way of prologue or Introduction, upon the occasion. In this he says, that a blackbird, grown old and feeble, droops his wings &c. &c., and gives up singing; but being called upon by the eagle, his voice recovers its powers, his spirits revive, he sets age at defiance, and sings better than ever. The application is obvious.

"There is not," said Dr. Johnson, "much of the spirit of *fabulosity* in this Fable; for the *call* of an eagle never yet had much tendency to restore the voice of a *black-bird!* 'Tis true that the fabulists frequently make the *wolves* converse with the *lambs;* but, when the conversation is over, the *lambs* are sure to be eaten! And so the *eagle* may entertain the *black-bird;* but the entertainment always ends in a feast for the *eagle.*"

"They say," cried Mrs. Thrale, "that Garrick was extremely hurt at the coolness of the King's applause, and did not find his reception such as he expected."

"He has been so long accustomed," said Mr. Seward, "to the thundering approbation of the Theatre, that a mere '*Very well,*' must necessarily and naturally disappoint him."

"Sir," said Dr. Johnson, "he should not, in a Royal apartment,

expect the hallowing and clamour of the One Shilling Gallery.
The King, I doubt not, gave him as much applause, as was ra-
tionally his due; and, indeed, great and uncommon as is the merit
of Mr. Garrick, no man will be bold enough to assert he has not
had his just proportion both of fame and profit. He has long
reigned the unequalled favourite of the public; and therefore nobody will mourn his hard fate, if the King and the Royal Family
were not transported into rapture, upon hearing him read
Lethe. Yet Mr. Garrick will complain to his friends, and his friends
will lament the King's want of feeling and taste;—and then Mr.
Garrick will kindly *excuse* the King. He will say that His
Majesty might be thinking of something else; that the affairs of
America might occur to him; or some subject of more importance
than Lethe; but, though he will say this himself, he will not forgive his friends, if they do not contradict him!"

But, now that I have written this satire, it is but just both to Mr.
Garrick and to Dr. Johnson, to tell you what he said of him afterwards, when he discriminated his character with equal candour
and humour.

"Garrick," said he, "is accused of vanity; but few men would
have borne such unremitting prosperity with greater, if with equal
moderation. He is accused, too, of avarice; but, were he not, he
would be accused of just the contrary; for he now lives rather as
a prince than an actor; but the frugality he practised, when he
first appeared in the world, and which, even then was perhaps
beyond his necessity, has marked his character ever since; and
now, though his table, his equipage, and manner of living, are all
the most expensive, and equal to those of a nobleman, yet the original stain still blots his name! Though, had he not fixed upon
himself the charge of avarice, he would long since have been re-
proached with luxury and with living beyond his station in
magnificence and splendour." . . .

[*April*]

O Yes!

Be it known to all whom it may concern, c'est à dire, in the first
place,—Nobody;—in the second place, the same person;—and in
the third place, *Ditto,*—That Frances Burney, Spinster, of the

Parish of Saint Martin's in the Fields, . . . did keep no Journal this unhappy year, till she wrote from Worcester to her Sister Susan of the same parish, and likewise a spinster.[54] There are who may live to mourn this. For my part, I shall not here enumerate all the particular misfortunes which this gap in literature may occasion, though I feel that they will be of a nature most serious and melancholy; but I shall merely scrawl down such matters of moment as will be requisite to mention, in order to make the Worcester Journal, which is a delicious morsel of learning and profound reasoning, intelligible to the three persons mentioned above.

When with infinite toil and labour, during the last year, I had transcribed in a feigned hand the second Volume of my new Essay,[55] I sent it by my brother Charles to Mr. Lowndes.[56] The fear of discovery, or of suspicion in the house, made the copying extremely laborious to me; for in the day time, I could only take odd moments, so that I was obliged to sit up the greatest part of many nights, in order to get it ready. And, after all this *fagging*, Mr. Lowndes sent me word, that he approved of the book; but could not think of printing it, till it was finished; that it would be a great disadvantage to it, and that he would wait my time, and hoped to see it again, as soon as it was completed.

Now, this man, knowing nothing of my situation, supposed, in all probability, that I could seat myself quietly at my bureau, and write on with all expedition and ease, till the work was finished. But so different was the case, that I had hardly time to write half a page in a day; and neither my health nor inclination would allow me to continue my *nocturnal* scribbling for so long a time, as to write first, and then copy, a whole volume. I was therefore obliged to give the attempt and affair entirely over for the present.

In March I made a long and happy visit to my ever-dear and ever-kind Mr. Crisp. There is no place where I more really *enjoy myself* than at Chessington. All the household are kind, hospitable, and partial to me; there is no sort of restraint; every body is disengaged, and at liberty to pursue their own inclinations; and my Daddy Crisp, who is the soul of the place, is at once so flatteringly affectionate to *me*, and so infinitely, so beyond comparison clever in *himself*, that were I to be otherwise than happy in his company, I must either be wholly without feeling or utterly destitute of understanding.

From this loved spot I was suddenly hurried by intelligence, that my uncle was coming to town. And the fear that he would be displeased at finding that I made a visit to Chessington nearly at the time I was invited to Barborne, made me not dare out-stay the intelligence of his intended journey. He brought with him his son James and his daughter Beckey. . . .

My uncle's professed intention in his journey, was to carry me back to Barborne; and he would not be denied; nor let my father rest, till he obtained his leave. And so, escorted by my uncle and cousin James, I set off for Worcester the beginning of April.

But, before I made this journey, while I was taking leave, I was so much penetrated by my dear father's kind parting embrace, that in the fullness of my heart I could not forbear telling him, that I had sent a manuscript to Mr. Lowndes; earnestly, however, beseeching him never to divulge it, nor to demand a sight of such trash as I could scribble; assuring him that Charles had managed to save me from being at all suspected. He could not help laughing; but I believe was much surprised at the communication. He desired me to acquaint him from time to time, how *my work* went on, called himself the *Pere confident,* and kindly promised to guard my secret as cautiously as I could wish.

So much to prelude the Worcester Journal.

But, when I told my dear father, I *never* wished or intended, that even he himself should see my essay, he forbore to ask me its name, or make any enquiries. I believe he is not sorry to be saved the giving me the pain of his criticism. He made no sort of objection to my having my own way in total secrecy and silence to all the world. Yet I am easier in not taking the step, without his having this little knowledge of it, as he is contented with my telling him I shall never have the courage to let him know its name.

FAME

[1778-1786]

[1778]

This year was ushered in by a grand and most important event! At the latter end of January the literary world was favoured with the first publication of the ingenious, learned, and most profound Fanny Burney! I doubt not but this memorable affair will, in future times, mark the period whence chronologers will date the zenith of the polite arts in this island!

This admirable authoress has named her most elaborate performance, *Evelina, or, a Young Lady's Entrance Into the World.*[1]

Perhaps this may seem a rather bold attempt and title, for a female whose knowledge of the world is very confined, and whose inclinations, as well as situation, incline her to a private and domestic life. All I can urge is, that I have only presumed to trace the accidents and adventures to which a "young woman" is liable; I have not pretended to show the world what it actually *is,* but what it *appears* to a girl of seventeen: and so far as that, surely any girl who is past seventeen may safely do? . . .

Chessington, June 18

. . . I came hither the first week in May.[2] My recovery from that time to this has been slow and sure, but as I could walk hardly three yards in a day at first, I found so much time to spare that I could not resist treating myself with a little private sport with *Evelina,* a young lady whom, I think, I have some right to make free with. I had promised *Hetty* that *she* should read it to Mr. Crisp, at her own particular request; but I wrote my excuses and introduced it myself.

I told him it was a book which Hetty had taken to Brompton to divert my cousin Richard during his confinement. He was so indifferent about it that I thought he would not give himself the trouble to read it, and often embarrassed me by unlucky questions, such as "If it was reckoned clever?" and "What I thought of it?" and "Whether folks laughed at it?" I always evaded any direct or satisfactory answer, but he was so totally free from any idea of suspicion that my perplexity escaped his notice.

At length he desired me to begin reading to him. I dared not trust my voice with the little introductory ode, for as *that* is no romance, but the sincere effusion of my heart, I could as soon read aloud my own letters, written in my own name and character: I therefore skipped it, and have so kept the book out of his sight that, to this day, he knows not it is there. Indeed, I have since heartily repented that I read *any* of the book to him, for I found it a much more awkward thing than I had expected: my voice quite faltered when I began it, which, however, I passed off for the effect of remaining weakness of lungs, and, in short, from an invincible embarrassment, which I could not for a page together repress, the book, by my reading, lost all manner of spirit.

Nevertheless, though he has by no means treated it with the praise so lavishly bestowed upon it from other quarters, I had the satisfaction to observe that he was even greedily eager to go on with it, so that I flatter myself the *story* caught his attention: and, indeed, allowing for my *mauling* reading, he gave it quite as much credit as I had any reason to expect. But, now that I was sensible of my error in being my own mistress of the ceremonies, I determined to leave to Hetty the third volume, and therefore pretended I had not brought it. He was in a delightful ill humour about it, and I enjoyed his impatience far more than I should have done his forbearance. Hetty, therefore, when she comes, has undertaken to bring it.

. . . I received from Charlotte a letter, the most interesting that could be written to me, for it acquainted me that my dear father was, at length, reading my book, which has now been published six months.

How this has come to pass I am yet in the dark; but it seems the very moment almost that my mother and Susan and Sally[3] left the house, he desired Charlotte to bring him the *Monthly Review;* she contrived to look over his shoulder as he opened it, which he did at the account of *Evelina, or, a Young Lady's Entrance Into the World.* He read it with great earnestness, then put it down; and presently after snatched it up, and read it again. Doubtless his paternal heart felt some agitation for his girl in reading a review of her publication!—how he got at the name I cannot imagine.

Soon after he turned to Charlotte, and bidding her come close to him, he put his finger on the word *Evelina,* and saying, *she knew what it was,* bade her write down the name, and send the man to Lowndes, as if for herself. This she did, and away went William. . . .

When William returned he took the books from him, and the moment he was gone, opened the first volume—and opened it upon the *ode!*[4]

How great must have been his astonishment at seeing himself so addressed! Indeed, Charlotte says, he looked all amazement, read a line or two with great eagerness, and then, stopping short, he seemed quite affected, and the tears started into his eyes: dear soul! I am sure they did into mine, nay, I even sobbed, as I read the account.

I believe he was obliged to go out before he advanced much further. But the next day I had a letter from Susan, in which I heard that he had begun reading it with Lady Hales and Miss Coussmaker,[5] and that they liked it vastly!

Lady Hales spoke of it very innocently, in the highest terms, declaring she was sure it was written by somebody in high life, and that it had all the marks of real genius! She added, "he must be a man of great abilities!" . . .

Ha! ha! ha! that's my answer. They little think how well they are already acquainted with the writer they so much honour! Susan begged to have, then, my father's *real* and *final* opinion;— and it is such as I almost blush to write, even for my own private reading; but yet is such as I can by no means suffer to pass unrecorded, as my whole journal contains nothing so grateful to me. I will copy his own words, according to Susan's solemn declaration of their authenticity.

"Upon my word, I think it the best novel I know, excepting Fielding's, and, in some respects, *better* than his! I have been excessively pleased with it; there are, perhaps, a few things that might have been otherwise. . . . Evelina is in a new style, too, so perfectly innocent and natural; and the scene between her and her father, Sir John Belmont, is a scene for a tragedy! I blubbered at it, and Lady Hales and Miss Coussmaker are not yet recovered from hearing it; it made them quite ill: it is, indeed, wrought up in a most extraordinary manner!"

This account delighted me more than I can express. How little did I dream of ever being so much honoured! But the approbation of all the world put together, would not bear any competition, in my estimation, with that of my beloved father. . . .

What will all this come to?—where will it end? and when, and how, shall I wake from the vision of such splendid success? for I hardly know how to believe it real.

Well, I cannot but rejoice that I published the book, little as I ever imagined how it would fare; for hitherto it has occasioned me no small diversion, and *nothing* of the disagreeable sort. But I often think a change *will* happen, for I am by no means so sanguine as to suppose such success will be uninterrupted. Indeed, in the midst of the greatest satisfaction that I feel, an inward *something* which I cannot account for, prepares me to expect a reverse; for the more the book is drawn into notice, the more exposed it becomes to criticism and remark.

July 25

Mrs. Cholmondeley[6] has been reading and praising *Evelina*, and my father is quite delighted at her approbation, and told Susan that I could not have had a greater compliment than making two such women my friends as Mrs. Thrale and Mrs. Cholmondeley, for they were severe and knowing, and afraid of praising *à tort et à travers*, as their opinions are liable to be quoted.

Mrs. Thrale said she had only to complain it was too short. She recommended it to my mother to read!—how droll!—and she told her she would be much entertained with it, for there was a great deal of human life in it, and of the manners of the present times, and added it was written "by somebody who knows the top and the bottom, the highest and the lowest of mankind." She has even lent her set to my mother, who brought it home with her! . . .

To Miss S. Burney

Chessington, July 5, 1778

My Dearest Susy— . . . I often think, when I am counting my laurels, what a pity it would have been had I popped off in my last illness, without knowing what a person of consequence I was! —and I sometimes think that, were I now to have a relapse, I could never go off with so much *éclat!* I am now at the summit of a high hill; my prospects on one side are bright, glowing, and invitingly beautiful; but when I turn round, I perceive, on the other side, sundry caverns, gulphs, pits, and precipices, that, to look at, make my head giddy and my heart sick. I see about me, indeed, many hills of far greater height and sublimity; but I have not the strength to attempt climbing them; if I move, it must be downwards. I have already, I fear, reached the pinnacle of my abilities, and therefore to stand still will be my best policy.

But there is nothing under heaven so difficult to do. Creatures who are formed for motion *must* move, however great their inducements to forbear. The wisest course I could take, would be to bid an eternal adieu to writing; then would the cry be, " 'Tis pity she does not go on!—she might do something better by and by," etc., etc. *Evelina,* as a first and a youthful publication, has been received with the utmost favour and lenity; but would a future attempt be treated with the same mercy?—no, my dear Susy, quite the contrary; there would not, indeed, be the same plea to save it; it would no longer be a young lady's *first* appearance in public; those who have met with less indulgence would all peck at any second work; and even those who most encouraged the first offspring might prove enemies to the second, by receiving it with expectations which it could not answer: and so, between either the friends or the foes of the eldest, the second would stand an equally bad chance, and a million of flaws which were overlooked in the former would be ridiculed as villainous and intolerable blunders in the latter. . . .

[F. B.]

July 20

. . . I have also had a letter from Susanne. She informs me that my father, when he took the books back to Streatham, actually acquainted Mrs. Thrale with my secret. . . .

A hundred handsome things, of course, followed; and she afterwards read some of the comic parts to Dr. Johnson, Mr. Thrale, and whoever came near her. How I should have quivered had I been there! but they tell me that Dr. Johnson laughed as heartily as my father himself did. . . .

August 3

. . . But Dr. Johnson's approbation!—it almost crazed me with agreeable surprise—it gave me such a flight of spirits, that I danced a jig to Mr. Crisp, without any preparation, music, or explanation—to his no small amazement and diversion. I left him, however, to make his own comments upon my friskiness, without affording him the smallest assistance. . . .

I now come to last Saturday evening, when my beloved father came to Chessington, in full health, charming spirits, and all kindness, openness, and entertainment. . . .

In his way hither he had stopped at Streatham, and he settled with Mrs. Thrale that he would call on her again in his way to town, and carry me with him! and Mrs. Thrale said, "We all long to know her."

I have been in a kind of twitter ever since, for there seems something very formidable in the idea of appearing as an authoress! I ever dreaded it, as it is a title which must raise more expectations than I have any chance of answering. Yet I am highly flattered by her invitation, and highly delighted in the prospect of being introduced to the Streatham society.[7]

She sent me some very serious advice to write for the theatre, as, she says, I so naturally run into conversations, that *Evelina* absolutely and plainly points out that path to me; and she hinted how much she should be pleased to be "honoured with my confidence."

My dear father communicated this intelligence, and a great deal more, with a pleasure that almost surpassed that with which I heard it, and he seems quite eager for me to make another attempt. He desired to take upon himself the communication to my daddy Crisp, and as it is now in so many hands that it is possible accident might discover it to him, I readily consented.

Sunday evening, as I was going into my father's room I heard him say, "The variety of characters—the variety of scenes—and the language—why she has had very little education but what she has given herself,—less than any of the others!" and Mr. Crisp exclaimed, "Wonderful—it's wonderful!"

I now found what was going forward, and therefore deemed it most fitting to decamp.

About an hour after, as I was passing through the hall, I met my daddy (Crisp). His face was all animation and archness; he doubled his fist at me, and would have stopped me, but I ran past him into the parlour.

Before supper, however, I again met him, and he would not suffer me to escape; he caught both my hands, and looked as if he would have looked me through, and then exclaimed, "Why you little hussy,—you young devil!—an't you ashamed to look me in the face, you *Evelina*, you! Why, what a dance have you led me about it! Young friend, indeed! Oh you little hussy, what tricks have you served me!" . . .

London, August

I have now to write an account of the most consequential day I have spent since my birth: namely, my Streatham visit.

Our journey to Streatham was the least pleasant part of the day, for the roads were dreadfully dusty, and I was really in the fidgets from thinking what my reception might be, and from fearing they would expect a less awkward and backward kind of person than I was sure they would find.

Mr. Thrale's house is white, and very pleasantly situated, in a fine paddock. Mrs. Thrale was strolling about, and came to us as we got out of the chaise. . . .

She then received me, taking both my hands, and with mixed politeness and cordiality welcoming me to Streatham. She led me into the house, and addressed herself almost wholly for a few minutes to my father, as if to give me an assurance she did not mean to regard me as a show, or to distress or frighten me by drawing me out. Afterwards she took me upstairs, and showed me the house, and said she had very much wished to see me at Streatham, and should always think herself much obliged to Dr. Burney for his goodness in bringing me, which she looked upon as a very great favour.

But though we were some time together, and though she was so very civil, she did not *hint* at my book, and I love her much more than ever for her delicacy in avoiding a subject which she could not but see would have greatly embarrassed me.

When we returned to the music-room we found Miss Thrale was with my father. Miss Thrale is a very fine girl, about fourteen years of age, but cold and reserved, though full of knowledge and intelligence.[8]

Soon after, Mrs. Thrale took me to the library; she talked a little while upon common topics, and then, at last, she mentioned *Evelina.*

"Yesterday at supper," said she, "we talked it all over, and discussed all your characters; but Dr. Johnson's favourite is Mr. Smith. He declares the fine gentleman *manqué* was never better drawn; and he acted him all the evening, saying he was 'all for the ladies!' He repeated whole scenes by heart. I declare I was astonished at him. Oh you can't imagine how much he is pleased with the book; he 'could not get rid of the rogue,' he told me. But was it not droll," said she, "that I should recommend it to Dr. Burney? and tease him, so innocently, to read it?"

I now prevailed upon Mrs. Thrale to let me amuse myself, and she went to dress. I then prowled about to choose some book, and I saw, upon the reading-table, *Evelina.*—I had just fixed upon a new translation of Cicero's *Lælius* when the library-door was opened, and Mr. Seward entered. I instantly put away my book, because I dreaded being thought studious and affected. He offered his service to find anything for me, and then, in the same breath, ran on to speak of the book with which I had myself "favoured the world!"

The exact words he began with I cannot recollect, for I was actually confounded by the attack; and his abrupt manner of letting me know he was *au fait* equally astonished and provoked me. How different from the delicacy of Mr. and Mrs. Thrale!

When we were summoned to dinner, Mrs. Thrale made my father and me sit on each side of her. I said that I hoped I did not take Dr. Johnson's place; for he had not yet appeared.

"No," answered Mrs. Thrale, "he will sit by you, which I am sure will give him great pleasure."

Soon after we were seated, this great man entered. I have so true a veneration for him, that the very sight of him inspires me with delight and reverence, notwithstanding the cruel infirmities to which he is subject; for he has almost perpetual convulsive movements, either of his hands, lips, feet, or knees, and sometimes of all together.

Mrs. Thrale introduced me to him, and he took his place. We had a noble dinner, and a most elegant dessert. Dr. Johnson, in the middle of dinner, asked Mrs. Thrale what was in some little pies that were near him.

"Mutton," answered she, "so I don't ask you to eat any, because I know you despise it."

"No, madam, no," cried he; "I despise nothing that is good of its sort; but I am too proud now to eat of it. Sitting by Miss Burney makes me very proud to-day!"

"Miss Burney," said Mrs. Thrale, laughing, "you must take great care of your heart if Dr. Johnson attacks it; for I assure you he is not often successless."

"What's that you say, madam?" cried he; "are you making mischief between the young lady and me already?"

A little while after he drank Miss Thrale's health and mine, and then added:

" 'Tis a terrible thing that we cannot wish young ladies well, without wishing them to become old women!"

"But some people," said Mr. Seward, "are old and young at the same time, for they wear so well that they never look old."

"No, sir, no," cried the Doctor, laughing; "that never yet was; you might as well say they are at the same time tall and short. . . . I remember an epitaph to that purpose, which is in——"

(I have quite forgot what,—and also the name it was made upon, but the rest I recollect exactly:)

> "—— lies buried here;
> So early wise, so lasting fair,
> That none, unless her years you told,
> Thought her a child, or thought her old."

Mrs. Thrale then repeated some lines in French, and Dr. Johnson some more in Latin. An epilogue of Mr. Garrick's to *Bonduca* was then mentioned, and Dr. Johnson said it was a miserable performance, and everybody agreed it was the worst he had ever made.

"And yet," said Mr. Seward, "it has been very much admired; but it is in praise of English valour, and so I suppose the subject made it popular."

"I don't know, sir," said Dr. Johnson, "anything about the subject, for I could not read on till I came to it; I got through half a dozen lines, but I could observe no other subject than eternal dulness. I don't know what is the matter with David; I am afraid he is grown superannuated, for his prologues and epilogues used to be incomparable."

"Nothing is so fatiguing," said Mrs. Thrale, "as the life of a wit: he and Wilkes are the two oldest men of their ages I know; for they have both worn themselves out, by being eternally on the rack to give entertainment to others."

"David, madam," said the Doctor, "looks much older than he is; for his face has had double the business of any other man's; it is never at rest; when he speaks one minute, he has quite a different countenance to what he assumes the next; I don't believe he ever kept the same look for half an hour together, in the whole course of his life; and such an eternal, restless, fatiguing play of the muscles, must certainly wear out a man's face before its real time."

"Oh yes," cried Mrs. Thrale, "we must certainly make some allowance for such wear and tear of a man's face."

The next name that was started, was that of Sir John Hawkins: and Mrs. Thrale said, "Why now, Dr. Johnson, he is another of those whom you suffer nobody to abuse but yourself; Garrick is one, too; for if any other person speaks against him, you browbeat him in a minute!"

"Why, madam," answered he, "they don't know when to abuse him, and when to praise him; I will allow no man to speak ill of David that he does not deserve; and as to Sir John, why really I believe him to be an honest man at the bottom: but to be sure he is penurious, and he is mean, and it must be owned he has a degree of brutality, and a tendency to savageness, that cannot easily be defended."

We all laughed, as he meant we should, at this curious manner of speaking in his favour, and he then related an anecdote that he said he knew to be true in regard to his meanness. He said that Sir John and he once belonged to the same club, but that as he eat no supper after the first night of his admission, he desired to be excused paying his share.

"And was he excused?"

"Oh yes; for no man is angry at another for being inferior to himself! we all scorned him, and admitted his plea. For my part I was such a fool as to pay my share for wine, though I never tasted any. But Sir John was a most *unclubable* man!". . .

"And this," continued he, "reminds me of a gentleman and lady with whom I travelled once; I suppose I must call them gentleman and lady, according to form, because they travelled in their own coach and four horses. But at the first inn where we stopped, the lady called for—a pint of ale! and when it came, quarrelled with the waiter for not giving full measure.—Now, Madame Duval 9 could not have done a grosser thing!"

Oh, how everybody laughed! and to be sure I did not glow at all, nor munch fast, nor look on my plate, nor lose any part of my usual composure! But how grateful do I feel to this dear Dr. Johnson, for never naming me and the book as belonging one to the other, and yet making an allusion that showed his thoughts led to it, and, at the same time, that seemed to justify the character as being natural! But, indeed, the delicacy I met with from him, and from all the Thrales, was yet more flattering to me than the praise with which I have heard they have honoured my book.

After dinner, when Mrs. Thrale and I left the gentlemen, we had a conversation that to me could not but be delightful, as she was all good-humour, spirits, sense and *agreeability*. Surely I may make words, when at a loss, if Dr. Johnson does. . . .

We left Streatham at about eight o'clock, and Mr. Seward, who handed me into the chaise, added his interest to the rest, that my father would not fail to bring me again next week to stay with them some time. In short I was loaded with civilities from them all. And my ride home was equally happy with the rest of the day, for my kind and most beloved father was so happy in *my* happiness, and congratulated me so sweetly, that he could, like myself, think on no other subject. . . .

Yet my honours stopped not here; for Hetty, who with her

sposo,[10] was here to receive us, told me she had lately met Mrs. Reynolds, sister of Sir Joshua;[11] and that she talked very much and very highly of a new novel called *Evelina;* though without a shadow of suspicion as to the scribbler; and not contented with her own praise, she said that Sir Joshua, who began it one day when he was too much engaged to go on with it, was so much caught, that he could think of nothing else, and was quite absent all the day, not knowing a word that was said to him: and, when he took it up again, found himself so much interested in it, that he sat up all night to finish it!

Sir Joshua, it seems, vows he would give fifty pounds to know the author! . . .

FROM MR. CRISP

August 16

MY DEAR FANNIKIN—"*If I wish to hear the sequel of the day?*" the question is injurious—both because I warmly interest myself in whatever concerns a Fannikin, and likewise that I must else be

duller than fat weed
That rots itself at ease on Lethe's wharf.[12]

The reception you met with at Streatham, though highly flattering, by no means surprises me; every article of it is most strictly your due. You have fairly earned it, and if your host and hostess had given you less, they had defrauded you. Flummery is a commodity I do not much deal in; but on this occasion I will subscribe with hand and heart to what I have now written. . . .

Well, the ice is now broke, and your perturbation ought to be in a great measure at an end. When you went into the sea at Teignmouth, did not you shiver and shrink at first, and almost lose your breath when the water came up to your chest? I suppose you afterwards learned to plunge in boldly, over head and ears at once, and then your pain was over. You must do the like now; and as the public have thought proper to put you on a cork jacket, your fears of drowning would be unpardonable.

S. C.

Streatham, Sunday, August 23

I know not how to express the fulness of my contentment at this sweet place. All my best expectations are exceeded, and you know they were not very moderate. If, when my dear father comes, Susan and Mr. Crisp were to come too, I believe it would require at least a day's pondering to enable me to form another wish.

Our journey was charming. The kind Mrs. Thrale would give courage to the most timid. She did not ask me questions, or catechise me upon what I knew, or use any means to draw me out, but made it her business to draw herself out—that is, to start subjects, to support them herself, and to take all the weight of the conversation, as if it behoved her to find me entertainment. But I am so much in love with her, that I shall be obliged to run away from the subject, or shall write of nothing else.

When we arrived here, Mrs. Thrale showed me my room, which is an exceeding pleasant one, and then conducted me to the library, there to divert myself while she dressed.

Miss Thrale soon joined me: and I begin to like her. Mr. Thrale was neither well nor in spirits all day. Indeed, he seems not to be a happy man, though he has every means of happiness in his power. But I think I have rarely seen a very rich man with a light heart and light spirits.

Dr. Johnson was in the utmost good humour.

There was no other company at the house all day. . . .

At night, Mrs. Thrale asked if I would have anything? I answered, "No"; but Dr. Johnson said,

"Yes: she is used, madam, to suppers; she would like an egg or two, and a few slices of ham, or a rasher—a rasher, I believe, would please her better."

How ridiculous! However, nothing could persuade Mrs. Thrale not to have the cloth laid: and Dr. Johnson was so facetious, that he challenged Mr. Thrale to get drunk! . . .

I ate nothing, that they might not again use such a ceremony with me. Indeed, their late dinners forbid suppers, especially as Dr. Johnson made me eat cake at tea, for he held it till I took it, with an odd or absent complaisance.

He was extremely comical after supper, and would not suffer Mrs. Thrale and me to go to bed for near an hour after we made the motion. . . .

Mrs. Thrale accompanied me to my room, and stayed chatting with me for more than an hour. . . .

Now for this morning's breakfast.

Dr. Johnson, as usual, came last into the library; he was in high spirits, and full of mirth and sport. I had the honour of sitting next to him: and now, all at once, he flung aside his reserve, thinking, perhaps, that it was time I should fling aside mine.

Mrs. Thrale told him that she intended taking me to Mr. T——'s.

"So you ought, madam," cried he; " 'tis your business to be Cicerone to her."

Then suddenly he snatched my hand, and kissing it,

"Ah!" he added, "they will little think what a tartar you carry to them!"

"No, that they won't!" cried Mrs. Thrale; "Miss Burney looks so meek and so quiet, nobody would suspect what a comical girl she is; but I believe she has a great deal of malice at heart."

"Oh, she's a toad!" cried the doctor, laughing—"a sly young rogue! with her Smiths and her Branghtons!"[13]

"Why, Mr. Johnson," said Mrs. Thrale, "I hope you are very well this morning! if one may judge by your spirits and good humour, the fever you threatened us with is gone off."

He had complained that he was going to be ill last night.

"Why no, madam, no," answered he, "I am not yet well; I could not sleep at all; there I lay restless and uneasy, and thinking all the time of Miss Burney. Perhaps I have offended her, thought I; perhaps she is angry; I have seen her but once, and I talked to her of a rasher!—Were you angry?"

I think I need not tell you my answer.

"I have been endeavouring to find some excuse," continued he, "and, as I could not sleep, I got up, and looked for some authority for the word; and I find, madam, it is used by Dryden: in one of his prologues, he says—'And snatch a homely rasher from the coals.' So you must not mind me, madam; I say strange things, but I mean no harm."

I was almost afraid he thought I was really idiot enough to have taken him seriously; but, a few minutes after, he put his hand on my arm, and shaking his head, exclaimed,

"Oh, you are a sly little rogue!—what a Holborn beau have you drawn!"[14]

"Ay, Miss Burney," said Mrs. Thrale, "the Holborn beau is Dr.

Johnson's favourite; and we have all your characters by heart, from Mr. Smith up to Lady Louisa."

"Oh, Mr. Smith, Mr. Smith is the man!" cried he, laughing violently. "Harry Fielding never drew so good a character!—such a fine varnish of low politeness!—such a struggle to appear a gentleman! Madam, there is no character better drawn anywhere—in any book or by any author."

I almost poked myself under the table. Never did I feel so delicious a confusion since I was born! But he added a great deal more, only I cannot recollect his exact words, and I do not choose to give him mine. . . .

Streatham, August 26

My opportunities for writing grow less and less, and my materials more and more. After breakfast I have scarcely a moment that I can spare all day.

Mrs. Thrale I like more and more. Of all the people I have ever seen since I came into this "gay and gaudy world," I never before saw the person who so strongly resembles our dear father. I find the likeness perpetually; she has the same natural liveliness, the same general benevolence, the same rare union of gaiety and of feeling in her disposition.

And so kind is she to me! She told me at first that I should have all my mornings to myself, and therefore I have studied to avoid her, lest I should be in her way; but since the first morning she seeks me, sits with me, saunters with me in the park, or compares notes over books in the library; and her conversation is delightful; it is so entertaining, so gay, so enlivening, when she is in spirits, and so intelligent and instructive when she is otherwise, that I almost as much wish to record all she says, as all Dr. Johnson says. . . .

When we were dressed for dinner, and went into the parlour, we had the agreeable surprise of seeing Mr. Seward there. . . .

There was also Mr. Lort, who is reckoned one of the most learned men alive, and is also a collector of curiosities, alike in literature and natural history. His manners are somewhat blunt and odd, and he is altogether out of the common road, without having chosen a better path.[15]

The day was passed most agreeably. In the evening we had, as usual, a literary conversation.

Mr. Lort produced several curious MSS. of the famous Bristol Chatterton; [16] among others, his will, and divers verses written against Dr. Johnson, as a placeman and pensioner; all which he read aloud, with a steady voice and unmoved countenance.

I was astonished at him; Mrs. Thrale not much pleased; Mr. Thrale silent and attentive; and Mr. Seward was slily laughing. Dr Johnson himself, listened profoundly and laughed openly. Indeed, I believe he wished his abusers no other thing than a good dinner, like Pope. [17]

Just as we had got our biscuits and toast-and-water, which make the Streatham supper, and which, indeed, is all there is any chance of eating after our late and great dinners, Mr. Lort suddenly said,

"Pray, ma'am, have you heard anything of a novel that runs about a good deal, called *Evelina?*"

What a ferment did this question, before such a set, put me in!

I did not know whether he spoke to me, or Mrs. Thrale; and Mrs. Thrale was in the same doubt, and as she owned, felt herself in a little palpitation for me, not knowing what might come next. Between us both, therefore, he had no answer.

"It has been recommended to me," continued he; "but I have no great desire to see it, because it has such a foolish name. Yet I have heard a great deal of it, too."

He then repeated *Evelina*—in a very languishing and ridiculous tone.

My heart beat so quick against my stays that I almost panted with extreme agitation, from the dread either of hearing some horrible criticism, or of being betrayed: and I munched my biscuit as if I had not eaten for a fortnight.

I believe the whole party were in some little consternation; Dr. Johnson began see-sawing; Mr. Thrale awoke; Mr. E——, [18] who I fear has picked up some notion of the affair from being so much in the house, grinned amazingly; and Mr. Seward, biting his nails and flinging himself back in his chair, I am sure had wickedness enough to enjoy the whole scene. . . .

"Why, have you had the book here?" cried Mr. Lort, staring.

"Ay, indeed, have we," said Mrs. Thrale; "I read it when I was last confined, and I laughed over it, and I cried over it!"

"Oh ho!" said Mr. Lort, "this is another thing! If you have had it here, I will certainly read it." . . .

"You need not go far for it," said Mrs. Thrale, "for it's now upon yonder table."

I could sit still no longer; there was something so awkward, so uncommon, so strange in my then situation, that I wished myself a hundred miles off; and, indeed, I had almost choked myself with the biscuit, for I could not for my life swallow it; and so I got up, and, as Mr. Lort went to the table to look for *Evelina,* I left the room, and was forced to call for water to wash down the biscuit, which literally stuck in my throat.

I heartily wished Mr. Lort at Jerusalem. Notwithstanding all this may read as nothing, because all that was said was in my favour, yet at the time, when I knew not what might be said, I suffered the most severe trepidation. . . .

When Mrs. Thrale and I retired, she not only, as usual, accompanied me to my room, but stayed with me at least an hour, talking over the affair. I seized with eagerness this favourable opportunity of conjuring her not merely not to tell Mr. Lort my secret, but ever after never to tell anybody. For a great while she only laughed, saying—

"Poor Miss Burney! so you thought just to have played and sported with your sisters and cousins, and had it all your own way; but now you are in for it! But if you will be an author and a wit, you must take the consequences!"

But when she found me seriously urgent and really frightened, she changed her note, and said,

"Oh, if I find you are in earnest in desiring concealment, I shall quite scold you; for if such a desire does not proceed from affectation, 'tis from something worse."

"No, indeed," cried I, "not from affectation; for my conduct has been as uniform in trying to keep snug as my words, and I never have wavered: I never have told anybody out of my own family, nor half the bodies in it. And I have so long forborne making this request to you for no other reason in the world but for fear you should think me affected."

"Well, I won't suspect you of affectation," returned she—"nay, I can't, for you have looked like your namesake in the *Clandestine Marriage*[19] all this evening, 'of fifty colours, I wow and purtest'; but when I clear you of that, I leave something worse."

"And what, dear madam, what can be worse?"

"Why, an over-delicacy that may make you unhappy all your life. Indeed you must check it—you must get the better of it: for why should you write a book, print a book, and have everybody read and like your book, and then sneak in a corner and disown it!"

"My printing it, indeed," said I, "tells terribly against me to all who are unacquainted with the circumstances that belonged to it, but I had so little notion of being discovered, and was so well persuaded that the book would never be heard of, that I really thought myself as safe, and meant to be as private, when the book was at Mr. Lowndes's, as when it was in my own bureau."

"Well, I don't know what we shall do with you! But indeed you must blunt a little of this delicacy, for the book has such success, that if you don't own it, somebody else will!"

Yet notwithstanding all her advice, and all her encouragement, I was so much agitated by the certainty of being known as a scribbler, that I was really ill all night and could not sleep. . . .

After breakfast on Friday, or yesterday, a curious trait occurred of Dr. Johnson's jocosity. It was while the talk ran so copiously upon their urgency that I should produce a comedy.[20] While Mrs. Thrale was in the midst of her flattering persuasions, the doctor, see-sawing in his chair, began laughing to himself so heartily as to almost shake his seat as well as his sides. We stopped our confabulation, in which he had ceased to join, hoping he would reveal the subject of his mirth; but he enjoyed it inwardly, without heeding our curiosity,—till at last he said he had been struck with a notion that "Miss Burney would begin her dramatic career by writing a piece called 'Streatham.'"

He paused, and laughed yet more cordially, and then suddenly commanded a pomposity to his countenance and his voice, and added, "Yes! 'Streatham—a Farce!'" . . .

Streatham, September

Tuesday morning, Mrs. Thrale asked me if I did not want to see Mrs. Montagu? I truly said, I should be the most insensible of all animals not to like to see our sex's glory.

"Well," said she, "we'll try to make you see her. Sir Joshua says she is in town, and I will write and ask her here. I wish you to see her of all things."

Mrs. Thrale wrote her note before breakfast. . . .

An answer came from Mrs. Montagu at noon. Mrs. Thrale gave it me to read: it was in a high strain of *politesse,* expressed equal admiration and regard for Mrs. Thrale, and accepted her invitation for the next day. But what was my surprise to read, at the bottom of the letter, "I have not yet seen *Evelina,* but will certainly get it: and if it should not happen to please me, the disgrace must be mine, not the author's."

"Oh, ma'am," cried I, "what does this mean?"

"Why, only," said she, "that, in my letter this morning I said, 'Have you seen the new work called *Evelina?* it was written by an amiable young friend of mine, and I wish much to know your opinion of it; for if you should not approve it, what signifies the approbation of a Johnson, a Burke, etc.?' " . . .

Before dinner, to my great joy, Dr. Johnson returned home from Warley Common. . . .

I was then looking over the *Life of Cowley,*[21] which he had himself given me to read, at the same time that he gave to Mrs. Thrale that of Waller. They are now printed, though they will not be published for some time. But he bade me put it away.

"Do," cried he, "put away that now, and prattle with us; I can't make this little Burney prattle, and I am sure she prattles well; but I shall teach her another lesson than to sit thus silent before I have done with her."

"To talk," cried I, "is the only lesson I shall be backward to learn from you, sir."

"You shall give me," cried he, "a discourse upon the passions: come, begin! Tell us the necessity of regulating them, watching over and curbing them! Did you ever read Norris's *Theory of Love?*"[22]

"No, sir," said I, laughing, yet staring a little.

Dr. J.—Well, it is worth your reading. He will make you see that inordinate love is the root of all evil: inordinate love of wealth brings on avarice; of wine, brings on intemperance; of power, brings on cruelty; and so on. He deduces from inordinate love all human frailty.

Mrs. T.—To-morrow, sir, Mrs. Montagu dines here, and then you will have talk enough.

Dr. Johnson began to see-saw, with a countenance strongly expressive of inward fun, and after enjoying it some time in silence, he suddenly, and with great animation, turned to me and cried,

"Down with her, Burney!—down with her!—spare her not!—attack her, fight her, and down with her at once! You are a rising wit, and she is at the top; and when I was beginning the world, and was nothing and nobody, the joy of my life was to fire at all the established wits! and then everybody loved to halloo me on. But there is no game now; everybody would be glad to see me conquered: but then, when I was new, to vanquish the great ones was all the delight of my poor little dear soul! So at her, Burney—at her, and down with her!"

Oh how we were all amused! By the way I must tell you that Mrs. Montagu is in very great estimation here, even with Dr. Johnson himself, when others do not praise her improperly. Mrs. Thrale ranks her as the first of women in the literary way. I should have told you that Miss Gregory, daughter of the Gregory who wrote the *Letters,* or, *Legacy of Advice,* lives with Mrs. Montagu, and was invited to accompany her.[23] . . .

Wednesday

. . . We could not prevail with him to stay till Mrs. Montagu arrived, though, by appointment, she came very early. She and Miss Gregory came by one o'clock. . . .

She is middle-sized, very thin, and looks infirm; she has a sensible and penetrating countenance, and the air and manner of a woman accustomed to being distinguished, and of great parts. Dr. Johnson, who agrees in this, told us that a Mrs. Hervey, of his acquaintance, says she can remember Mrs. Montagu *trying* for this same air and manner. Mr. Crisp has said the same: however, nobody can now impartially see her, and not confess that she has extremely well succeeded.

My expectations, which were compounded of the praise of Mrs. Thrale, and the abuse of Mr. Crisp, were most exactly answered, for I thought her in a medium way.

Miss Gregory is a fine young woman, and seems gentle and well-bred.

A bustle with the dog Presto—Mrs. Thrale's favourite—at the

entrance of these ladies into the library, prevented any formal reception; but as soon as Mrs. Montagu heard my name, she inquired very civilly after my father, and made many speeches concerning a volume of *Linguet*,[24] which she has lost; but she hopes soon to be able to replace it. I am sure he is very high in her favour, because she did me the honour of addressing herself to me three or four times.

But my ease and tranquillity were soon disturbed: for she had not been in the room more than ten minutes, ere, turning to Mrs. Thrale, she said—

"Oh, ma'am—but your *Evelina*—I have not yet got it—I sent for it, but the bookseller had it not. However, I will certainly have it."

"Ay, I hope so," answered Mrs. Thrale, "and I hope you will like it too; for 'tis a book to be liked."

I began now a vehement nose-blowing, for the benefit of handkerchiefing my face.

"I hope though," said Mrs. Montagu drily, "it is not in verse? I can read anything in prose, but I have a great dread of a long story in verse."

"No, ma'am, no; 'tis all in prose. I assure you. 'Tis a novel; and an exceeding——but it does nothing good to be praised too much, so I will say nothing more about it; only this, that Mr. Burke sat up all night to read it."

"Indeed? Well, I propose myself great pleasure from it; and I am gratified by hearing it is written by a woman."

"And Sir Joshua Reynolds," continued Mrs. Thrale, "has been offering fifty pounds to know the author."

"Well, I will have it to read on my journey; I am going to Berkshire, and it shall be my travelling book."

"No, ma'am, if you please you shall have it now. Queeny, do look for it for Mrs. Montagu, and let it be put in her carriage, and go to town with her."

Miss Thrale rose to look for it, and involuntarily I rose too, intending to walk off, for my situation was inexpressibly awkward; but then I recollected that if I went away, it might seem like giving Mrs. Thrale leave and opportunity to tell my tale, and therefore I stopped at a distant window, where I busied myself in contemplating the poultry.

"And Dr. Johnson, ma'am," added my kind puffer, "says Fielding never wrote so well—never wrote equal to this book; he says it is a better picture of life and manners than is to be found anywhere in Fielding."

"Indeed?" cried Mrs. Montagu surprised; "that I did not expect, for I have been informed it is the work of a young lady, and therefore, though I expected a very pretty book, I supposed it to be a work of mere imagination, and the name I thought attractive; but life and manners I never dreamt of finding."

"Well, ma'am, what I tell you is literally true; and for my part, I am never better pleased than when good girls write clever books—and that this is clever—But all this time we are killing Miss Burney, who wrote the book herself."

What a clap of thunder was this!—the last thing in the world I should have expected before my face! I know not what bewitched Mrs. Thrale, but this was carrying the jest farther than ever. All *retenue* being now at an end, I fairly and abruptly took to my heels, and ran out of the room with the utmost trepidation, amidst astonished exclamations from Mrs. Montagu and Miss Gregory. . . .

I determined not to make my appearance again till dinner was upon table; yet I could neither read nor write, nor indeed do anything but consider the new situation in life into which I am thus hurried—I had almost said forced—and if I had, methinks it would be no untruth.

Miss Thrale came laughing up after me, and tried to persuade me to return. She was mightily diverted all the morning, and came to me with repeated messages of summons to attend the company; but I could not *brave* it again into the room, and therefore entreated her to say I was finishing a letter. Yet I was sorry to lose so much of Mrs. Montagu.

When dinner was upon table, I followed the procession, in a tragedy step, as Mr. Thrale will have it, into the dining-parlour. Dr. Johnson was returned.

The conversation was not brilliant, nor do I remember much of it; but Mrs. Montagu behaved to me just as I could have wished, since she spoke to me very little, but spoke that little with the utmost politeness. But Miss Gregory, though herself a very modest girl, quite stared me out of countenance, and never took her eyes off my face.

When Mrs. Montagu's new house was talked of, Dr. Johnson, in a jocose manner, desired to know if he should be invited to see it.

"Ay, sure," cried Mrs. Montagu, looking well pleased; "or else I shan't like it: but I invite you all to a house warming; I shall hope for the honour of seeing all this company at my new house next Easter day: I fix the day now that it may be remembered."

Everybody bowed and accepted the invite but me, and I thought fitting not to hear it; for I have no notion at snapping at invites from the eminent. But Dr. Johnson, who sat next to me, was determined I should be of the party, for he suddenly clapped his hand on my shoulder, and called out aloud—

"Little Burney, you and I will go together!"

"Yes, surely," cried Mrs. Montagu, "I shall hope for the pleasure of seeing 'Evelina.' "

"*Evelina?*" repeated he; "has Mrs. Montagu then found out *Evelina?*"

"Yes," cried she, "and I am proud of it: I am proud that a work so commended should be a woman's."

Oh, how my face burnt! . . .

They went away very early, because Mrs. Montagu is a great coward in a carriage.[25] She repeated her invitation as she left the room. So now that I am invited to Mrs. Montagu's, I think the measure of my glory full! . . .

Monday, September 21

I am more comfortable here than ever; Dr. Johnson honours me with increasing kindness; Mr. Thrale is much more easy and sociable than when I was here before; I am quite jocose, whenever I please, with Miss Thrale; and the charming head and life of the house, her mother, stands the test of the closest examination, as well and as much to her honour as she does a mere cursory view. She is, indeed, all that is excellent and desirable in woman.

I have had a thousand delightful conversations with Dr. Johnson, who, whether he loves me or not, I am sure seems to have some opinion of my discretion, for he speaks of all this house to me with unbounded confidence, neither diminishing faults, nor exaggerating praise. Whenever he is below stairs he keeps me a prisoner, for he does not like I should quit the room a moment; if I rise he constantly calls out, "Don't you go, little Burney!" . . .

FROM MR. CRISP

November 6

MY DEAR FANNIKIN— . . . I do entirely acquit you of all wish or design of being known to the world as an author. I believe it is ever the case with writers of real merit and genius, on the appearance of their first productions: as their powers are finer and keener than other people's, so is their sensibility. On these occasions they are as nervous as Lady Louisa in *Evelina*. But surely these painful feelings ought to go off when the salts of general applause are continually held under their nose. It is then time to follow your friend Dr. Johnson's advice, and learn to be a swaggerer, at least so far as to be able to face the world, and not be ashamed of the distinction you have fairly earned, especially when it is apparent you do not court it.

I now proceed to assume the daddy, and consequently the privilege of giving counsel. Your kind and judicious friends are certainly in the right in wishing you to make your talents turn to something more solid than empty praise. When you come to know the world half so well as I do, and what yahoos mankind are, you will then be convinced that a state of independence is the only basis on which to rest your future ease and comfort. You are now young, lively, gay. You please, and the world smiles upon you—this is your time. Years and wrinkles in their due season (perhaps attended with want of health and spirits) will succeed. You will then be no longer the same Fanny of 1778, feasted, caressed, admired, with all the soothing circumstances of your present situation. The Thrales, the Johnsons, the Sewards, Cholmondeleys, etc., etc., who are now so high in fashion, and might be such powerful protectors as almost to insure success to anything that is tolerable, may then themselves be moved off the stage. I will no longer dwell on so disagreeable a change of the scene; let me only earnestly urge you to act vigorously (what I really believe is in your power) a distinguished part in the present one—"now while it is yet day, and before the night cometh, when no man can work." . . .

Your loving daddy,
S. C.

FROM MR. CRISP

Chessington, December 8

MY DEAR FANNIKIN— . . . 'Tis true, I have more than once, Fanny, whispered in your ear a gentle caution—that you have much to lose. Why is that?—because much you have gained. Now you have gone so far, and so rapidly, you will not be allowed to slacken your pace. This is so far from being meant as a discouragement, that it is intended to animate you. But it will explain what was in my head when I threw out those (perhaps useless, perhaps too officious) hints.[26] I plainly foresaw (what has since happened) that, as your next step, you would be urged, strongly urged, by your many friends and admirers, to undertake a comedy. I think you capable, highly capable of it; but in the attempt there are great difficulties in the way; some more particularly and individually in the way of a Fanny, than of most people.

I will instantly name these, lest you should misapprehend. I need not observe to you that in most of our successful comedies there are frequent lively freedoms (and waggeries that cannot be called licentious, neither) that give a strange animation and vigour to the style, and of which if it were to be deprived it would lose wonderfully of its salt and spirit. I mean such freedoms as ladies of the strictest character would make no scruple, openly, to laugh at, but at the same time, especially if they were prudes (and you know you are one), perhaps would shy at being known to be the authors of. Some comic characters would be deficient without strokes of this kind; in scenes where gay men of the world are got together, they are natural and expected; and the business would be mighty apt to grow *fade* without them. . . .

I find myself forestalled by the intelligent Mrs. Montagu in another observation I was going to make, and which she very justly and judiciously enforces by the instance she gives of Fielding, who, though so eminent in characters and descriptions, did by no means succeed in comedy.

'Tis certain, different talents are requisite for the two species of writing, though they are by no means incompatible; I fear, however, the labouring oar lies on the comic author.

In these little entertaining elegant histories, the writer has his full scope; as large a range as he pleases to hunt in—to pick, cull, select whatever he likes: he takes his own time—he may be as minute as he pleases, and the more minute the better, provided that taste, a deep and penetrating knowledge of human nature, and the world, accompany that minuteness. When this is the case, the very soul, and all its most secret recesses and workings, are developed and laid as open to the view, as the blood globules circulating in a frog's foot, when seen through a microscope. The exquisite touches such a work is capable of (of which *Evelina* is, without flattery, a glaring instance), are truly charming. But of these great advantages, these resources, you are strangely curtailed the moment you begin a comedy. . . . There all must be compressed into quintessence; the moment the scene ceases to move on briskly, and business seems to hang, sighs and groans are the consequence. Dreadful sound!—In a word, if the plot, the story of the comedy does not open and unfold itself in the easy, natural, unconstrained flow of the dialogue—if that dialogue does not go on with spirit, wit, variety, fun, humour, repartee, and—and all in short into the bargain—*serviteur!*—good-bye, t'ye!

One more: now, Fanny, don't imagine that I am discouraging you from the attempt: or that I am retracting or shirking back from what I have said above—*i.e.* that I think you highly capable of it. On the contrary, I reaffirm it: I affirm that in common conversation I observe in you a ready choice of words, with a quickness and conciseness that have often surprised me. This is a lucky gift for a comic writer, and not a very common one: so that if you have not the united talents I demand, I don't know who has: for if you have your familiar, your sprite, for ever thus at your elbow without calling for, surely it will not desert you, when in deep conjuration raising your genius in your closet.

God bless you, Adieu,—Your loving daddy—

S. C.

[1779]

To Mr. Crisp

January

. . . Every word you have urged concerning the salt and spirit of gay, unrestrained freedom in comedies, carries conviction along with it,—a conviction which I feel, in trembling; should I ever venture in that walk publicly, perhaps the want of it might prove fatal to me. I do, indeed, think it most likely that such would be the event, and my poor piece, though it might escape catcalls and riots, would be fairly slept off the stage. I cannot, however, attempt to avoid this danger, though I see it, for I would a thousand times rather forfeit my character as a writer, than risk ridicule or censure as a female. I have never set my heart on fame, and therefore would not, if I could, purchase it at the expense of all my own ideas of propriety. You who know me for a prude will not be surprised, and I hope not offended, at this avowal, for I should deceive you were I not to make it. If I should try, I must e'en take my chance, and all my own expectations may be pretty easily answered. . . .

—Yours affectionately,
F. B.

[January (?)]

. . . And now, my dear Susan, to relate the affairs of an evening, perhaps the most important of my life. To say that, is, I am sure, enough to interest you, my dearest girl, in all I can tell you of it.

On Monday last, my father sent a note to Mrs. Cholmondeley, to propose our waiting on her the Wednesday following; she accepted the proposal, and accordingly on Wednesday evening, my father, mother, and self went to Hertford Street. . . .

Mr. and the Misses Cholmondeley and Miss Forrest were with

her; but who else think you?—why Mrs. Sheridan![27] I was absolutely charmed at the sight of her. I think her quite as beautiful as ever, and even more capitivating; for she has now a look of ease and happiness that animates her whole face.

Miss Linley[28] was with her; she is very handsome, but nothing near her sister: the elegance of Mrs. Sheridan's beauty is unequalled by any I ever saw, except Mrs. Crewe.[29] I was pleased with her in all respects. She is much more lively and agreeable than I had any idea of finding her; she was very gay, and very unaffected, and totally free from airs of any kind.

Miss Linley was very much out of spirits; she did not speak three words the whole evening, and looked wholly unmoved at all that passed. Indeed she appeared to be heavy and inanimate.

Mrs. Cholmondeley sat next me. She is determined, I believe, to make me like her; and she will, I believe, have full success; for she is very clever, very entertaining, and very much unlike anybody else.

The first subject started was the Opera, and all joined in the praise of Pacchierotti.[30] Mrs. Sheridan declared she could not hear him without tears, and that he was the first Italian singer who ever affected her to such a degree.

They then talked of the intended marriage of the Duke of Dorset with Miss Cumberland, and many ridiculous anecdotes were related. The conversation naturally fell upon Mr. Cumberland, and he was finely cut up!

"What a man is that!" said Mrs. Cholmondeley: "I cannot bear him—so querulous, so dissatisfied, so determined to like nobody and nothing but himself!"

"What, Mr. Cumberland?" exclaimed I.

"Yes," answered she; "I hope you don't like him?"

"I don't know him, ma'am. I have only seen him once, at Mrs. Ord's."[31]

"Oh, don't like him for your life! I charge you not! I hope you did not like his looks?"

"Why," quoth I, laughing, "I went prepared and determined to like him; but, perhaps, when I see him next, I may go prepared for the contrary."

After this, Miss More[32] was mentioned; and I was asked what I thought of her?

"Don't be formal with me; if you are, I shan't like you!"

"I have no hope that you will anyway!"

"Oh, fie! fie! but as to Miss More—I don't like her at all; that is, I detest her! She does nothing but flatter and fawn; and then she thinks ill of nobody. Don't you hate a person who thinks ill of nobody?"

My father then told what Dr. Johnson had said to her on the occasion of her praising him.

"This rejoices, this does me good!" cried she; "I would have given the world to have heard that. Oh, there's no supporting the company of professed flatterers. She gives me such doses of it, that I cannot endure her; but I always sit still and make no answer, but receive it as if I thought it my due: that is the only way to quiet her. She is really detestable. I hope, Miss Burney, you don't think I admire all geniuses? The only person I flatter," continued she, "is Garrick; and he likes it so much, that it pays one by the spirits it gives him. Other people that I like, I dare not flatter." . . .

Just then the door opened, and Mr. Sheridan entered.[33]

Was I not in luck? Not that I believe the meeting was accidental; but I had more wished to meet him and his wife than any people I know not. . . .

Mr. Sheridan has a very fine figure, and a good though I don't think a handsome face. He is tall, and very upright, and his appearance and address are at once manly and fashionable, without the smallest tincture of foppery or modish graces. In short, I like him vastly, and think him every way worthy his beautiful companion.

And let me tell you what I know will give you as much pleasure as it gave me,—that, by all I could observe in the course of the evening, and we stayed very late, they are extremely happy in each other: he evidently adores her, and she as evidently idolises him. The world has by no means done him justice. . . .

Some time after this, my eyes happening to meet his, he waived the ceremony of introduction, and in a low voice said,

"I have been telling Dr. Burney that I have long expected to see in Miss Burney a lady of the gravest appearance, with the quickest parts."

I was never much more astonished than at this unexpected address, as among all my numerous puffers the name of Sheridan has never reached me, and I did really imagine he had never deigned to look at my trash.

Of course I could make no verbal answer, and he proceeded then to speak of *Evelina* in terms of the highest praise; but I was in such a ferment from surprise (not to say pleasure), that I have no recollection of his expressions. I only remember telling him that I was much amazed he had spared time to read it, and that he repeatedly called it a most surprising book; and sometime after he added, "But I hope, Miss Burney, you don't intend to throw away your pen?"

"You should take care, sir," said I, "what you say: for you know not what weight it may have."

He wished it might have any, he said, and soon after turned again to my father.

I protest, since the approbation of the Streathamites, I have met with none so flattering to me as this of Mr. Sheridan, and so very unexpected. . . .

Some time after, Sir Joshua returning to his standing-place, entered into confab with Miss Linley and your slave, upon various matters, during which Mr. Sheridan, joining us, said,

"Sir Joshua, I have been telling Miss Burney that she must not suffer her pen to lie idle—ought she?"

Sir Joshua.—No, indeed, ought she not.

Mr. Sheridan.—Do you then, Sir Joshua, persuade her. But perhaps you have begun something? May we ask? Will you answer a question candidly?

F. B.—I don't know, but as candidly as *Mrs. Candour* [34] I think I certainly shall.

Mr. Sheridan.—What then are you about now?

F. B.—Why, twirling my fan, I think!

Mr. Sheridan.—No, no; but what are you about at home? However, it is not a fair question, so I won't press it.

Yet he looked very inquisitive; but I was glad to get off without any downright answer.

Sir Joshua.—Anything in the dialogue way, I think, she must succeed in; and I am sure invention will not be wanting.

Mr. Sheridan.—No, indeed; I think, and say, she should write a comedy.

Sir Joshua.—I am sure I think so; and hope she will.

I could only answer by incredulous exclamations.

"Consider," continued Sir Joshua, "you have already had all the applause and fame you can have given you in the closet; but the acclamation of a theatre will be new to you."

And then he put down his trumpet, and began a violent clapping of his hands.

I actually shook from head to foot! I felt myself already in Drury Lane, amidst the hubbub of a first night.

"Oh no!" cried I, "there may be a noise, but it will be just the reverse." And I returned his salute with a hissing.

Mr. Sheridan joined Sir Joshua very warmly.

"Oh, sir!" cried I, "you should not run on so,—you don't know what mischief you may do!"

Mr. Sheridan.—I wish I may—I shall be very glad to be accessory.

Sir Joshua.—She has, certainly, something of a knack at characters;—where she got it, I don't know,—and how she got it, I can't imagine; but she certainly has it. And to throw it away is——

Mr. Sheridan.—Oh, she won't,—she will write a comedy,—she has promised me she will!

F. B.—Oh!—if you both run on in this manner, I shall——

I was going to say get under the chair, but Mr. Sheridan, interrupting me with a laugh, said,

"Set about one? very well, that's right!"

"Ay," cried Sir Joshua, "that's very right. And you (to Mr. Sheridan) would take anything of hers, would you not?—unsight, unseen?"

What a point-blank question! who but Sir Joshua would have ventured it!

"Yes," answered Mr. Sheridan, with quickness, "and make her a bow and my best thanks into the bargain."

Now, my dear Susy, tell me, did you ever hear the fellow to such a speech as this!—it was all I could do to sit it.

"Mr. Sheridan," I exclaimed, "are you not mocking me?"

"No, upon my honour! this is what I have meditated to say to you the first time I should have the pleasure of seeing you."

To be sure, as Mrs. Thrale says, if folks are to be spoilt, there is nothing in the world so pleasant as spoiling! But I was never so much astonished, and seldom have been so much delighted, as by this attack of Mr. Sheridan. Afterwards he took my father aside, and formally repeated his opinion that I should write for the stage, and his desire to see my play,—with encomiums the most flattering of *Evelina*.

And now, my dear Susy, if I should attempt the stage, I think

I may be fairly acquitted of presumption, and however I may fail, that I was strongly pressed to try by Mrs. Thrale, and by Mr. Sheridan, the most successful and powerful of all dramatic living authors, will abundantly excuse my temerity.

In short,—this evening seems to have been decisive; my many and increasing scruples all gave way to encouragement so warm, from so experienced a judge, who is himself interested in not making such a request *par complaisance.* . . .

To Mr. Crisp

Streatham, May 4

Oh! My Dear Daddy—Ah!—alas!—woe is me!—In what terms may I venture to approach you? I don't know, but the more I think of it, the more guilty I feel. I have a great mind, instead of tormenting you with apologies, and worrying myself with devising them, to tell you the plain, honest, literal truth. Indeed, I have no other way any chance of obtaining your forgiveness for my long silence. Honestly, then, my time has, ever since the receipt of your most excellent letter, been not merely occupied, but burthened, with much employment. I have lived almost wholly at Streatham, and the little time I have spent at home, has been divided between indispensable engagements, and preparations for returning hither.

But you will say there is no occasion to exert much honesty in owning this much; therefore now to the secret of the disposal of my private hours. The long and the short is, I have devoted them to writing, and I have finished a play.[35] I must entreat you, my dearest daddy, to keep this communication to yourself, or, at least, if you own it to Kitty, whose long friendship for me I am sure deserves my confidence, make her vow not to reveal it to anybody whatsoever.

This is no capricious request, as I will explain; my own secret inclination leads me forcibly and involuntarily to desire concealment; but that is not all, for Dr. Johnson himself enjoins it; he says, that nothing can do so much mischief to a dramatic work as previous expectation, and that my wisest way will be to endeavour to have it performed before it is known, except to the managers, to be written. . . .

I wish with all my heart it was in my power to take a trip to Chessington for a few days; I have so many things I long to talk over, and I wish so sincerely to see you again. The homely home, as you call it, will never be forgotten while I keep aloof from my last home.

But I forgot to mention, that another and a very great reason for secrecy in regard to my new attempt, is what you have your-self mentioned—avoiding the interference of the various Mæ-cenases who would expect to be consulted. Of these, I could not confide in one without disobliging all the rest; and I could not confide in all, without having the play read all over the town before it is acted. Mrs. Montagu, Mrs. Greville,[36] Mrs. Crewe, Sir Joshua Reynolds, Mrs. Cholmondeley, and many inferior etc.'s, think they have an equal claim, one with the other, to my confidence: and the consequence of it all would be, that, instead of having it, in your words, all my own, and all of a piece, every-body would have a stroke at it, and it would become a mere patch-work of all my acquaintance. The only way to avoid this, is to keep to myself that such a thing exists. Those to whom I have owned it seem all of the same opinion, and I am resolutely de-termined to own it no more.

Evelina continues to sell in a most wonderful manner; a fourth edition is preparing, with cuts, designed by Mortimer just before he died, and executed by Hall and Bartolozzi.[37]

To Dr. Burney

[August (?)]

The fatal knell, then, is knolled, and "down among the dead men" sink the poor *Witlings*—for ever, and for ever, and for ever!

I give a sigh, whether I will or not, to their memory! for, however worthless, they were *mes enfans,* and one must do one's nature, as Mr. Crisp will tell you of the dog.

You, my dearest sir, who enjoyed, I really think, even more than myself, the astonishing success of my first attempt, would, I believe, even more than myself, be hurt at the failure of my second; and I am sure I speak from the bottom of a very honest heart, when I most solemnly declare, that upon your account any disgrace would mortify and afflict me more than upon my own; for whatever appears with your knowledge, will be naturally supposed to have met with your approbation, and, perhaps, your assistance; therefore, though all particular censure would fall where it ought—upon me—yet any general censure of the whole, and the plan, would cruelly, but certainly involve you in its severity.

Of this I have been sensible from the moment my "authorshipness" was discovered, and, therefore, from that moment I determined to have no opinion of my own in regard to what I should thenceforth part with out of my own hands. I would long since have burnt the fourth act, upon your disapprobation of it, but that I waited, and was by Mrs. Thrale so much encouraged to wait, for your finishing the piece.

You have finished it now in every sense of the word. Partial faults may be corrected; but what I most wished was, to know the general effect of the whole; and as that has so terribly failed, all petty criticisms would be needless. I shall wipe it all from my memory, and endeavour never to recollect that I ever wrote it.

You bid me open my heart to you,—and so, my dearest sir, I will, for it is the greatest happiness of my life that I dare be sincere to you. I expected many objections to be raised—a thousand errors to be pointed out—and a million of alterations to be proposed; but the suppression of the piece were words I did not expect; indeed, after the warm approbation of Mrs. Thrale, and the repeated commendations and flattery of Mr. Murphy,[38] how could I?

I do not, therefore, pretend to wish you should think a decision, for which I was so little prepared, has given me no disturbance; for I must be a far more egregious witling than any of those I tried to draw, to imagine you could ever credit that I wrote without some remote hope of success now—though I literally did when I composed *Evelina!*

But my mortification is not at throwing away the characters, or the contrivance;—it is all at throwing away the time,—which

I with difficulty stole, and which I have buried in the mere trouble of writing.

What my daddy Crisp says, "that it would be the best policy, but for pecuniary advantages, for me to write no more," is exactly what I have always thought since *Evelina* was published. But I will not now talk of putting it in practice,—for the best way I can take of showing that I have a true and just sense of the spirit of your condemnation, is not to sink sulky and dejected under it, but to exert myself to the utmost of my power in endeavours to produce something less reprehensible. And this shall be the way I will pursue as soon as my mind is more at ease about Hetty and Mrs. Thrale,[39] and as soon as I have read myself into a forgetfulness of my old *dramatis personæ*—lest I should produce something else as witless as the last.

Adieu, my dearest, kindest, truest, best friend. I will never proceed so far again without your counsel, and then I shall not only save myself so much useless trouble, but you, who so reluctantly blame, the kind pain which I am sure must attend your disapprobation. The world will not always go well, as Mrs. Sapient[40] might say, and I am sure I have long thought I have had more than my share of success already. . . .

FRANCES BURNEY

Brighthelmstone, October 12[41]

. . . On Tuesday Mr., Mrs., Miss Thrale, and "yours, ma'am, yours," set out on their expedition. The day was very pleasant, and the journey delightful; but that which chiefly rendered it so was Mr. Thrale's being apparently the better for it.[42]

I need not tell you how sweet a county for travelling is Kent, as you know it so well. We stopped at Sevenoaks, which is a remarkably well-situated town; and here, while dinner was preparing, my kind and sweet friends took me to Knowle,[43] though they had seen it repeatedly themselves. . . .

We dined very comfortably at Sevenoaks, and thence made but one stage to Tunbridge.[44] It was so dark when we went through the town that I could see it very indistinctly. The Wells, however, are about seven miles yet farther,—so that we saw that night nothing; but I assure you, I felt that I was entering into a new country pretty roughly, for the roads were so *sidelum* and *jumblum,* as Miss L—— called those of Teignmouth, that I expected an overturn every minute. Safely, however, we reached the Sussex Hotel, at Tunbridge Wells. . . .

Tunbridge Wells is a place that to me appeared very singular: the coutry is all rock, and every part of it is either up or down hill, scarce ten yards square being level ground in the whole place: the houses, too, are scattered about in a strange wild manner, and look as if they had been dropped where they stand by accident, for they form neither streets nor squares, but seem strewed promiscuously, except, indeed, where the shopkeepers live who have got two or three dirty little lanes, much like dirty little lanes in other places. . . .

We left Tunbridge Wells, and got, by dinner time, to our first stage, Uckfield, which afforded me nothing to record, except two lines of a curious epitaph which I picked up in the churchyard:—

> A wife and eight little children had I,
> And two at a birth who never did cry.

Our next stage brought us to Brighthelmstone, where I fancy we shall stay till the Parliament calls away Mr. Thrale. . . .

October 20

. . . I must now have the honour to present to you a new acquaintance, who this day dined here—Mr. B[lackne]y, an Irish gentleman, late a commissary in Germany. He is between sixty and seventy, but means to pass for about thirty; gallant, complaisant, obsequious, and humble to the fair sex, for whom he has an awful reverence; but when not immediately addressing them, swaggering, blustering, puffing, and domineering. These are his two apparent characters; but the real man is worthy, moral, religious, though conceited and parading.

He is as fond of quotations as my poor *"Lady Smatter,"*[45] and, like her, knows little beyond a song, and always blunders about the author of that. His language greatly resembles Rose Fuller's, who, as Mrs. Thrale well says, when as old, will be much such another personage. His whole conversation consists in little French phrases, picked up during his residence abroad, and in anecdotes and story-telling, which are sure to be retold daily and daily in the same words.

Having given you this general sketch, I will endeavour to illustrate it by some specimens; but you must excuse their being unconnected, and only such as I can readily recollect.

Speaking of the ball in the evening, to which we were all going, "Ah, madam!" said he to Mrs. Thrale, "there was a time when—tol-de-rol, tol-de-rol (rising, and dancing, and singing), tol-de-rol! —I could dance with the best of them; but, now a man, forty and upwards, as my Lord Ligonier used to say—but—tol-de-rol! —there was a time!"

"Ay, so there was, Mr. B[lackne]y," said Mrs. Thrale, "and I think you and I together made a very venerable appearance!"

"Ah! madam, I remember once, at Bath, I was called out to dance with one of the finest young ladies I ever saw. I was just preparing to do my best, when a gentleman of my acquaintance was so cruel as to whisper me, 'B[lackne]y! the eyes of all Europe are upon you!'—for that was the phrase of the times. 'B[lackne]y!' says he, 'the eyes of all Europe are upon you!'—I vow, ma'am, enough to make a man tremble!—tol-de-rol, tol-de-rol! dancing— the eyes of all Europe are upon you!—I declare, ma'am, enough to put a man out of countenance!" . . .

After this, Dr. Johnson being mentioned, "Ay," said he, "I'm sorry he did not come down with you. I liked him better than those others: not much of a fine gentleman, indeed, but a clever fellow—a deal of knowledge—got a deuced good understanding!" . . .

"I am glad, Mr. Thrale," continued this hero, "you have got your fireplace altered. Why, ma'am, there used to be such a wind, there was no sitting here. Admirable dinners—excellent company—*très bon* fare—and, all the time, 'Signor Vento' coming down the chimney! Do you remember, Miss Thrale, how, one day at dinner, you burst out a-laughing, because I said a *très bon* goose?"

But if I have not now given you some idea of Mr. B[lackne]y's conversation, I never can, for I have written almost as many words as he ever uses, and given you almost as many ideas as he ever starts! And as he almost lives here, it is fitting I let you know something of him. . . .

November 3

. . . However, I have never yet told you his most favourite story, though we have regularly heard it three or four times a day!—And this is about his health.

"Some years ago," he says,—"let's see, how many? in the year '71—ay, '71, '72—thereabouts—I was taken very ill, and, by ill-luck, I was persuaded to ask advice of one of these Dr. Gallipots: —oh, how I hate them all! Sir, they are the vilest pick-pockets— know nothing, sir! nothing in the world! poor ignorant mortals! and then they pretend——In short, sir, I hate them all; I have suffered so much by them, sir—lost four years of the happiness of my life—let's see, '71, '72, '73, '74—ay, four years, sir!—mistook my case sir!—and all that kind of thing. Why, sir, my feet swelled as big as two horses' heads! I vow I will never consult one of these Dr. Gallipot fellows again! lost, me, sir, four years of the happiness of my life!—why I grew quite an object!—you would hardly have known me!—lost all the calves of my legs!—had not an ounce of flesh left!—and as to the rouge—why, my face was the colour of that candle!—those —— Gallipot fellows!—why they robbed me of four years—let me see, ay, '71, '72——"

And then it all goes over again!

This story is always *à propos;* if health is mentioned, it is instanced to show its precariousness; if life, to bewail what he has lost of it; if pain, to relate what he has suffered; if pleasure, to recapitulate what he has been deprived of; but if a physician is hinted at, eagerly, indeed, is the opportunity seized of inveighing against the whole faculty.

[1780]

TO MR. CRISP

St. Martin's Street, January 22

MY DEAREST DADDY —. . . You make a *comique* kind of inquiry about my "incessant and uncommon engagements." Now, my dear daddy, this is an inquiry I feel rather small in answering, for I am sure you expect to hear something respectable in that sort of way, whereas I have nothing to enumerate that commands attention, or that will make a favourable report. For the truth is, my "uncommon" engagements have only been of the *visiting system,* and my "incessant" ones only of the *working party;*—for perpetual dress requires perpetual replenishment, and that replenishment actually occupies almost every moment I spend out of company.[46]

"Fact! fact!" I assure you,—however paltry, ridiculous, or inconceivable it may sound. Caps, hats, and ribbons make, indeed, no venerable appearance upon paper;—no more do eating and drinking;—yet the one can no more be worn without being made, than the other can be swallowed without being cooked; and those who can neither pay milliners nor keep scullions, must either toil for themselves, or go capless and dinnerless. So, if you are for a high-polished comparison, I'm your man!

Now, insteady of furbelows and gewgaws of this sort, my dear daddy probably expected to hear of duodecimos, octavos, or quartos!—*Hélas!* I am sorry that is not the case,—but not one word, no, not one syllable did I write to any purpose, from the time you left me at Streatham, till Christmas, when I came home. . . .

F. B.

Bath, April 7

. . . Don't be angry that I have been absent so long without writing, for I have been so entirely without a moment to myself, except for dressing, that I really have not had it in my power. This morning, being obliged to have my hair dressed early, I am a prisoner, that I may not spoil it by a hat, and therefore I have made use of my captivity in writing to my dear Susy. . . .

I shall now skip to our arrival at this beautiful city, which I really admire more than I did, if possible, when I first saw it.[47] The houses are so elegant, the streets are so beautiful, the prospects so enchanting. I could fill whole pages upon the general beauty of the place and country, but that I have neither time for myself, nor incitement for you, as I know nothing tires so much as description.

We alighted at York House, and Mrs. Thrale sent immediately to Sir Philip Jennings Clerke,[48] who spent the Easter holidays here. He came instantly, with his usual alacrity to oblige, and

told us of lodgings upon the South Parade, whither in the afternoon we all hied, and Mr. Thrale immediately hired a house at the
left corner. It was most deliciously situated; we have meadows,
hills, Prior Park, "the soft-flowing Avon"—whatever Nature has to
offer, I think, always in our view. My room commands all these;
and more luxury for the eye I cannot form a notion of. . . .

Bath, April 9

Tuesday morning we spent in walking all over the town,
viewing the beautiful Circus, the company-crowded Pump-room,
and the exquisite Crescent, which, to all the excellence of archi-
tecture that adorns the Circus, adds all the delights of nature
that beautify the Parades. We also made various visits, and I
called upon Mrs. Cholmley,[49] but was not admitted, and also
upon Miss Bowdler, who was also invisible. We then went to
Mrs. Lambart's,[50] where we again met Miss Lewis, and heard
abundance of Bath chit-chat and news, and were all invited for
Friday to cards. I am, however, determined never to play but
when we are quite alone, and a fourth is indispensably wanted.
I have, therefore, entreated Mrs. Thrale not to make known that
I can.

In the evening we went to the play, and saw *The School for
Scandal* and *The Critic;* both of them admirably well acted, and
extremely entertaining. . . .

Thursday Morning, April 13

. . . Our party to-night at the Dean of Ossory's has by no means
proved enchanting, yet Mrs. Montagu was there, and Hoare, the
painter,[51] and the agreeable Mrs. Lambart. But I was unfortunate
enough not to hear one word from any of them, by being pestered
with witlings all the night.

First I was seated next the eldest Miss L——, not the pretty
girl I have mentioned, Charlotte, who is the second daughter.
This Miss L—— is very heavy and tiresome, though she was
pleased to promise to call upon me, and to cultivate acquaintance
with me, in most civil terms.

This was my fag till after tea, and then Mr. E—— joined us;
I have always endeavoured to shirk this gentleman, who is about
as entertaining and as wise as poor Mr. Pugh, but for whom not
having the same regard, I have pretty soon enough of him; and
so, as I rather turned away, he attacked Miss L——, and I spent
another half-hour in hearing them. . . .

Soon after we went to join the party in the next room. And
then two hours, I believe, were consumed in the most insipid
manner possible. I will give you a specimen, though, to judge of.

Mr. E.—"I never had the pleasure of being in company with
Mrs. Montagu before—I was quite pleased at it."

And yet the booby could not stay where she was!

"Mrs. Montagu! let's see," he continued, "pray, Miss Burney,
did she not write *Shakespeare Moralised?*"

I simpered a little, I believe, but turned to Miss Gregory to
make the answer.

"No, sir," said she, "only an *Essay on the Genius of Shakespeare.*"

"I think," said this wight, "nobody must have so much pleasure at a play as Mrs. Montagu, if it's well done; if not, nobody
must suffer so much, for that's the worst of too much knowledge,
it makes people so difficult."

"Ay, that is to say," said the other wiseacre, "that the more
wisdom, the less happiness."

"That's all the better," said Miss L——, "for there are more
people in the world ignorant than wise."

"Very true," said Mr. E——; "for, as Pope says,

"If ignorance is bliss,
'Tis folly to be wise."

Pope says! Did you ever hear such "witlings"?

But I won't write a word more about the evening—it was
very stupid, and that's enough. . . .

We see Mrs. Montagu very often, and I have already spent six
evenings with her at various houses.

I am very glad at this opportunity of seeing so much of her;
for, allowing a little for parade and ostentation, which her power
in wealth, and rank in literature, offer some excuse for, her conversation is very agreeable; she is always reasonable and sensible,
and sometimes instructive and entertaining. . . .

FROM MR. CRISP

April 27

MY DEAR FANNIKIN—I am very glad you are now with the Thrales, in the midst of the Bath circle. Your time could not be better employed, for all your St. Martin's daddy wanted to retain you for some other purpose. You are now at school, the great school of the world, where swarms of new ideas and new characters will continually present themselves before you,

which you'll draw in,
As we do air, fast as 'tis ministered![52]

. . . You take no notice of several particulars I want to hear of. Your unbeautiful, clever heroine, beset all round for the sake of her great fortune—what is become of her?[53] I am persuaded she'd make her own fortune, whatever were the fate of her hunters. The idea is new and striking, and presents a large field for unhackneyed characters, observations, subjects for satire and ridicule, and numberless advantages you'd meet with by walking in such an untrodden path. . . .

Your loving daddy,
S. C.

Friday

. . . In the evening we went to visit Mrs. K——.

Mrs. K—— is a Welsh lady, of immense fortune, who has a house in the Crescent, and lives in a most magnificent style. She is about fifty, very good-humoured, well-bred, and civil, and her waist does not measure above a hogshead. She is not very deep, I must own; but what of that? If all were wits, where would be the admirers at them?

She received me very graciously, having particularly desired Mrs. Thrale to bring me: for she is an invalid, and makes no visits herself. . . .

Soon after this, arrived Mrs. Montagu and Miss Gregory. Miss

Gregory brought a chair next to mine, and filled up the rest of my evening. . . .

Afterwards, who should be announced but the author of the *Bath Guide*, Mr. Anstey.[54] I was now all eye; but not being able to be all ear, I heard but little that he said, and that little was scarce worth hearing. He had no opportunity of shining and was as much like another man as you can imagine. It is very unfair to expect wonders from a man all at once; yet it was impossible to help being disappointed, because his air, look, and manner are mighty heavy and unfavourable to him.

But here see the pride of riches! and see whom the simple Mrs. K—— can draw to her house! However, her party was not thrown away upon her,—as I ought to say, because highly honoured by her exultingly whispering to Mrs. Thrale,

"Now, ma'am, now, Mrs. Thrale, I'm quite happy; for I'm surrounded with people of sense! Here's Mrs. Montagu, and Mrs. Thrale, and Mr. Anstey, and Miss Burney. I'm quite surrounded, as I may say, by people of sense!"

Thursday

We were appointed to meet the Bishop of Chester[55] at Mrs. Montagu's. This proved a very gloomy kind of grandeur; the Bishop waited for Mrs. Thrale to speak, Mrs. Thrale for the Bishop; so neither of them spoke at all!

Mrs. Montagu cared not a fig, as long as she spoke herself, and so she harangued away. Meanwhile Mr. Melmoth, the Pliny Melmoth,[56] as he is called, was of the party, and seemed to think nobody half so great as himself, and, therefore, chose to play first-violin without further ceremony. But, altogether, the evening was not what it was intended to be, and I fancy nobody was satisfied. It is always thus in long-projected meetings. . . .

[May], Sunday

We went to the abbey, to hear the bishop preach. He gave us a very excellent sermon, upon the right use of seeking knowledge, namely, to know better the Creator by his works, and to learn our own duty in studying his power. . . .

Monday

We went to Mrs. Lambart. Here we met Lady Dorothy Inglish, a Scotchwoman; Sir Robert Pigot, an old Englishman; Mrs. North, the Bishop of Worcester's handsome wife, and many nameless others.

Mrs. North, who is so famed for tonishness, exhibited herself in a more perfect undress than I ever before saw any lady, great or small, appear in upon a visit. Anything alike worse as better than other folks, that does but obtain notice and excite remark, is sufficient to make happy ladies and gentlemen of the *ton*. I always long to treat them as daddy Crisp does bad players (when his own partners) at whist, and call to them, with a nod of contemptuous anger, "Bless you! bless you!" . . .

Saturday

. . . In the afternoon we all went to the Whalleys', where we found a large and a highly-dressed company: at the head of which sat Lady Miller.[57] Among the rest were Mr. Anstey, his lady, and two daughters, Miss Weston, Mrs. Aubrey, the thin quaker-like woman I saw first at Mrs. Lawes', Mrs. Lambart, and various others, male and female, that I knew not. . . .

Do you know now that, notwithstanding Bath Easton is so much laughed at in London, nothing here is more tonish than to visit Lady Miller, who is extremely curious in her company, admitting few people who are not of rank or of fame, and excluding of those all who are not people of character very unblemished.[58]

Some time after, Lady Miller took a seat next mine on the sofa, to play at cards, and was excessively civil indeed—scolded Mrs. Thrale for not sooner making us acquainted, and had the politeness to offer to take me to the balls herself, as she heard Mr. and Mrs. Thrale did not choose to go.

After all this, it is hardly fair to tell you what I think of her. However, the truth is, I always, to the best of my intentions, speak honestly what I think of the folks I see, without being biassed either by their civilities or neglect; and that you will allow is being a very faithful historian.

Well, then, Lady Miller is a round, plump, coarse-looking dame of about forty, and while all her aim is to appear an elegant woman of fashion, all her success is to seem an ordinary woman in very common life, with fine clothes on. Her manners are bustling, her air is mock-important, and her manners very inelegant.

So much for the lady of Bath Easton; who, however, seems extremely good-natured, and who is I am sure extremely civil. . . .

To Dr. Burney

Bath, June 9

My Dearest Sir—How are you? where are you? and what is to come next? These are the questions I am dying with anxiety to have daily announced. The accounts from town are so frightful, that I am uneasy, not only for the city at large, but for every individual I know in it. I hope to Heaven that ere you receive this, all will be once more quiet; but till we hear that it is so, I cannot be a moment in peace.[59] . . .

A private letter to Bull, the bookseller, brought word this morning that much slaughter has been made by the military among the mob. Never, I am sure, can any set of wretches less deserve quarter or pity; yet it is impossible not to shudder at hearing of their destruction. Nothing less, however, would do; they were too outrageous and powerful for civil power.

But what is it they want? who is going to turn papist? who, indeed, is thinking in an alarming way of religion—this pious mob, and George Gordon excepted?

I am very anxious indeed about our dear Etty. Such disturbance in her neighbourhood I fear must have greatly terrified her; and I am sure she is not in a situation or state of health to bear terror. I have written and begged to hear from her.

All the stage-coaches that come into Bath from London are chalked over with "No Popery," and Dr. Harrington called here just now, and says the same was chalked this morning upon his door, and is scrawled in several places about the town. Wagers have been laid that the popish chapel here will be pulled or burnt down in a few days; but I believe not a word of the matter, nor do I find that anybody is at all alarmed. Bath, indeed, ought to be held sacred as a sanctuary for invalids; and I doubt not but the news of the firing in town will prevent all tumults out of it. . . .

Friday Night

The above I writ this morning, before I recollected this was not post-day, and all is altered here since. The threats I despised were but too well grounded, for, to our utter amazement and consternation, the new Roman Catholic chapel in this town was set on fire at about nine o'clock. It is now burning with a fury that is dreadful, and the house of the priest belonging to it is in flames also. The poor persecuted man himself has, I believe, escaped with life, though pelted, followed, and very ill-used. Mrs. Thrale and I have been walking about with the footmen several times. The whole town is still and orderly. The rioters do their work with great composure, and though there are knots of people in every corner, all execrating the authors of such outrages, nobody dares oppose them. An attempt, indeed, was made, but it was ill-conducted, faintly followed, and soon put an end to by a secret fear of exciting vengeance. . . .

Saturday Afternoon, June 10

I was most cruelly disappointed in not having one word today. I am half crazy with doubt and disturbance in not hearing. Everybody here is terrified to death. We have intelligence that Mr. Thrale's house in town is filled with soldiers, and threatened by the mob with destruction.[60] Perhaps he may himself be a marked man for their fury. We are going directly from Bath, and intend to stop only at villages. To-night we shall stop at Warminster, not daring to go to Devizes. This place is now well guarded, but still we dare not await the event of to-night; all the Catholics in the town have privately escaped.

I know not now when I shall hear from you. I am in agony for news. Our headquarters will be Brighthelmstone, where I do most humbly and fervently entreat you to write—do, dearest sir, write, if but one word—if but only you name YOURSELF! . . .

Salisbury, June 11

Here we are, dearest sir, and here we mean to pass this night.

We did not leave Bath till eight o'clock yesterday evening, at which time it was filled with dragoons, militia, and armed constables, not armed with muskets, but bludgeons: these latter were all chairmen, who were sworn by the mayor in the morning for petty constables. A popish private chapel, and the houses of all the Catholics, were guarded between seven and eight, and the inhabitants ordered to keep house.

We set out in the coach-and-four, with two men on horseback, and got to Warminster, a small town in Somersetshire, a little before twelve.

This morning two more servants came after us from Bath, and brought us word that the precautions taken by the magistrates last night had had good success, for no attempt of any sort had been renewed towards a riot.

But the happiest tidings to me were contained in a letter which they brought, which had arrived after our departure, by the diligence, from Mr. Perkins,[61] with an account that all was quiet in London, and that Lord G. Gordon was sent to the Tower.

I am now again tolerably easy, but I shall not be really comfortable, or free from some fears, till I hear from St. Martin's Street. . . .

F. B.

FROM DR. BURNEY

1 St. Martin's Street, Monday Afternoon, June 1780
Your letter just received.

MY DEAR FANNY—We are all safe and well, after our heartaches and terrors. London is now the most secure residence in the kingdom.

I wrote a long letter to our dear Mrs. T. on Friday night, with a kind of detail of the week's transactions. I am now obliged to go out, and shall leave the girls to fill up the rest of the sheet. All is safe and quiet in the Borough.[62] We sent William[63] thither on Saturday. God bless you! . . .

[1781]

To Mr. Crisp

Streatham, April 29

Have you not, my dearest daddy, thought me utterly lost? and, indeed, to all power of either giving or taking comfort, I certainly have been for some time past. I did not, it is true, *hope* that poor Mr. Thrale could live very long, as the alteration I saw in him only during my absence while with you had shocked and astonished me. Yet, still the suddenness of the blow gave me a horror from which I am not even now recovered.[64] The situation of sweet Mrs. Thrale, added to the true concern I felt at his loss, harassed my mind till it affected my health, which is now again in a state of precariousness and comfortless restlessness that will require much trouble to remedy.

You have not, I hope, been angry at my silence; for, in truth, I have had no spirits to write, nor, latterly, ability of *any* kind, from a headache that has been incessant. . . .

Mrs. Thrale flew immediately upon this misfortune to Brighthelmstone, to Mr. Scrase—*her* Daddy Crisp—both for consolation and counsel; [65] and she has but just quitted him, as she deferred returning to Streatham till her presence was indispensably necessary upon account of proving the will. I offered to accompany her to Brighthelmstone; but she preferred being alone, as her mind was cruelly disordered, and she saw but too plainly I was too sincere a mourner myself to do much besides adding to her grief. The moment, however, she came back, she solicited me to meet her,—and I am now here with her, and endeavour, by every possible exertion, to be of some use to her. She looks wretchedly indeed, and is far from well; but she bears up, though not with calm intrepidity, yet with flashes of spirit that rather, I fear, spend than relieve her. Such, however, is her character, and were this exertion repressed, she would probably sink quite.

Miss Thrale is steady and constant, and very sincerely grieved for her father.

The four executors, Mr. Cator, Mr. Crutchley, Mr. Henry Smith,[66] and Dr. Johnson, have all behaved generously and honourably, and seem determined to give Mrs. Thrale all the comfort and assistance in their power. She is to carry on the business jointly with them. Poor soul! it is a dreadful toil and worry to her.

Adieu, my dearest daddy. I will write again in a week's time. I have now just been blooded; but am by no means *restored* by that loss. But well and ill, equally and ever, your truly affectionate child,

F. B.

Streatham, May

Miss Owen and I arrived here without incident, which, in a journey of six or seven miles, was really marvellous! Mrs. Thrale came from the Borough with two of the executors, Dr. Johnson and Mr. Crutchley, soon after us. She had been sadly worried, and in the evening frightened us all by again fainting away. Dear creature! she is all agitation of mind and of body: but she is now wonderfully recovered, though in continual fevers about her affairs, which are mightily difficult and complicate indeed.[67] Yet the behaviour of all the executors is exactly to her wish. Mr. Crutchley, in particular, was he a darling son or only brother, could not possibly be more truly devoted to her. Indeed, I am very happy in the revolution in my own mind in favour of this young man, whom formerly I so little liked; for I now see so much of him, business and inclination uniting to bring him hither continually, that if he were disagreeable to me, I should spend my time in a most comfortless manner. . . .

Sunday morning nobody went to church but Mr. Crutchley, Miss Thrale, and myself; and some time after, when I was sauntering upon the lawn before the house, Mr. Crutchley joined me. We were returning together into the house, when Mrs. Thrale, popping her head out of her dressing-room window, called out, "How nicely these men domesticate among us, Miss Burney! Why, they take to us as natural as life!"

"Well, well," cried Mr. Crutchley, "I have sent for my horse, and I shall release you early to-morrow morning. I think yonder comes Sir Philip."

"Oh! you'll have enough to do with *him,*" cried she, laughing; "he is well prepared to plague you, I assure you."

"Is he?—and what about?"

"Why, about Miss Burney. He asked me the other day what was my present establishment. 'Mr. Crutchley and Miss Burney,' I answered. 'How well these two names go together,' cried he; 'I think they can't do better than make a match of it: *I* will consent, I am sure,' he added; and to-day, I daresay, you will hear enough of it."

I leave you to judge if I was pleased at this stuff thus communicated; but Mrs. Thrale, with all her excellence, can give up no occasion of making sport, however unseasonable, or even painful.

"I am very much obliged to him, indeed!" cried I drily; and Mr. Crutchley called out, "*Thank him!—thank him!*" in a voice of pride and of pique that spoke him mortally angry.

I instantly came into the house, leaving him to talk it out with Mrs. Thrale, to whom I heard him add, "So this is Sir Philip's kindness!" and her answer, "I wish you no worse luck!"

Now, what think you of this? was it not highly insolent?—and from a man who has behaved to me hitherto with the utmost deference, good nature, and civility, and given me a thousand reasons, by every possible opportunity, to think myself very high indeed in his good opinion and good graces? But these rich men think themselves the constant prey of all portionless girls, and are always upon their guard, and suspicious of some design to take them in. This sort of disposition I had very early observed in Mr. Crutchley, and therefore I had been more distant and cold with him than with anybody I ever met with; but latterly his character had risen so much in my mind, and his behaviour was so much improved, that I had let things take their own course, and no more shunned than I sought him; for I evidently saw his doubts concerning *me* and *my* plots were all at an end, and his civility and attentions were daily increasing, so that I had become very comfortable with him, and well pleased with his society.

I need not, I think, add that I determined to see as little of this most fearful and haughty gentleman in future as was in my power, since no good qualities can compensate for such arrogance of suspicion; and, therefore, as I had reason enough to suppose he would, in haste, resume his own reserve, I resolved, without much effort, to be beforehand with him in resuming mine. . . .

I was obliged, at dinner, to be seated between Miss O'Riley and Mr. Crutchley, to whom you may believe I was not very courteous, especially as I had some apprehensions of Sir Philip. Mr. Crutchley, however, to my great surprise, was quite as civil as ever, and endeavoured to be as chatty; but there I begged to be excused, only answering *upon the reply*, and that very drily, for I was indeed horribly provoked with him.

Indeed, all his behaviour would have been natural and good-humoured, and just what I should have liked, had he better concealed his chagrin at the first accusation; but that, still dwelling by me, made me very indifferent to what followed, though I found he had no idea of having displeased me, and rather sought to be more than less sociable than usual. . . .

Wednesday, June 26

Dr. Johnson, who had been in town some days, returned, and Mr. Crutchley came also, as well as my father. I did not see the two latter till summoned to dinner; and then Dr. Johnson seizing my hand, while with one of his own he gave me a no very gentle tap on the shoulder, half drolly and half reproachfully called out,

"Ah, you little baggage, you! and have you known how long I have been here, and never to come to me?"

And the truth is, in whatever sportive mode he expresses it, he really likes not I should be absent from him half a minute whenever he is here, and not in his own apartment. . . . Mr. Crutchley, however, continues the least fathomable, . . . of all the men I have seen. I will give you, therefore, having, indeed, nothing better to offer, some further specimens to judge of. . . .

. . . [We] began more seriously to talk upon happiness and misery; and I accused him of having little sense of either, from the various strange and desperate speeches which he is continually making; such as those I told you, of his declaring he cared not if he was to be shut up in the Exchequer for the rest of his life; and as to Mrs. Plumbe [68]—the stupidest of all women—he had as lieve as not pass the rest of his days with her: and during this last visit, when the horrors of a convent were enumerating by Mrs. Thrale, he asserted that there was nothing but prejudice in preferring any other mode of life, since every mode was, in fact, alike.

"Well," said he, "and custom will make anything endured; though a great deal of all this must be given to mere talk without meaning; for as to living with Mrs. Plumbe, I protest I would not spend an hour with her to save me from ruin, nor with anybody I did not like. I cannot even make common visits to people unless I like them. But the few I *do* like, perhaps nobody ever liked equally. I have, indeed, but one wish or thought about them; and that is, to be with them not only every day, but every hour. And I never change, and never grow tired: nobody in the world has less taste for variety."

Afterwards he asserted that nobody ever died of grief. I did not agree with him; for I do, indeed, believe it is a death but too possible.

"I judge," said he, "as people are too apt to judge, by myself; I am sure *I* have no affections that can kill me."

"I can easily believe that," said I, "and I fancy very few people have; but, among them, I should certainly never number those who settle themselves into a philosophic coldness and apathy that renders all things equal to them, and the Convent or the Exchequer the same as any other places."

"Why, a little use would make them so," said he, laughing. "However, I believe I have had as much delight *one* way as any man breathing; and that is, in hunting. I have pursued that with an enthusiasm that has been madness. I have been thrown from my horse and half killed, and mounted her again and gone on. I have been at it till every one has been tired out; but myself never. I have jumped from my horse to catch a dirty hound in my arms and kiss it!"

"Well," cried I, "and does this last?"

"Why, no," cried he, "thank Heaven! not quite so bad now. To be sure, 'tis the most contemptible delight that ever man took, and I never knew three men in the world who pursued it with equal pleasure that were not idiots. Those, however," said he afterwards, "are, I believe, the most happy who have most affections; even the pain of such has pleasure with it."

This from a man whose evident effort is to stifle every affection, nay, every feeling, of the soul!

"I do not," continued he, "believe that any grief in the world ever out-lasted a twelvemonth."

"A twelvemonth," said I, "spent in real sorrow is a long, long time indeed. I question myself if it almost *can* last or be supported longer."

After this, upon my saying I supposed him hardly a fair judge of affliction, as I believed him a man determined to extinguish every feeling that led to it, he grew very unexpectedly grave and communicative, and told me he had had two calamities as heavy and as bitter as anybody could have or could feel.

"And yet," said he, "I found I got the better of them. I was ill—I lost my appetite—I could not sleep—I had a fever; yet in time all these complaints were gone, and I got well, and lived on much as usual."

One of these calamities he then explained to have been the loss of his mother, whom I find he quite adored; and he seems still to wonder how he survived her. The other he seemed half inclined to mention, but I did not venture to lead to it, as it occurred to me that it was possibly an affair of the heart; in which, if, notwithstanding all his assertions of ignorance of *la belle passion,* he has had a disappointment, I think much of the strangeness of his character accounted for. . . .

Streatham

. . . Mr. Crutchley arrived, who came to spend two or three days, as usual. Sir Philip Clerke also was here; but I have no time now to write any account of what passed, except that I must and ought to mention that Mr. Crutchley, in the presence of Sir Philip, is always more respectful to me than at any other time; indeed, only then, for he troubles not himself with too much ceremony. . . .

The day he ended his visit, Sir Philip also ended his, having only come from Hampshire for a few days; and, as I wanted much to go down and see my sister, Mrs. Thrale ordered her coach, and took us all thither herself.

In our way Mr. Crutchley, who was in uncommon spirits, took

it in his head to sing the praises of wine (though no man drinks less), and afterwards of smoking; Mrs. Thrale all the time combating all he said, Sir Philip only laughing, and I, I suppose, *making faces.* At last he called out,

"Look at Miss Burney, how she sits wondering at my impudence!"

He expected, I fancy, I should contradict this; but not a word did I say: so then, with a little *dépit,* he added,

"I suppose, now, I shall have *impudence* added to the—the *vanity* you gave my character before."

This mistake I am pretty sure was a *wilful* one, by way of passing for only slightly remembering the accusation.

"Vanity!" cried I; "when did I charge you with vanity?"

"Well, what was it then?—*pride!*"

I said nothing; neither choosing to confirm what he has taken so seriously to heart, nor to contradict what I think as strongly as ever.

"Pride and impudence!" continued he, with a look at once saucy and mortified—"a pretty composition, upon my life!"

"Nay, nay," said I, "this is an addition of your own. I am sure I never called, or thought, you impudent."

It would be strange if I had; for, on the contrary, he is an actual *male prude!*

"No, no; she gave you nothing but the pride," said Mrs. Thrale, "she left all the vanity for me! Saucy that she is! So you have, at least, the higher fault; for vanity is much the meaner of the two. Lord Bacon says, 'A beggar of bread is a better man than a beggar of a bow; for the bread is of more worth.' So see if you are not best off."

"Me best off!" cried he—"no, indeed; Miss Burney thinks better of vanity than pride, by her giving one to you and t'other to me."

To this, again, I would not speak; for I could not well without a new argument, and the old one is so long remembered that I am determined to have no more.

"If Miss Burney," said he presently, "thought as well of me as of you, I believe I should have reason to be very well contented. Should not I?"

"As well of you as of me!" cried Mrs. Thrale; "why, if ever I heard such a speech! No, indeed, I hope not! I have always heard her called a very wise girl!" . . .

Friday, September 14

And now, if I am not mistaken, I come to relate the conclusion of Mr. Crutchley's most extraordinary summer career at Streatham, which place, I believe, he has now left without much intention to frequently revisit. However, this is mere conjecture; but he really had a run of ill-luck not very inviting to a man of his cold and splenetic turn, to play the same game.[69]

When we were just going to supper, we heard a disturbance among the dogs; and Mrs. and Miss Thrale went out to see what was the matter, while Dr. Johnson and I remained quiet. Soon returning, "A friend! a friend!" she cried, and was followed by Mr. Crutchley.

He would not eat with us, but was chatty and in good-humour, and as usual, when in spirits, saucily sarcastic. For instance, it is generally half my employment in hot evenings here to rescue some or other poor buzzing idiot of an insect from the flame of a candle. This, accordingly, I was performing with a Harry Longlegs,[70] which, after much trial to catch, eluded me, and escaped, nobody could see how. Mr. Crutchley vowed I had caught and squeezed him to death in my hand.

"No, indeed," cried I, "when I catch them, I put them out of the window."

"Ay, their bodies," said he, laughing; "but their legs, I suppose, you keep."

"Not I, indeed; I hold them very safe in the palm of my hand."

"Oh!" said he, "the palm of your hand! why, it would not hold a fly! But what have you done with the poor wretch—thrown him under the table slyly?"

"What good would that do?"

"Oh, help to establish your full character for mercy."

Now, was not that a speech to provoke Miss Grizzle herself?[71] However, I only made up a saucy lip.

"Come," cried he, offering to take my hand, "where is he? Which hand is he in? Let me examine?"

"No, no, I thank you; I shan't make *you* my confessor, whenever I take one."

He did not much like this; but I did not mean he should.

Afterwards he told us a most unaccountably ridiculous story of a *crying wife*. A gentleman, he said, of his acquaintance had married lately his own kept mistress; and last Sunday he had dined with the bride and bridegroom; but, to his utter astonishment, without any apparent reason in the world, in the middle of dinner or tea, she burst into a violent fit of crying, and went out of the room, though there was not the least quarrel, and the *sposo* seemed all fondness and attention!

"What, then," said I, somewhat maliciously, I grant, "had *you* been saying to her?"

"Oh, thank you!" said he, with a half-affronted bow, "I expected this! I declare I thought you would conclude it was me!" . . .

Dr. Johnson has been very unwell indeed. Once I was quite frightened about him; but he continues his strange discipline— starving, mercury, opium; and though for a time half demolished by its severity, he always, in the end, rises superior both to the disease and the remedy,—which commonly is the most alarming of the two. His kindness for me, I think, if possible, still increased: he actually *bores* everybody so about me that the folks even complain of it. I must, however, acknowledge I feel but little pity for their fatigue.

[1782]

To Mrs. Phillips[72]

February 25

Are you quite *enragée* with me, my dearest Susy? Indeed, I think I am with myself, for not sooner and oftener writing to you; and every night when I go to bed, and every morning when I wake, I determine shall be the last I will do either again till I have written to you. But, *hélas!* my pens get so fagged, and my hands so crippled, when I have been up two or three hours, that my resolution wavers, and I sin on, till the time of rest and meditation, and then I repent again.[73] Forgive me, however, my dearest girl, and pray pay me not in kind; for, as Charlotte would say, *kind* that would not be, however deserved and just.

My work is too long in all conscience for the hurry of my people to have it produced. I have a thousand million of fears for it. The mere copying, without revising and correcting, would take at least ten weeks, for I cannot do more than a volume in a fortnight, unless I scrawl short hand and rough hand, as badly as the original. Yet my dear father thinks it will be published in a month! Since you went I have copied one volume and a quarter —no more! Oh, I am sick to think of it! Yet not a little reviving is my father's very high approbation of the first volume, which is all he has seen. . . .

Would you ever believe, bigoted as he was to *Evelina,* that he now says he thinks this a superior design and superior execution?

You can never half imagine the delight this has given me. It is answering my first wish and first ambition in life. And though I am certain, and though he thinks himself, it will never be so popular as *Evelina,* his so warm satisfaction will make me amends for almost any mortification that may be in store for me.

I would to Heaven it were possible for me to have a reading *de suite* of it with you, my Susy, more than with anybody; but I could not admit Captain Phillips, dearly as I love him; I could not for my life read myself to Mr. Burney, and was obliged to make Etty. It is too awkward a thing to do to any human beings but my sisters, and poor auntys, and Kitty Cooke. I have let the first *tome* also run the gauntlet with Mrs. Thrale.

From Mrs. Thrale

Tuesday Night

My eyes red with reading and crying, I stop every moment to kiss the book and to wish it was my Burney! 'Tis the sweetest book, the most interesting, the most engaging. Oh! it beats every other book, even your own other vols., for *Evelina* was a baby to it.[74] . . .

Such a novel! Indeed, I am seriously and sensibly touched by it, and am proud of her friendship who so knows the human heart. May mine long bear the inspection of so penetrating, so discriminating an eye!

This letter is written by scraps and patches, but every scrap is admiration, and every patch thanks you for the pleasure I have received. I will say no more; I cannot say half I think with regard to praise. . . .

My most ingenious, my most admirable friend, adieu! If I had more virtue than *Cecilia*, I should half fear the censures of such an insight into the deepest recesses of the mind. Since I have read this volume, I have seriously thanked Heaven that all the litter of mine was in sight; none hoarded in holes, nor hastily stuffed into closets. You have long known the worst of your admiring

H. L. T.

June

. . . So much has passed since I lost you [75]—for I cannot use any other word—that I hardly know what first to record; but I think 'tis best to begin with what is uppermost in my mind, Mr. Burke.[76]

Among the many I have been obliged to shirk this year, for the sake of living almost solely with *Cecilia*, none have had less patience with my retirement than Miss Palmer,[77] who, bitterly believing I intended never to visit her again, has forborne sending me any invitations: but, about three weeks ago, my father had a note from Sir Joshua Reynolds, to ask him to dine at Richmond, and meet the Bishop of St. Asaph: and, therefore, to make my peace, I scribbled a note to Miss Palmer to this purpose,—

"After the many kind invitations I have been obliged to refuse, will you, my dear Miss Palmer, should I offer to accompany my father to-morrow, bid me remember the old proverb,—

"Those who will not when they may,
When they will, they shall have nay?

F. B."

This was graciously received; and the next morning Sir Joshua and Miss Palmer called for my father and me, accompanied by Lord Corke. We had a mighty pleasant ride. Miss Palmer and I *made up*, though she scolded most violently about my long absence, and attacked me about the book without mercy. The book, in short, to my great consternation, I find is talked of and expected all the town over. My dear father himself, I do verily believe, mentions it to everybody; he is fond of it to enthusiasm, and does not foresee the danger of raising such general expectation, which fills *me* with the horrors every time I am tormented with the thought.

Sir Joshua's house is delightfully situated, almost at the top of Richmond Hill. We walked till near dinner-time upon the terrace, and there met Mr. Richard Burke, the brother of the orator. . . .

Miss Palmer soon joined us; and, in a short time, entered more company, three gentlemen and one lady; but there was no more ceremony used of introductions. The lady, I concluded, was Mrs. Burke, wife of *the* Mr. Burke, and was not mistaken. One of the gentlemen I recollected to be young Burke, her son, whom I once met at Sir Joshua's in town, and another of them I knew for Mr. Gibbon: [78] but the third I had never seen before. I had been told that *the* Burke was not expected; yet I could conclude this gentleman to be no other; he had just the air, the manner, the appearance, I had prepared myself to look for in him, and there was an evident, a striking superiority in his demeanour, his eye, his motions, that announced him no common man.

I could not get at Miss Palmer to satisfy my doubts, and we were soon called downstairs to dinner. Sir Joshua and the *unknown* stopped to speak with one another upon the stairs; and, when they followed us, Sir Joshua, in taking his place at the table, asked me to sit next to him; I willingly complied. "And then," he added, "Mr. Burke shall sit on the other side of you." . . .

He is tall, his figure is noble, his air commanding, his address graceful; his voice is clear, penetrating, sonorous, and powerful; his language is copious, various, and eloquent; his manners are attractive, his conversation is delightful. . . .

I can give you, however, very little of what was said, for the conversation was not *suivie*, Mr. Burke darting from subject to subject with as much rapidity as entertainment. Neither is the charm of his discourse more in the matter than the manner; all, therefore, that is related *from* him loses half its effect in not being related *by* him. . . .

From the Right Honorable Edmund Burke

Whitehall, July 29

MADAM—I should feel exceedingly to blame if I could refuse to myself the natural satisfaction, and to you the just but poor return, of my best thanks for the very great instruction and entertainment I have received from the new present you have bestowed on the public. There are few—I believe I may say fairly there are none at all—that will not find themselves better informed concerning human nature, and their stock of observation enriched, by reading your *Cecilia*. They certainly will, let their experience in life and manners be what it may. The arrogance of age must submit to be taught by youth. You have crowded into a few small volumes an incredible variety of characters; most of them well planned, well supported, and well contrasted with each other. If there be any fault in this respect, it is one in which you are in no great danger of being imitated. Justly as your characters are drawn, perhaps they are too numerous. But I beg pardon; I fear it is quite in vain to preach economy to those who are come young to excessive and sudden opulence.

I might trespass on your delicacy if I should fill my letter to you with what I fill my conversation to others. I should be troublesome to you alone if I should tell you all I feel and think on the natural vein of humour, the tender pathetic, the comprehensive and noble moral, and the sagacious observation, that appear quite throughout that extraordinary performance.

In an age distinguished by producing extraordinary women, I hardly dare to tell you where my opinion would place you amongst them. I respect your modesty, that will not endure the commendations which your merit forces from everybody.

I have the honour to be, with great gratitude, respect, and esteem, madam, your most obedient and most humble servant,

EDM. BURKE

Brighthelmstone, October 26

My journey was incidentless; but the moment I came into Brighthelmstone I was met by Mrs. Thrale, who had most eagerly been waiting for me a long while, and therefore I dismounted, and walked home with her. It would be very superfluous to tell you how she received me, for you cannot but know, from her impatient letters, what I had reason to expect of kindness and welcome. . . .

Oh, but let me not forget that a fine note came from Mr. Pepys,[79] who is here with his family, saying he was *pressé de vivre,* and entreating to see Mrs. and Miss T.,[80] Dr. Johnson, and Cecilia, at his house the next day. I hate mightily this method of naming me from my heroines, of whose honour I think I am more jealous than of my own.

October 27

The Pepyses came to visit me in form, but I was dressing; in the evening, however, Mrs. and Miss T. took me to them. Dr. Johnson would not go; he told me it was my day, and I should be crowned, for Mr. Pepys was wild about *Cecilia.* . . .

We found at Mr. Pepys' nobody but his wife, his brother, Dr. Pepys, and Dr. Pepys' lady, Countess of Rothes. Mr. Pepys received me with such distinction, that it was very evident how much the book, with the most flattering opinion of it, was in his head; however, he behaved very prettily, and only mentioned it by allusions. . . .

We did not stay with them long, but called upon Miss Benson, and proceeded to the Rooms. Mr. Pepys was very unwilling to part with us, and wanted to frighten me from going, by saying,

"And has Miss Burney courage to venture to the Rooms? I wonder she dares!"

I did not seem to understand him, though to mistake him was impossible. However, I thought of him again when I was at the Rooms, for most violent was the staring and whispering as I passed and repassed; insomuch that I shall by no means be in any haste to go again to them. Susan and Sophy Thrale, who were with their aunt, Mrs. Scot, told Queeny, upon our return, that they heard nothing said, whichever way they turned, but "That's she!" "That's the famous Miss Burney!" I shall certainly escape going any more, if it is in my power. . . .

Monday, October 28

Mr. Pepys had but just left me, when Mrs. Thrale sent Susan with a particular request to see me in her dressing-room, where I found her with a milliner.

"Oh, Miss Burney," she cried, "I could not help promising Mrs. Cockran that she should have a sight of you—she has begged it so hard."

You may believe I stared; and the woman, whose eyes almost looked ready to eat me, eagerly came up to me, exclaiming,

"Oh, ma'am, you don't know what a favour this is, to see you! I have longed for it so long! It is quite a comfort to me, indeed. Oh, ma'am, how clever you must be! All the ladies I deal with are quite distracted about *Cecilia*,—and I got it myself. Oh, ma'am, how sensible you must be! It does my heart good to see you."

Did you ever hear the like? 'Twas impossible not to laugh, and Mrs. Thrale has done nothing else ever since.

At dinner we had Dr. Delap [81] and Mr. Selwyn, [82] who accompanied us in the evening to a ball; as did also Dr. Johnson, to the universal amazement of all who saw him there;—but he said he had found it so dull being quite alone the preceding evening, that he determined upon going with us; "for," he said, "it cannot be worse than being alone."

Strange that he should think so! I am sure I am not of his mind.

Mr. H. Cotton and Mr. Swinerton [83] of course joined us immediately. We had hardly been seated five minutes before Mr. Selwyn came to me, from some other company he had joined, and said,

"I think you don't choose dancing, ma'am?"

"No," I answered.

"There is a gentleman," he added, "who is very ambitious of the honour of dancing with you; but I told him I believed you would not dance."

I assured him he was right.

There was, indeed, no need of my dancing by way of attraction, as I saw, again, so much staring, I scarce knew which way to look; and every glance I met was followed by a whisper from the glancer to his or her party. It was not, indeed, quite so bad as on Sunday, as the dancers were something to look at besides me: but I was so very much watched, and almost pointed at, that I have resolved to go no more, neither to balls nor Rooms, if I can possibly avoid it. . . .

Saturday, November 2

. . . [W]e went to Lady Shelley's.[84] Dr. Johnson, again, excepted in the invitation. He is almost constantly omitted, either from too much respect or too much fear. I am sorry for it, as he hates being alone, and as, though he scolds the others, he is well enough satisfied himself; and, having given vent to all his own occasional anger or ill-humour, he is ready to begin again, and is never aware that those who have so been "downed" by him, never can much covet so triumphant a visitor. In contests of wit, the victor is as ill off in future consequences as the vanquished in present ridicule.

Monday, November 4

. . . When all our company was gone, late as it was, it was settled we should go to the ball, the last for the season being this night. My own objections about going not being strong enough to combat the ado my mentioning them would have occasioned, I joined in the party without demur. We all went but Dr. Johnson.

The ball was half over, and all the company seated to tea. Mr. Wade [85] came to receive us all, as usual, and we had a table procured for us, and went to tea ourselves, for something to do. When this repast was over, the company returned to their recreation. The room was very thin, and almost half the ladies danced with one another, though there were men enough present, I believe, had they chosen such exertion; but the Meadowses at balls are in crowds. Some of the ladies were in riding habits, and they made admirable men. 'Tis *tonnish* to be so much undressed at the last ball.

None of our usual friends, the Shelleys, Hatsels, Dickens, or

Pepys, were here, and we, therefore, made no party; but Mrs. Thrale and I stood at the top of the room to look on the dancing, and as we were thus disengaged, she was seized with a violent desire to make one among them, and I felt myself an equal inclination. She proposed, as so many women danced together, that we two should, and nothing should I have liked so well; but I begged her to give up the scheme, as that would have occasioned more fuss and observation than our dancing with all the men that ever were born. . . .

Here [Mr. Wade] was called away by some gentleman, but presently came to me again.

"Miss Burney," he said, "shall you dance?"

"No, sir, not to-night."

"A gentleman," he added, "has desired me to speak to you for him."

Now, Susanna, for the grand moment!—the height—the zenith of my glory in the *ton* meridian! I again said I did not mean to dance, and to silence all objection, he expressively said,

" 'Tis Captain Kaye who sends me."[86]

Is not this magnificent? Pray congratulate me!

I was really very much surprised, but repeated my refusal, with all customary civilities to soften it. He was leaving me with this answer, when this most flashy young officer, choosing to trust his cause to himself, came forward, and desired to be introduced to me. Mr. Metcalf [87] performed that ceremony, and he then, with as much respect and deference as if soliciting a countess, said,

"May I flatter myself you will do me the honour of dancing with me?"

I thanked him, and said the same thing over again. He looked much disappointed, and very unwilling to give up his plan.

"If you have not," he said, "any particular dislike to dancing, it will be doing, not only me, but the whole room much honour, if you will make one in a set."

"You do me much honour, sir," I answered, "but I must beg you to excuse me."

"I hope not," cried he; "I hope out of charity you will dance, as it is the last ball, and the company is so thin." . . .

I was a little thrown off my guard at this unexpected earnestness, so different to the *ton* of the day, and I began hardly to know what to answer, my real objection being such as I could by no means publish, though his urgency and his politeness joined would have made me give up any other.

"This is a very quiet dance," he continued; "there is nothing fatiguing in it."

"You are very good," said I, "but I cannot really dance to-night."

I was sorry to seem so obstinate, but he was just the man to make everybody inquire whom he danced with; and any one who wished for general attention could do no better than to be his partner. . . .

Monday, [December 23]

. . . I begin to grow most heartily sick and fatigued of this continual round of visiting, and these eternal new acquaintances. I am now arranging matters in my mind for a better plan; and I mean, henceforward, never to go out more than three days in the week; and, as I am now situated, with Mrs. Thrale to seize every moment I do not hide from her, it will require all the management I can possibly make use of to limit my visits to only half the week's days. But yet, I am fixed in resolving to put it in practice, except upon some very singular and unforeseen occasions, as I really have at present no pleasure in any party, from the trouble and tiresomeness of being engaged to so many.

For my own part, if I wished to prescribe a cure for dissipation, I should think none more effectual than to give it a free course. The many who have lived so from year to year amaze me now more than ever; for now more than ever I can judge what dissipation has to offer. I would not lead a life of daily engagements even for another month, for any pay short of the most serious and substantial benefit. I have been tired some time, though I have only now broke out: but I will restore my own spirit and pleasure by getting more courage in making refusals, and by giving that zest to company and diversion which can only be given by making them subservient to convenience, and by taking them in turn with quietness and retirement.

This is my intention, and I shall never, by inclination, alter it. . . .

. . . Our evening was really a charming one. The two Mr. Cambridges [88] came at about eight o'clock, and the good Mr. Hoole was here. My father came downstairs to them in high spirits and good humour, and he and the elder Mr. Cambridge not only talked enough for us all, but so well and so pleasantly that no person present had even a wish to speak for himself. Mr. Cambridge has the best stock of good stories I almost ever heard; and, though a little too precise in his manner, he is always well bred, and almost always entertaining. Our sweet father kept up the ball with him admirably, whether in anecdotes, serious disquisitions, philosophy, or fun; for all which Mr. Cambridge has both talents and inclination.

The son rises extremely in my opinion and liking. He is sensible, rational, and highly cultivated; very modest in all he asserts, and attentive and pleasing in his behaviour; and he is wholly free from the coxcombical airs, either of impertinence, or negligence and nonchalance, that almost all the young men I meet, except also young Burke, are tainted with. What chiefly, however, pleased me in him was observing that he quite adores his father. He attended to all his stories with a face that never told he had heard them before; and, though he spoke but little himself, he seemed as well entertained as if he had been the leading person in the company,—a post which, nevertheless, I believe he could extremely well sustain; and, no doubt, much the better for being in no haste to aspire to it. I have seldom, altogether, had an evening with which I have been better pleased. . . .

[1783]

January

Young Mr. Cambridge need not complain of my taciturnity, whatever his father may do. Who, indeed, of all my new acquaintances, has so well understood me? The rest all talk of *Evelina*

and *Cecilia,* and turn every other word into some compliment;
while he talks of Chessington, or Captain Phillips,[89] and pays me,
not even by implication, any compliments at all. He neither looks
at me with any curiosity, nor speaks to me with any air of expectation; two most insufferable honours, which I am continually receiving. He is very properly conscious he has at least as much to
say as to hear, and he is above affecting a ridiculous deference to
which he feels I have no claim. If I met with more folks who
would talk to me upon such rational terms,—considering, like him,
their own dignity of full as much value as my ladyship's vanity,—
with how infinitely more ease and pleasure should I make one in
those conversations!

Sunday, January 19

And now for Mrs. Delany.[90] I spent one hour with Mrs. Thrale,
and then called for Mrs. Chapone,[91] and we proceeded together
to St. James's Place.

Mrs. Delany was alone in her drawing-room, which is entirely
hung round with pictures of her own painting, and ornaments of
her own designing. She came to the door to receive us. She is still
tall, though some of her height may be lost: not much, however,
for she is remarkably upright. She has no remains of beauty in
feature, but in countenance I never but once saw more, and that
was in my sweet maternal grandmother. Benevolence, softness,
piety, and gentleness are all resident in her face; and the resemblance with which she struck me to my dear grandmother, in her
first appearance, grew so much stronger from all that came from
her mind, which seems to contain nothing but purity and native
humility, that I almost longed to embrace her; and I am sure if
I had, the recollection of that saint-like woman would have been so
strong that I should never have refrained from crying over her.

Mrs. Chapone presented me to her, and taking my hand, she
said,

"You must pardon me if I give you an old-fashioned reception,
for I know nothing new."

And she saluted me. I did not, as with Mrs. Walsingham,[92] retreat from her.

"Can you forgive, Miss Burney," she continued, "this great

liberty I have taken with you, of asking for your company to dinner? I wished so impatiently to see one from whom I have received such extraordinary pleasure, that, as I could not be alone
this morning, I could not bear to put it off to another day; and, if
you had been so good to come in the evening, I might, perhaps,
have had company; and I hear so ill that I cannot, as I wish to do,
attend to more than one at a time; for age makes me stupid even
more than I am by nature; and how grieved and mortified I
must have been to know I had Miss Burney in the room, and not
to hear her!"

She then mentioned her regret that we could not stay and spend
the evening with her, which had been told her in our card of
accepting her invitation, as we were both engaged, which, for my
part, I heartily regretted.

"I am particularly sorry," she added, "on account of the
Duchess Dowager of Portland, who is so good as to come to me
in an evening, as she knows I am too infirm to wait upon her
Grace myself: and she wished so much to see Miss Burney.[93] But
she said she would come as early as possible, and you won't, I
hope, want to go very soon?"

My time, I answered, was Mrs. Chapone's, and Mrs. Chapone
said she could not stay later than half-past seven. . . .

Soon after we went to dinner, which was plain, neat, well
cooked, and elegantly served. When it was over, I began to speak;
and now, my Chessington auditors, look to yourselves!

"Will you give me leave, ma'am, to ask if you remember anybody of the name of Crisp?"

"Crisp?" cried she; "what! Mrs. Ann Crisp?"[94]

"Yes, ma'am."

"Oh surely! extremely well! a charming, an excellent woman
she was; we were very good friends once; I visited her at Burford,
and her sister Mrs. Gast."

Then came my turn, and I talked of the brother; but I won't
write what I said. . . .

This Chessingtonian talk lasted till we went upstairs, and then
she showed me the new art which she has invented. It is staining
paper of all possible colours, and then cutting it out, so finely and
delicately, that when it is pasted on paper or vellum, it has all
the appearance of being pencilled, except that, by being raised, it
has still a richer and more natural look. The effect is extremely
beautiful. She invented it at seventy-five! She told me she did four

flowers the first year; sixteen the second; and the third, 160; and after that many more. They are all from nature, and consist of the most curious flowers, plants, and weeds, that are to be found. She has been supplied with patterns from all the great gardens, and all the great florists in the kingdom. Her plan was to finish 1000; but, alas! her eyes now fail her, though she has only twenty undone of her task.[95]

She has marked the places whence they all came, on the back, and where she did them, and the year; and she has put her cypher, M. D., at the corner of each, in different coloured letters for every different year—such as red, blue, green, etc.

"But," said she, "the last year, as I found my eyes grew very dim and threatened to fail before my work was completed, I put my initials in white, for I seemed to myself already working in my winding-sheet."

I could almost have cried at the mingled resignation and spirit with which she made this melancholy speech. . . .

At about seven o'clock, the Duchess Dowager of Portland came. She is not near so old as Mrs. Delany, nor, to me, is her face by any means so pleasing; but yet there is sweetness, and dignity, and intelligence in it. Mrs. Delany received her with the same respectful ceremony as if it was her first visit, though she regularly goes to her every evening. But what she at first took as an honour and condescension, she has so much of true humility of mind, that no use can make her see in any other light. She immediately presented me to her. Her Grace courtesied and smiled with the most flattering air of pleasure, and said she was particularly happy in meeting with me. . . .

In the course of this conversation I found her very charming, high-bred, courteous, sensible, and spirited; not merely free from pride, but free from affability—its most mortifying deputy.

After this she asked me if I had seen Mrs. Siddons,[96] and what I thought of her. I answered that I admired her very much.

"If Miss Burney approves her," said the Duchess, "no approbation, I am sure, can do her so much credit; for no one can so perfectly judge of characters or of human nature."

"Ah, ma'am," cried Mrs. Delany archly, "and does your Grace remember protesting you would never read *Cecilia?*"

"Yes," said she, laughing; "I declared that five volumes could never be attacked; but since I began I have read it three times."

"Oh, terrible!" cried I, "to make them out fifteen!" . . .

I think I need now write no more. I could, indeed, hear no more: for this last so serious praise, from characters so respectable, so moral, and so aged, quite affected me; and though I had wished a thousand times during the discourse to run out of the room, when they gave me finally this solemn sanction to the meaning and intention of my writing, I found it not without difficulty that I could keep the tears out of my eyes; and when I told what had passed to our sweet father, his quite ran over. . . .

To Mr. Crisp

April 12

MY DEAREST—DEAREST DADDY—I am more grieved at the long and most disappointing continuation of your illness than I know how to tell you; and though my last account, I thank Heaven, is better, I find you still suffer so much, that my congratulations in my letter to Susan, upon what I thought your recovery, must have appeared quite crazy, if you did not know me as well as you do, and were not sure what affliction the discovery of my mistake would bring to myself.

I think I never yet so much wished to be at Chessington, as at this time, that I might see how you go on, and not be kept in such painful suspense from post to post. . . .

God bless and restore you, my most dear daddy! You know not how kindly I take your thinking of me, and inquiring about me, in an illness that might so well make you forget us all: but Susan assures me your heart is as affectionate as ever to your ever and ever faithful and loving child,

F. B.

From Dr. Burney

[April (?)]

I am much more afflicted than surprised at the violence and duration of your sorrow for the terrible scenes and events at Chessington, and not only pity you, but participate in all your feelings.[97]

Not an hour in the day has passed, as you will some time or other find, since the fatal catastrophe, in which I have not felt a pang for the irreparable loss I have sustained. However, as something is due to the living, there is, perhaps, a boundary at which it is right to endeavour to stop in lamenting the dead. It is very hard, as I have found it all my life, to exceed these bounds in our duty or attention, without its being at the expense of others. I have lost in my time persons so dear to me, as to throw me into the utmost affliction and despondency which can be suffered without insanity; but I had claims on my life, my reason, and activity, which drew me from the pit of despair, and forced me, though with great difficulty, to rouse and exert every nerve and faculty in answering them. It has been very well said of mental wounds, that they must digest, like those of the body, before they can be healed. Necessity can alone, perhaps, in some cases, bring on this digestion; but we should not prevent it by caustics or corrosion; let the wound be open a due time, but not treated with violence. To quit all metaphor, we must, alas! try to diminish our sorrow for our calamity, to enable us to support another; as a national peace is but time to refit, a mental is no more. So far, however, am I from blaming your indulgence of sorrow on the present occasion, that I both love and honour you for it; and therefore shall add no more on that melancholy subject.

C. B.

Thursday, June 19

We heard to-day that Dr. Johnson had been taken ill, in a way that gave a dreadful shock to himself, and a most anxious alarm to his friends. Mr. Seward brought the news here, and my father and I instantly went to his house. He had earnestly desired me, when we lived so much together at Streatham, to see him frequently if he should be ill. He saw my father, but he had medical people with him, and could not admit me upstairs, but he sent me down a most kind message, that he thanked me for calling, and when he was better should hope to see me often. I had the satisfaction to hear from Mrs. Williams[98] that the physicians had pronounced him to be in no danger, and expected a speedy recovery.

The stroke was confined to his tongue. Mrs. Williams told me a most striking and touching circumstance that attended the attack. It was at about four o'clock in the morning: he found himself with a paralytic affection; he rose, and composed in his own mind a Latin prayer to the Almighty, "that whatever were the sufferings for which he must prepare himself, it would please Him, through the grace and mediation of our blessed Saviour, to spare his intellects, and let them all fall upon his body." When he had composed this, internally, he endeavoured to speak it aloud, but found his voice was gone. . . .

Wednesday, July 1

I was again at Mrs. Vesey's,[99] where again I met Mr. Walpole,[100] Mr. Pepys, Miss Elliott, Mr. Burke, his wife and son, Sir Joshua Reynolds, and some others.

Mr. Burke was extremely kind to me, but not at all in spirits. He is tormented by the political state of affairs; and loses, I really believe, all the comfort of his life, at the very time he is risen to the station his ambition has long pointed out to him.

I had the satisfaction to hear from Sir Joshua that Dr. Johnson had dined with him at the Club.[101] I look upon him, therefore, now, as quite recovered. I called the next morning to congratulate him, and found him very gay and very good-humoured.

Friday, July 18

I called in the morning upon my dear Mrs. Delany, who received me with the utmost kindness, and whom I really love even more than I admire. I appointed to spend Tuesday with her. And so I would any other day she had named, or even any week. It is sweet, it is consolatory to me to be honoured with so much of her favour as to see her always eager to fix a time for our next and next meeting. . . .

Wednesday, November 19

I received a letter from Dr. Johnson, which I have not by me, but will try to recollect.

To Miss Burney

Bolt Court, November 19

MADAM—You have now been at home this long time, and yet I have neither seen nor heard from you. Have we quarrelled?

I have met with a volume of the *Philosophical Transactions*, which I imagine to belong to Dr. Burney. Miss Charlotte will please to examine.

Pray send me a direction where Mrs. Chapone lives; and pray, some time, let me have the honour of telling you how much I am, madam, your most humble servant,

SAM. JOHNSON

Now if ever you read anything more dry, tell me. I was shocked to see him undoubtedly angry, but took courage, and resolved to make a serious defence; therefore thus I answered,

To Dr. Johnson

St. Martin's Street, November 19

DEAR SIR—May I not say dear? for quarrelled I am sure we have not. The bad weather alone has kept me from waiting upon you; but now you have condescended to give me a summons, no lion shall stand in the way of my making your tea this afternoon, unless I receive a prohibition from yourself, and then I must submit; for what, as you said of a certain great lady, signifies the barking of a lap-dog, if once the lion puts out his paw?

The book was very right. Mrs. Chapone lives at either No. 7 or 8 in Dean Street, Soho.

I beg you, sir, to forgive a delay for which I can only 'tax the elements with unkindness,' and to receive, with your usual goodness and indulgence, your most obliged and most faithful humble servant,

F. BURNEY

My dear father spared me the coach, and to Bolt Court, therefore, I went, and with open arms was I received. Nobody was there but Charles[102] and Mr. Sastres,[103] and Dr. Johnson was, if possible, more instructive, entertaining, good-humoured, and exquisitely fertile, than ever. He thanked me repeatedly for coming, and was so kind I could hardly ever leave him. . . .

[1784]

FROM MRS. THRALE

Bath, Wednesday, February 18

Thanks, thanks, a thousand, my prettiest, dearest Burney! This charming letter makes amends for all. And you remember last winter, do you? and remember it with tenderness? What then must have passed in my mind, on the dreadful anniversary of a day which, instead of killing me as it ought to have done, gave to two innocent, unfortunate people, a cruel and lingering death,— like the arrows tipped with African poison, which slowly and gradually retarding the vital powers, at length (in about three years, I think) wholly put a stop to their exertion![104] . . .

Johnson is in a sad way, doubtless; yet he may still with care last another twelvemonth, and every week's existence is gain to him, who, like good Hezekiah, wearies Heaven with entreaties for life. I wrote him a very serious letter the other day. . . .

Well you have lost some of the old treason-plotters, to be sure, by whom you were and are dearly loved and valued; but when friends are once parted in this wide world, 'tis so strange if they ever meet again, that no one ought to wonder should they see each other no more. There is a place, however, where we shall meet those we love, and enjoy their society in peace and comfort. To such as have fully experienced the agonies of absence, sure that will be heaven enough.

Adieu, my precious friend, and don't forget one on whose heart time and distance have no other effect than to engrave affection and affliction the deeper. Adieu! I am really almost drawn together from emptiness and sinking. Love me, however, while I am your

H. L. T.

Saturday, April 17

The sight of your paw any way, my dearest Susy, my heart's ever dearest friend, would be well worth all the pence I have in the world, could I see it on no other condition. Indeed I have not been really in spirits, nor had one natural laugh, since I lost you; there seems such an insipidity, such a vacuity in all that passes. I know not, in truth, whether I most miss you when happy or when sad. That I wish for you most when happy is certain; but that nothing upon earth can do me so much good, when sad, as your society, is certain too. Constantly to hear from you, and to write to you, is the next best thing; so now, with as little murmuring as I am able, I return to our paper conversations. . . .

Friday, April 23

The sweet and most bewitching Mrs. Locke[105] called upon me in the evening, with her son George. I let her in, and did so rejoice I had not gone to Mrs. Vesey's. But I rejoiced for only a short time; she came but to take leave, for she was going to Norbury the very next morning. I was quite heavy all the evening. She does truly interest both head and heart. I love her already. And she was so kind, so caressing, so soft; pressed me so much to fix a time for going to Norbury; said such sweet things of Mrs. Phillips; and kissed me so affectionately in quitting me, that I was quite melted by her.

What a charm has London lost for me by her departure! sweet creature that she is; born and bred to dispense pleasure and delight to all who see or know her! She, Mrs. Thrale, and Mrs. Delany, in their several ways all excellent, possess the joint powers of winning the affections, while they delight the intellects, to the highest summit I can even conceive of human attraction. . . .

FROM MRS. THRALE

Mortimer Street, Cavendish Square
Tuesday Night, May

I am come, dearest Burney. It is neither dream nor fiction; though I love you dearly, or I would not have come. Absence and distance do nothing towards wearing out real affection; so you shall always find it in your true and tender

H. L. T.

I am somewhat shaken bodily, but 'tis the mental shocks that have made me unable to bear the corporeal ones. 'Tis past ten o'clock, however, and I must lay myself down with the sweet expectation of seeing my charming friend in the morning to breakfast. I love Dr. Burney too well to fear him, and he loves me too well to say a word which should make me love him less.

May 17

Let me now, my Susy, acquaint you a little more connectedly than I have done of late how I have gone on. The rest of that week I devoted almost wholly to sweet Mrs. Thrale, whose society was truly the most delightful of cordials to me, however, at times, mixed with bitters the least palatable. . . .

I parted most reluctantly with my dear Mrs. Thrale, whom, when or how, I shall see again, Heaven only knows! but in sorrow we parted—on *my* side in real affliction.[106] . . .

[Norbury Park], Wednesday, November 3

. . . Nothing can be more truly pleasant than our present lives. I bury all disquietudes in immediate enjoyment; an enjoyment more fitted to my secret mind than any I had ever hoped to attain. We are so perfectly tranquil, that not a particle of our whole frames seems ruffled or discomposed. Mr. Locke is gayer and more sportive than I ever have seen him; his Fredy seems made up of happiness; and the two dear little girls are in spirits almost ecstatic; and all from that internal contentment which Norbury Park seems to have gathered from all corners of the world into its own sphere.

Our mornings, if fine, are to ourselves, as Mr. Locke rides out; if bad, we assemble in the picture room. We have two books in public reading, Madame de Sévigné's *Letters* and Cook's last voyage. Mrs. Locke reads the French, myself the English.

Our conversations, too, are such as I could almost wish to last for ever. Mr. Locke has been all himself,—all instruction, information, and intelligence,—since we have been left alone; and the invariable sweetness, as well as judgment, of all he says, leaves, indeed, nothing to wish.

They will not let me go while I can stay, and I am now most willing to stay till I *must* go. The serenity of a life like this smoothes the whole internal surface of the mind. My own, I assure you, begins to feel quite glossy. . . .

Norbury Park, Sunday, November 28

How will my Susan smile at sight of this date! Let me tell her how it has all happened. Last Thursday, Nov. 25, my father set me down at Bolt Court, while he went on upon business. I was anxious to again see poor Dr. Johnson, who has had terrible health since his return from Lichfield. He let me in, though very ill. He was alone, which I much rejoiced at; for I had a longer and more satisfactory conversation with him than I have had for many months. He was in rather better spirits, too, than I have lately seen him; but he told me he was going to try what sleeping out of town might do for him.

"I remember," said he, "that my wife, when she was near her end, poor woman, was also advised to sleep out of town; and when she was carried to the lodgings that had been prepared for her, she complained that the staircase was in very bad condition—for the plaster was beaten off the walls in many places. 'Oh,' said the man of the house, 'that's nothing but by the knocks against it of the coffins of the poor souls that have died in the lodgings!' "

He laughed, though not without apparent secret anguish, in telling me this. I felt extremely shocked, but, willing to confine my words at least to the literal story, I only exclaimed against the unfeeling absurdity of such a confession.

"Such a confession," cried he, "to a person then coming to try his lodging for her health, contains, indeed, more absurdity than we can well lay our account for." . . .

Yet, all brilliant as he was, I saw him growing worse, and offered to go, which, for the first time I ever remember, he did not oppose; but, most kindly pressing both my hands,

"Be not," he said, in a voice of even tenderness, "be not longer in coming again for my letting you go now."

I assured him I would be the sooner, and was running off, but he called me back, in a solemn voice, and, in a manner the most energetic, said,

"Remember me in your prayers!"

I longed to ask him to remember me, but did not dare. I gave him my promise, and, very heavily indeed, I left him. Great, good, and excellent that he is, how short a time will he be our boast! Ah, my dear Susy, I see he is going! . . .

St. Martin's Street, Wednesday, December 10

I went in the evening to poor Dr. Johnson. Frank[107] told me he was very ill, but let me in. He would have taken me upstairs, but I would not see him without his direct permission. I desired Frank to tell him I called to pay my respects to him, but not to disturb him if he was not well enough to see me. Mr. Strahan,[108] a clergyman, he said, was with him alone.

In a few minutes, this Mr. Strahan came to me himself. He told me Dr. Johnson was very ill, very much obliged to me for coming, but so weak and bad he hoped I would excuse his not seeing me. . . .

Dear, dear, and much-reverenced Dr. Johnson! how ill or how low must he be, to decline seeing a creature he has so constantly, so fondly, called about him! If I do not see him again I shall be truly afflicted. And I fear, I almost know, I cannot! . . .

At night my father brought us the most dismal tidings of dear Dr. Johnson. Dr. Warren[109] had seen him, and told him to take what opium he pleased! He had thanked and taken leave of all his physicians. Alas!—I shall lose him, and he will take no leave of me! . . .

December 11

. . . This morning, after church time, I went. Frank said he was very ill, and saw nobody; I told him I had understood by my father the day before that he meant to see me. He then let me in. I went into his room upstairs; he was in his bedroom. I saw it crowded, and ran hastily down. Frank told me his master had refused seeing even Mr. Langton. I told him merely to say I had called, but by no means to press my admission. His own feelings were all that should be consulted; his tenderness, I knew, would be equal, whether he was able to see me or not.

I went into the parlour, preferring being alone in the cold, to any company with a fire. Here I waited long, here and upon the stairs, which I ascended and descended to meet again with Frank, and make inquiries; but I met him not. At last, upon Dr. Johnson's ringing his bell, I saw Frank enter his room, and Mr. Langton follow. "Who's that?" I heard him say; they answered, "Mr. Langton," and I found he did not return.

Soon after, all the rest went away but a Mrs. Davis, a good sort of woman, whom this truly charitable soul had sent for to take a dinner at his house. I then went and waited with her by the fire: it was, however, between three and four o'clock before I got any answer. Mr. Langton then came himself. He could not look at me and I turned away from him. Mrs. Davis asked how the Doctor was? "Going on to death very fast!" was his mournful answer. "Has he taken," said she, "anything?" "Nothing at all! We carried him some bread and milk—he refused it, and said—'*The less the better.*'" She asked more questions, by which I found his faculties were perfect, his mind composed, and his dissolution was quick drawing on.[110] . . .

December 20

This day was the ever-honoured, ever-lamented Dr. Johnson committed to the earth. Oh, how sad a day to me! My father attended, and so did Charles. I could not keep my eyes dry all day; nor can I now, in the recollecting it; but let me pass over what to mourn is now so vain! . . .

[1785]

[Windsor], Friday, December 16

. . . After dinner, while Mrs. Delany was left alone, as usual, to take a little rest,—for sleep it but seldom proves,—Mr. B. Dewes, his little daughter, Miss Port, and myself, went into the drawing-room.[111] And here, while, to pass the time, I was amusing the little girl with teaching her some Christmas games, in which her father and cousin joined, Mrs. Delany came in. We were all in the middle of the room, and in some confusion;—but she had but just come up to us to inquire what was going forwards, and I was disentangling myself from Miss Dewes, to be ready to fly off if any one knocked at the street-door, when the door of the drawing-room was again opened, and a large man, in deep mourning, appeared at it, entering and shutting it himself without speaking.

A ghost could not more have scared me, when I discovered, by its glitter on the black, a star! The general disorder had prevented his being seen, except by myself, who was always on the watch, till Miss P——, turning round, exclaimed, "The King!—Aunt, the King!"[112]

Oh, mercy! thought I, that I were but out of the room! which way shall I escape? and how pass him unnoticed? There is but the single door at which he entered, in the room! Every one scampered out of the way: Miss P——, to stand next the door; Mr. Bernard Dewes to a corner opposite it; his little girl clung to me; and Mrs. Delany advanced to meet His Majesty, who, after quietly looking on till she saw him, approached, and inquired how she did.

He then spoke to Mr. Bernard, whom he had already met two or three times here.

I had now retreated to the wall, and purposed gliding softly, though speedily, out of the room; but before I had taken a single step, the King, in a loud whisper to Mrs. Delany, said, "Is that Miss Burney?"—and on her answering, "Yes, sir," he bowed, and with a countenance of the most perfect good humour came close up to me.

A most profound reverence on my part arrested the progress of my intended retreat.

"How long have you been come back, Miss Burney?"

"Two days, sir."

Unluckily he did not hear me, and repeated his question; and whether the second time he heard me or not, I don't know, but he made a little civil inclination of his head, and went back to Mrs. Delany. . . .

During this discourse, I stood quietly in the place where he had first spoken to me. His quitting me so soon, and conversing freely and easily with Mrs. Delany, proved so delightful a relief to me, that I no longer wished myself away; and the moment my first panic from the surprise was over, I diverted myself with a thousand ridiculous notions, of my own situation. . . .

. . . It seemed to me we were acting a play. There is something so little like common and real life, in everybody's standing, while talking, in a room full of chairs, and standing, too, so aloof from each other, that I almost thought myself upon a stage, assisting in the representation of a tragedy,—in which the King played his own part, of the king; Mrs. Delany that of a venerable confidante; Mr. Dewes, his respectful attendant; Miss P——, a suppliant virgin, waiting encouragement to bring forward some petition; Miss Dewes, a young orphan, intended to move the royal compassion; and myself,—a very solemn, sober, and decent mute.

These fancies, however, only regaled me while I continued a quiet spectator, and without expectation of being called into play. But the King, I have reason to think, meant only to give me time to recover from my first embarrassment; and I feel myself infinitely obliged to his good breeding and consideration, which perfectly answered, for before he returned to me I was entirely recruited. . . .

Then coming up close to me, he said,

"But what?—what?—how was it?"

"Sir?"—cried I, not well understanding him.

"How came you—how happened it—what?—what?"

"I—I only wrote, sir, for my own amusement,—only in some odd, idle hours."

"But your publishing—your printing—how was that?"

"That was only, sir,—only because——"

I hesitated most abominably, not knowing how to tell him a long story, and growing terribly confused at these questions:—besides,—to say the truth, his own "what? what?" so reminded me of those vile *Probationary Odes*,[113] that, in the midst of all my flutter, I was really hardly able to keep my countenance.

The *What!* was then repeated, with so earnest a look, that, forced to say something, I stammeringly answered,

"I thought—sir—it would look very well in print!".

I do really flatter myself this is the silliest speech I ever made! I am quite provoked with myself for it; but a fear of laughing made me eager to utter anything, and by no means conscious, till I had spoken, of what I was saying. . . .

While this was talking over, a violent thunder was made at the door. I was almost certain it was the Queen.[114] Once more I would have given anything to escape; but in vain. I had been informed that nobody ever quitted the royal presence, after having been conversed with, till motioned to withdraw.

Miss P——, according to established etiquette on these occasions, opened the door which she stood next, by putting her hand behind her, and slid out, backwards, into the hall, to light the Queen in. The door soon opened again, and Her Majesty entered.

Immediately seeing the King, she made him a low curtsey, and cried,

"Oh, your Majesty is here!"

"Yes," he cried, "I ran here, without speaking to anybody."

The Queen had been at the lower Lodge,[115] to see the Princess Elizabeth, as the King had before told us.

She then hastened up to Mrs. Delany, with both her hands held out, saying,

"My dear Mrs. Delany, how are you?"

Instantly after, I felt her eye on my face. I believe, too, she curtsied to me; but though I saw the bend, I was too near-sighted to be sure it was intended for me. I was hardly ever in a situation more embarrassing; I dared not return what I was not certain I had received, yet considered myself as appearing quite a monster, to stand stiff-necked, if really meant.

Almost at the same moment, she spoke to Mr. Bernard Dewes, and then nodded to my little clinging girl.

I was now really ready to sink, with horrid uncertainty of what I was doing, or what I should do,—when His Majesty, who I fancy saw my distress, most good-humouredly said to the Queen something, but I was too much flurried to remember what, except these words,—"I have been telling Miss Burney——"

Relieved from so painful a dilemma, I immediately dropped a curtsey. She made one to me in the same moment, and, with a very smiling countenance, came up to me; but she could not speak, for the King went on talking, eagerly, and very gaily, repeating to her every word I had said during our conversation upon *Evelina*, its publication, etc. etc. . . .

Almost instantly upon his leaving me, a very gentle voice called out—"Miss Burney!"

It was the Queen's. I walked a little nearer her, and a gracious inclination of her head made me go quite up to her.

"You have been," she said, "at Mrs. Walsingham's?"

"Yes, ma'am."

"She has a pretty place, I believe?"

"Yes, ma'am."

"Were you ever there before?"

"Yes, ma'am."

Oh, shocking! shocking! thought I; what will Mrs. Delany say to all these monosyllables?

"Has not she lately made some improvements?"

"Yes, ma'am; she has built a conservatory."

Then followed some questions about its situation, during which the King came up to us; and she then, ceasing to address me in particular, began a general sort of conversation, with a spirit and animation that I had not at all expected, and which seemed the result of the great and benevolent pleasure she took in giving entertainment to Mrs. Delany. . . .

Her accent is a little foreign, and very prettily so; and her emphasis has that sort of changeability, which gives an interest to everything she utters. But her language is rather peculiar than foreign. . . .

. . . She chiefly addressed herself to Mrs. Delany; and to me, certainly, she would not, separately, have been so communicative; but she contrived, with great delicacy, to include me in the little party, by frequently looking at me, and always with an expression that invited my participation in the conversation. And, indeed, though I did not join in words, I shared very openly in the pleasure of her recital. . . .

. . . A pause ensuing, I, too, drew back, meaning to return to my original station, which, being opposite the fire, was never a bad one. But the moment I began retreating, the Queen, bending forward, and speaking in a very low voice, said, "Miss Burney!"—and, upon my coming up to her, almost in a whisper, cried, "But shall we have no more—nothing more?"

I could not but understand her, and only shook my head.

The Queen then, as if she thought she had said too much, with great sweetness and condescension, drew back herself, and, very delicately, said,

"To be sure it is, I own, a very home question, for one who has not the pleasure to know you."

I was quite ashamed of this apology, but did not know what to say to it. But how amiable a simplicity in her speaking of herself in such a style,—"for one who has not the pleasure to know you."

"But, indeed," continued she presently, "I would not say it, only that I think from what has been done, there is a power to do so much good—and good to young people—which is so very good a thing—that I cannot help wishing it could be."

I felt very grateful for this speech, and for the very soft manner in which she said it; and I very much wished to thank her, and was trying to mutter something, though not very intelligibly, when the King suddenly coming up to us, inquired what was going forward.

The Queen readily repeated her kind speech.

The King eagerly undertook to make my answer for me, crying, "Oh, but she will write!—she only waits for *inclination*—she told me so." Then, speaking to me, he said, "What—is it not so?"

I only laughed a little; and he again said to the Queen,

"She will write! She told me, just now, she had made no vow against it."

"No, no," cried the Queen, "I hope not, indeed!" . . .

I was quite ashamed of all this, and quite sorry to make no acknowledgment of their great condescension in pressing such a subject, and pressing it so much in earnest. But I really could get out nothing, so that's the truth; and I wish I could give a better account of my eloquence, my dear Padre and Susan. . . .

The King then, looking at his watch, said, "It is eight o'clock, and if we don't go now, the children will be sent to the other house."[116]

"Yes, your Majesty," cried the Queen, instantly rising.

Mrs. Delany put on Her Majesty's cloak, and she took a very kind leave of her. She then curtsied separately to us all, and the King handed her to the carriage.

It is the custom for everybody they speak to to attend them out, but they would not suffer Mrs. Delany to move. Miss P——, Mr. Dewes, and his little daughter, and myself, all accompanied them, and saw them in their coach, and received their last gracious nods. . . .

Upon the whole, and for me, don't you think, my dear father and Susan, I comported myself mighty well in my grand interview? Indeed, except quite at the first, I was infinitely more easy than I usually am with strangers; and the great reason of that was, that I had no fear of being frightened, nor shame of being ashamed; for they, I was sure, were more accustomed to see people frightened and confused, than to find them composed and undisturbed. But that is not the case with others, who cannot, therefore, make the same allowance. . . .

COURT

[1786-1791]

[1786]

A vacancy at this time occurred in the royal household, from the resignation of Madame Haggerdorn, one of the Queen's German attendants who, together with Madame Schwellenberg, held the office of Keeper of the Robes.[1] The place was much sought after, but Her Majesty had been so well pleased with what she saw of Miss Burney, that she graciously empowered Mr. Smelt[2] to offer her this situation, allowing her time to consider and weigh its advantages.

Miss Burney, though deeply grateful for such a distinction, foresaw with alarm the separation from her family and the total confinement it would occasion; and, in her perplexity how to decide, she wrote the following letter to her judicious and faithful friend, the late Miss Cambridge.[3]

To Miss Cambridge

Monday, June

. . . I now see the end—I see it next to inevitable. I can suggest nothing upon earth that I dare say for myself, in an audience so generously meant. I cannot even to my father utter my reluctance, —I see him so much delighted at the prospect of an establishment he looks upon as so honourable. But for the Queen's own word *permanent*,—but for her declared desire to attach me entirely to herself and family,—I should share in his pleasure; but what can make *me* amends for all I shall forfeit? But I must do the best I can. Write me a comforting and strengthening letter, my dearest Miss Cambridge. I have no heart to write to Mickleham, or Norbury. I know how they will grieve:—they have expected me to spend the whole summer with them. My greatest terror is, lest the Queen, from what Mr. Smelt hinted, should make me promise myself to her for a length of years. What can I do to avoid that? Anything that has a period is endurable; but what can I object that will not sound ungrateful, to the honour she is doing me and meaning me? She has given the most highly flattering reasons for making this application, in preference to listening to that of others; she has put it upon terms of commendation the most soothing; she is, indeed, one of the sweetest characters in the world. Will you, too, condemn me, then, that I feel thus oppressed by her proposal? I hope not,—I think not;—but be very honest if you really do. I wish I could see you! It is not from nervousness;—I have always and uniformly had a horror of a life of attendance and dependence. . . .

To Mrs. Francis, Aylsham, Norfolk

St. Martin's Street, June 27

. . . Her Majesty has sent me a message, express, near a fortnight ago, with an offer of a place at Court, to succeed Mrs. Haggerdorn, one of the Germans who accompanied her to England, and who is now retiring into her own country. 'Tis a place of being constantly about her own person, and assisting in her toilette, —a place of much confidence, and many comforts; apartments in the palace; a footman kept for me; a coach in common with Mrs. Schwellenberg; £200 a-year, etc. etc.

I have been in a state of extreme disturbance ever since, from the reluctance I feel to the separation it will cause me from all my friends. Those, indeed, whom I most love, I shall be able to invite to me in the palace; but I see little or no possibility of being able to make, what I most value, excursions into the country.

When you come, however, my dearest Charlotte, I shall certainly take measures for seeing you, either in Town, or at Windsor, or both.

So new a scene, so great a change, so uncertain a success, frightens and depresses me; though the extreme sweetness of the Queen, in so unsolicited an honour, so unthought-of a distinction, binds me to her with a devotion that will make an attendance upon her light and pleasant. I repine only at losing my loved visits to the country, Mickleham, Norbury, Chessington, Twickenham, and Aylsham,[4] as I had hoped; all these I must now forego.

Everybody so violently congratulates me, that it seems as if *all* was gain. However, I am glad they are all so pleased. My dear father is in raptures; that is my first comfort. Write to wish him joy, my Charlotte, without a hint to him, or any one but Susan, of my confessions of my internal reluctance and fears.

You may believe how much I am busied. I have been presented at the Queen's Lodge in Windsor, and seen Mrs. Haggerdorn in office, and find I have a place of really nothing to do, but to *attend;* and on Thursday I am appointed by Her Majesty to go to St. James's, to see all that belongs to me there. And I am now *fitting out* just as you were, and all the maids and workers suppose I am going to be married, and snigger every time they bring in any of my new attire. I do not care to publish the affair, till it is made known by authority; so I leave them to their conjectures, and I fancy their greatest wonder is, *who* and *where* is the *sposo;* for they must think it odd he should never appear!

F. B.

Queen's Lodge, Windsor, Monday, July 17

With what hurry of mind and body did I rise this morning! Everything had already been arranged for Mrs. Ord's carrying us to Windsor, and my father's carriage was merely to go as baggage-waggon for my clothes. But I wept not then. I left no one behind me to regret; my dear father accompanied me, and all my dear sisters had already taken their flight, never more to return. Even poor little Sarah, whom I love very dearly, was at Chessington.

Between nine and ten o'clock we set off. We changed carriage in Queen Ann Street, and Mrs. Ord conveyed us thence to Windsor. With a struggling heart, I kept myself tolerably tranquil during the little journey. My dear father was quite happy, and Mrs. Ord felt the joy of a mother in relinquishing me to the protection of a Queen so universally reverenced. Had I been in better spirits, their ecstasy would have been unbounded; but alas!—what I was approaching was not in my mind; what I was leaving had taken possession of it solely.

Miss P——[5] flew out to us as the carriage stopped—the youthful blush of pleasure heightening her complexion, and every feature showing her kind happiness. Mrs. Delany, she said, was gone out with the Queen. I took leave of my good Mrs. Ord, whose eyes overflowed with maternal feelings—chiefly of contentment. Mrs. Delany came home in about an hour. A chastened satisfaction was hers; she rejoiced in the prospect before me; she was happy we should now be so much united, but she felt for my deprivations, she saw the hard conflict within me, and the tenderest pity checked her delight. . . .

Oh, my dear Susan! in what an agony of mind did I obey the summons! I was still in my travelling dress, but could not stay to change it. My father accompanied me. Mrs. Delany, anxiously and full of mixed sensations, gave me her blessing. We walked; the Queen's Lodge is not fifty yards from Mrs. Delany's door. My dear father's own courage all failed him in this little step; for as I was now on the point of entering—probably for ever—into an entire new way of life, and of forgoing by it all my most favourite schemes,[6] and every dear expectation my fancy had ever indulged of happiness adapted to its taste—as now all was to be given up—I could disguise my trepidation no longer—indeed I never had disguised, I had only forborne proclaiming it. But my dear father now, sweet soul! felt it all, as I held by his arm, without power to say one word, but that if he did not hurry along I should drop by the way. I heard in his kind voice that he was now really alarmed; he would have slackened his pace, or have made me stop to breathe; but I could not; my breath seemed gone, and I could only hasten with all my might, lest my strength should go too. . . .

The page came in a minute or two to summon me to the Queen. The Queen was in her dressing-room. Mrs. Schwellenberg[7] was standing behind her: nobody else present.

She received me with a most gracious bow of the head, and a smile that was all sweetness. She saw me much agitated, and attributed it, no doubt, to the awe of her presence. Oh, she little knew my mind had no room in it for feelings of that sort! She talked to me of my journey, my father, my sisters, and my brothers; the weather, the roads, and Mrs. Delany—any, everything she could suggest, that could best tend to compose and to make me easy; and when I had been with her about a quarter of an hour, she desired Mrs. Schwellenberg to show me my apartment, and, with another graceful bow, motioned my retiring.

Not only to the sweet Queen, but to myself let me here do justice, in declaring that though I entered her presence with a heart filled with everything but herself, I quitted it with sensations much softened. The condescension of her efforts to quiet me, and the elegance of her receiving me, thus, as a visitor, without naming to me a single direction, without even the most distant hint of business, struck me to show so much delicacy, as well as graciousness, that I quitted her with a very deep sense of her goodness, and a very strong conviction that she merited every exertion on my part to deserve it.

Mrs. Schwellenberg left me at the room door, where my dear father was still waiting for me, too anxious to depart till he again saw me.

We spent a short time together, in which I assured him I would from that moment take all the happiness in my power, and banish all the regret. I told him how gratifying had been my reception, and I omitted nothing I could think of to remove the uneasiness that this day seemed first to awaken in him. Thank God! I had the fullest success; his hopes and gay expectations were all within call, and they ran back at the first beckoning. . . .

I now took the most vigorous resolutions to observe the promise I had made my dear father. Now all was finally settled, to borrow my own words, I needed no monitor to tell me it would be foolish, useless, even wicked, not to reconcile myself to my destiny.

The many now wishing for just the same—Oh! could they look within me. I am *married,* my dearest Susan—I look upon it in that light—I was averse to forming the union, and I endeavoured to escape it; but my friends interfered—they prevailed—and the knot is tied. What then now remains but to make the best wife in my power? I am bound to it in duty, and I will strain every nerve to succeed. . . .

Monday, July 18

. . . My Windsor apartment is extremely comfortable. I have a large drawing-room, as they call it, which is on the ground-floor, as are all the Queen's rooms, and which faces the Castle and the venerable Round Tower, and opens at the further side, from the windows, to the Little Park. It is airy, pleasant, clean, and healthy.

My bedroom is small, but neat and comfortable; its entrance is only from the drawing-room, and it looks to the garden. These two rooms are delightfully independent of all the rest of the house, and contain everything I can desire for my convenience and comfort.[8] . . .

Monday, July 24

. . . [L]et me endeavour to give you, more connectedly, a concise abstract of the general method of passing the day, that then I may only write what varies, and occurs occasionally.

I rise at six o'clock, dress in a morning gown and cap, and wait my first summons, which is at all times from seven to near eight, but commonly in the exact half-hour between them.

The Queen never sends for me till her hair is dressed. This, in a morning, is always done by her wardrobe-woman, Mrs. Thielky, a German, but who speaks English perfectly well.

Mrs. Schwellenberg, since the first week, has never come down in a morning at all. The Queen's dress is finished by Mrs. Thielky and myself. No maid ever enters the room while the Queen is in it. Mrs. Thielky hands the things to me, and I put them on. 'Tis fortunate for me I have not the handing them! I should never know which to take first, embarrassed as I am, and should run a prodigious risk of giving the gown before the hoop, and the fan before the neck-kerchief.

By eight o'clock, or a little after, for she is extremely expeditious, she is dressed. She then goes out to join the King, and be joined by the Princesses, and they all proceed to the King's chapel in the Castle, to prayers, attended by the governesses of the Princesses, and the King's equerry. Various others at times attend; but only these indispensably.

I then return to my own room to breakfast. I make this meal the most pleasant part of the day; I have a book for my companion, and I allow myself an hour for it. My present book is Gilpin's description of the *Lakes of Cumberland and Westmoreland*. Mrs. Delany has lent it me. It is the most picturesque reading I ever met with: it shows me landscapes of every sort, with tints so bright and lively, I forget I am but reading, and fancy I see them before me, coloured by the hand of Nature.

At nine o'clock I send off my breakfast things, and relinquish

my book, to make a serious and steady examination of everything
I have upon my hands in the way of business—in which preparations for dress are always included, not for the present day alone,
but for the court-days, which require a particular dress; for the
next arriving birthday of any of the Royal Family, every one of
which requires new apparel; for Kew, where the dress is plain-
est; and for going on here, where the dress is very pleasant to me,
requiring no show nor finery, but merely to be neat, not inelegant,
and moderately fashionable.

That over, I have my time at my own disposal till a quarter before twelve, except on Wednesdays and Saturdays, when I have it
only to a quarter before eleven.

My rummages and business sometimes occupy me uninterruptedly to those hours. When they do not, I give till ten to necessary letters of duty, ceremony, or long arrears;—and now, from
ten to the times I have mentioned, I devote to walking.

These times mentioned call me to the irksome and quick-re-
turning labours of the toilette. The hour advanced on the Wednesdays and Saturdays is for curling and craping the hair, which it
now requires twice a week.

A quarter before one is the usual time for the Queen to begin
dressing for the day. Mrs. Schwellenberg then constantly attends;
so do I; Mrs. Thielky, of course, at all times. We help her off with
her gown, and on with her powdering things, and then the hair-
dresser is admitted. She generally reads the newspapers during
that operation.

When she observes that I have run to her but half dressed, she
constantly gives me leave to return and finish as soon as she is
seated. If she is grave, and reads steadily on, she dismisses me,
whether I am dressed or not; but at all times she never forgets to
send me away while she is powdering, with a consideration not to
spoil my clothes, that one would not expect belonged to her high
station. Neither does she ever detain me without making a point
of reading here and there some little paragraph aloud.

When I return, I finish, if anything is undone, my dress, and
then take Baretti's *Dialogues*, my dearest Fredy's *Tablet of
Memory*,[9] or some such disjointed matter, for the few minutes
that elapse ere I am again summoned.

I find her then always removed to her state dressing-room, if
any room in this private mansion can have the epithet of state.
There, in a very short time, her dress is finished. She then says

she won't detain me, and I hear and see no more of her till bed-time.

It is commonly three o'clock when I am thus set at large. And I have then two hours quite at my own disposal: but, in the natural course of things, not a moment after! These dear and quiet two hours, my only quite sure and undisturbed time in the whole day, after breakfast is over, I shall henceforward devote to thus talking with my beloved Susan, my Fredy, my other sisters, my dear father, or Miss Cambridge; with my brothers, cousins, Mrs. Ord, and other friends, in such terms as these two hours will occasionally allow me. Henceforward, I say; for hitherto dejection of spirits, with uncertainty how long my time might last, have made me waste moment after moment as sadly as unprofitably.

At five, we have dinner. Mrs. Schwellenberg and I meet in the eating-room. We are commonly *tête-à-tête:* when there is anybody added, it is from her invitation only. Whatever right my place might afford me of also inviting my friends to the table I have now totally lost, by want of courage and spirits to claim it originally.

When we have dined, we go upstairs to her apartment, which is directly over mine. Here we have coffee till the *terracing* is over:[10] this is at about eight o'clock. Our *tête-à-tête* then finishes, and we come down again to the eating-room. There the equerry,[11] whoever he is, comes to tea constantly, and with him any gentleman that the King or Queen may have invited for the evening; and when tea is over, he conducts them, and goes himself, to the concert-room.

This is commonly about nine o'clock.

From that time, if Mrs. Schwellenberg is alone, I never quit her for a minute, till I come to my little supper at near eleven.

Between eleven and twelve my last summons usually takes place, earlier and later occasionally. Twenty minutes is the customary time then spent with the Queen: half an hour, I believe, is seldom exceeded.

I then come back, and after doing whatever I can to forward my dress for the next morning, I go to bed—and to sleep, too, believe me: the early rising, and a long day's attention to new affairs and occupations, cause a fatigue so bodily, that nothing mental stands against it, and to sleep I fall the moment I have put out my candle and laid down my head.

Such is the day to your F. B. in her new situation at Windsor; such, I mean, is its usual destination, and its intended course. I make it take now and then another channel, but never stray far enough not to return to the original stream after a little meandering about and about it.

I think now you will be able to see and to follow me pretty closely.

With regard to those summonses I speak of, I will now explain myself. My summons, upon all regular occasions—that is, morning, noon, and night toilets—is neither more nor less than a bell. Upon extra occasions a page is commonly sent.

At first, I felt inexpressibly discomfited by this mode of call. A bell!—it seemed so mortifying a mark of servitude, I always felt myself blush, though alone, with conscious shame at my own strange degradation. But I have philosophised myself now into some reconcilement with this manner of summons, by reflecting that to have some person always sent would be often very inconvenient, and that this method is certainly less an interruption to any occupation I may be employed in, than the entrance of messengers so many times in the day. It is, besides, less liable to mistakes. So I have made up my mind to it as well as I can; and now I only feel that proud blush when somebody is by to revive my original dislike of it.

Tuesday, July 25

. . . Mrs. Schwellenberg, Miss Planta,[12] and myself travelled to Kew[13] together. I have two rooms there; both small, and up two pairs of stairs; but tidy and comfortable enough. Indeed all the apartments but the King's and Queen's, and one of Mrs. Schwellenberg's, are small, dark, and old-fashioned. There are staircases in every passage, and passages to every closet. I lost myself continually, only in passing from my own room to the Queen's. . . .

Friday, July 28

. . . The Kew life, you will perceive, is different from the Windsor. As there are no early prayers, the Queen rises later; and as there is no form or ceremony here of any sort, her dress is plain, and the hour for the second toilette extremely uncertain. The Royal family are here always in so very retired a way, that they live as the simplest country gentlefolks. The King has not even an equerry with him, nor the Queen any lady to attend her when she goes her airings.

Miss Planta belongs here to our table; so does anybody that comes, as there is no other kept.

There is no excuse for parting after dinner, and therefore I live unremittingly with Mrs. Schwellenberg after the morning.

It is a still greater difficulty to see company here than at Windsor, for as my apartments are upstairs, there is a greater danger of encountering some of the Royal family; and I find all the household are more delicate in inviting or admitting any friends here than elsewhere, on account of the very easy and unreserved way in which the family live, running about from one end of the house to the other, without precaution or care. . . .

Monday, August 7

. . . In the evening, for the first time since my arrival, I went upon the terrace, under the wing and protection of my dear Mrs. Delany, who was tempted to walk there herself, in order to pay her respects on the little Princess's birthday. She was carried in her chair to the foot of the steps. . . .

It was really a mighty pretty procession. The little Princess, just turned of three years old, in a robe-coat covered with fine muslin, a dressed close cap, white gloves, and a fan, walked on alone and first, highly delighted in the parade, and turning from side to side to see everybody as she passed: for all the terracers stand up against the walls, to make a clear passage for the Royal Family, the moment they come in sight. Then followed the King and Queen, no less delighted themselves with the joy of their little darling. The Princess Royal, leaning on Lady Elizabeth Waldegrave,[14] followed at a little distance.

This Princess, the second female in the kingdom, shows, I think, more marked respect and humility toward the King and Queen than any of the family.

Next the Princess Augusta, holding by the Duchess of Ancaster;

and next the Princess Elizabeth, holding by Lady Charlotte Bertie. Office here takes place of rank, which occasioned Lady Elizabeth Waldegrave, as lady of her bedchamber, to walk with the Princess Royal.

Then followed the Princess Mary with Miss Goldsworthy, and the Princess Sophia with Mademoiselle Monmoulin and Miss Planta; then General Budé and the Duke of Montagu; and, lastly, Major Price, who, as equerry, always brings up the rear, walks at a distance from the group, and keeps off all crowd from the Royal Family.[15]

On sight of Mrs. Delany, the King instantly stopped to speak to her. The Queen, of course, and the little Princess, and all the rest, stood still, in their ranks. They talked a good while with the sweet old lady; during which time the King once or twice addressed himself to me. I caught the Queen's eye, and saw in it a little surprise, but by no means any displeasure, to see me of the party.

The little Princess went up to Mrs. Delany, of whom she is very fond, and behaved like a little angel to her: she then, with a look of inquiry and recollection, slowly, of her own accord, came behind Mrs. Delany to look at me. "I am afraid," said I, in a whisper, and stooping down, "your Royal Highness does not remember me?"

What think you was her answer? An arch little smile, and a nearer approach, with her lips pouted out to kiss me. I could not resist so innocent an invitation; but the moment I had accepted it I was half afraid it might seem, in so public a place, an improper liberty: however, there was no help for it. She then took my fan, and, having looked at it on both sides, gravely returned it me, saying, "Oh! a brown fan!"

The King and Queen then bid her curtsey to Mrs. Delany, which she did most gracefully, and they all moved on; each of the Princesses speaking to Mrs. Delany as they passed, and condescending to curtsey to her companion. . . .

August 8

. . . At the second toilette to-day, Mrs. Schwellenberg, who left the dressing-room before me, called out at the door, "Miss Bernar, when you have done from the Queen, come to my room."

There was something rather more peremptory in the order than was quite pleasant to me, and I rather drily answered, "Very well, Mrs. Schwellenberg." . . .

When I went to Mrs. Schwellenberg, she said, "You might know I had something to say to you, by my calling you before the Queen." She then proceeded to a long prelude, which I could but ill comprehend, save that it conveyed much of obligation on my part, and favour on hers; and then ended with, "I might tell you now, the Queen is going to Oxford, and you might go with her; it is a secret—you might not tell it nobody. But I tell you once, I shall do for you what I can; you are to have a gown."

I stared, and drew back, with a look so undisguised of wonder and displeasure at this extraordinary speech, that I saw it was understood, and she then thought it time, therefore, to name her authority, which, with great emphasis, she did thus: "The Queen will give you a gown! The Queen says you are not rich," etc.

There was something in the manner of this quite intolerable to me; and I hastily interrupted her with saying, "I have two new gowns by me, and therefore do not require another."

Perhaps a proposed present from Her Majesty was never so received before; but the grossness of the manner of the messenger swallowed up the graciousness of the design in the principal; and I had not even a wish to conceal how little it was to my taste. . . .

Seeing the wonder and displeasure now hers, I calmly added, "The Queen is very good, and I am very sensible of Her Majesty's graciousness; but there is not, in this instance, the least occasion for it."

"Miss Bernar," cried she, quite angrily, "I tell you once, when the Queen will give you a gown, you must be humble, thankful, when you are Duchess of Ancaster!"[16]

She then enumerated various ladies to whom Her Majesty had made the same present, many of them of the first distinction, and all, she said, great secrets. Still I only repeated again the same speech. . . .

When she had finished her list of secret ladies, I told her I must beg to speak to the Queen, and make my own acknowledgments for her gracious intention.

This she positively forbid; and said it must only pass through her hands. "When I give you the gown," she added, "I will tell you when you may make your curtsey."

I was not vexed at this prohibition, not knowing what etiquette I might offend by breaking it; and the conversation concluded with nothing being settled. . . .

To Mrs. Phillips

August 20

Has my dear Susan thought me quite dead?—not to write so long! and after such sweet converse as she has sent me. O my beloved Susan, 'tis a refractory heart I have to deal with!—it struggles so hard to be sad—and silent—and fly from you entirely, since it cannot fly entirely to you. . . .

If to you alone I show myself in these dark colours, can you blame the plan that I have intentionally been forming—namely, to wean myself from myself—to lessen all my affections—to curb all my wishes—to deaden all my sensations?—This design, my Susan, I formed so long ago as the first day my dear father accepted my offered appointment: I thought that what demanded a complete new system of life, required, if attainable, a new set of feelings for all enjoyment of new prospects, and for lessening regrets at what were quitted, or lost. Such being my primitive idea, merely from my grief of separation, imagine but how it was strengthened and confirmed when the interior of my position became known to me! —when I saw myself expected by Mrs. Schwellenberg, not to be her colleague, but her dependent deputy! not to be her visitor at my own option, but her companion, her humble companion, at her own command! This has given so new a character to the place I had accepted under such different auspices, that nothing but my horror of disappointing, perhaps displeasing, my dearest father, has deterred me, from the moment that I made this mortifying discovery, from soliciting his leave to resign. But oh my Susan,— kind, good, indulgent as he is to me, I have not the heart so cruelly to thwart his hopes—his views—his happiness, in the honours he conceived awaiting my so unsolicited appointment. The Queen, too, is all sweetness, encouragement, and gracious goodness to me, and I cannot endure to complain to her of her old servant. You see, then, my situation; here I must remain!—The die is cast, and that struggle is no more.—To keep off every other, to support the loss of the dearest friends, and best society, and bear, in exchange, the tyranny, the *exigeance,* the *ennui,* and attempted indignities of their greatest contrast,—this must be my constant endeavour. . . .

What erasures! Can you read me? I blot, and re-write—yet know not how to alter or what to send; I so fear to alarm your tender kindness.

[F. B.]

[Wednesday], September 20

A grand incident, for my new life, happened. Mrs. Schwellenberg finding herself very unwell, and wishing for advice from a physician, went on to town, and I remained, for the first time, with the Queen by myself.

Nothing could be more gracious and encouraging than her behaviour upon this occasion. We were at Kew only two days, and her sweetness, in sundry particulars, rendered them, with respect to my attendance, the most pleasant of any I had witnessed.

Friday, September 22

We all went to town for keeping the anniversary of the King's coronation,[17] on which there is always a drawing-room. We found Mrs. Schwellenberg still very unwell, and uncertain whether she should be able to return with us to Windsor the next day.

Early the following morning, Miss Planta sent to me, to know whether we went back alone, or with Mrs. Schwellenberg: I could give her no satisfaction. Soon after she came herself; but, while she was apologising for her inquiries, a message came to me, to let me know that Mrs. Schwellenberg meant to continue in town. Miss Planta took a hasty leave, to prepare for our journey; but, turning round as she opened the door, she made a sort of involuntary exclamation, "Ah Miss Burney, if Mrs. Schwellenberg was not so sick—and so cross—how happily we might all live!" . . .

Tuesday, November 28

Miss Planta and Mr. de Luc[18] accompanied me to Kew, where, as soon as I arrived, I had the honour of a little call from the Princess Royal, with a most gracious message from the Queen, to desire me to invite my friends the Smelts to dinner. You may imagine with what pleasure I obeyed.

They came,—as did, afterwards, Mr. Turbulent,[19] and the dinner was enlivened with very animated conversation, in which this gentleman took a part so principal, that I now began to attend, and now, first, to be surprised by him.

The subject was female character. Miss Planta declared her opinion that it was so indispensable to have it without blemish, that nothing upon earth could compensate, or make it possible to countenance one who wanted it. Mrs. Smelt agreed that compassion alone was all that could be afforded upon such an occasion, not countenance, acquaintance, nor intercourse. Mr. de Luc gave an opinion so long and confused, that I could not sufficiently attend to make it out. Mr. Smelt spoke with mingled gentleness and irony, upon the nature of the debate. I said little, but that little was, to give every encouragement to penitence, and no countenance to error.

The hero, however, of the discourse was Mr. Turbulent. With a warmth and fervour that broke forth into exclamations the most vehement, and reflections the most poignant, he protested that many of the women we were proscribing were amongst the most amiable of the sex—that the fastidiousness we recommended was never practised by even the best part of the world—and that we ourselves, individually, while we spoke with so much disdain, never acted up to our doctrines, by using, towards *all* fair failers, such severity.

This brought me forth. I love not to be attacked for making professions beyond my practice; and I assured him, very seriously, that I had not one voluntary acquaintance, nor one with whom I kept up the smallest intercourse of my own seeking or wilful concurrence, that had any stain in their characters that had ever reached my ears.

"Pardon me, ma'am," cried he, warmly, "there are amongst your acquaintance, and amongst everybody's, many of those the most admired, and most charming, that have neither been spared by calumny, nor been able to avoid reproach and suspicion." . . .

I boldly protested I knew not, as an acquaintance of my own, a single person his description suited. Those whom I might see or meet or know at the houses of others, I could not pretend to assert might all be blameless; but however I might compassionate, or even admire, some who could not be vindicated, I began no such acquaintances—I wished them well, and wished them better, —but I distanced them to the best of my power, as I had not weight enough to do good to them, and avoided, therefore, the danger of being supposed to approve them.

"Yes, ma'am," cried he, in a high tone, "you also know, visit, receive, caress, and distinguish a lady in this very class!"

"Do I?" cried I, amazed.

"You do, ma'am! You all do!" . . .

I assured him I was quite in a wood, and begged him to be more explicit. He hung back, but we all called upon him, and I declared I should regard the description as fabulous unless he spoke out, and this piqued him to be categorical; but what was my concern to hear him then name—almost whispering with his own reluctance—Madame de Genlis![20] I was quite thunderstruck, and everybody was silent.

He was then for closing the discourse, but I could not consent to it. I told him that I pretended not to say the character of that lady had never, in my hearing, been attacked; but that I could, and would, and hoped I ever should, say I believed her perfectly innocent of the charges brought against her.

He smiled a little provokingly, and said, "We agree here, ma'am,—I think her innocent too."

"No, sir, we do not agree!—I should not think her innocent if I believed the charge!"

"Circumstances," cried he, "may make her mind innocent."

I could say nothing to this, I think it so true; but I would not venture such a concession, where my wishes led me to aim at a full defence. Accordingly, with all the energy in my power, I attempted it; assuring him that there was an evidence of her untainted worth in her very countenance, and written there so strongly, that to mistake the characters was impossible.

"True," cried he, again smiling, "the countenance speaks all that captivating sweetness that belongs—if she has them—to the very frailties of her character."

I could not bear this. "No, sir," I cried, as warmly as himself, " 'tis a countenance that announces nothing but the openness of virtue and goodness! There would be more reserve and closeness if she failed in them. I saw her myself, at first, with a prejudice in her disfavour, from the cruel reports I had heard; but the moment I looked at her, it was removed. There was a dignity with her sweetness, and a frankness with her modesty, that assured, that convinced me, beyond all power of report, of her real worth and innocence." . . .

Here the matter was forced to drop. I was vexed at the instance he brought, and grieved to have nothing more positive than my own opinion to bring forward in her defence: for it is most true I do believe her innocent, though I fear she has been imprudent. . . .

Christmas Day

. . . I think I have omitted to mention, in its place, Mr. Mathias.²¹ . . .

If you will not laugh at me too much, I will also acknowledge that I liked Mr. Mathias all the more for observing him as awkward and embarrassed how to present me my salary as I felt myself in receiving it.

There is something, after all, in money, by itself money, that I can never take possession of it without a secret feeling of something like a degradation: money in its effects, and its produce, creates far different and more pleasant sensations. But here it made me feel so like—what I am, in short—a servant! We are all servants, to be sure, in the red book,²² but still—— . . .

[1787]

Tuesday, January 16

[This] was the day appointed for removing to town for the winter; from which time we were only to come to Windsor for an occasional day or two every week.

I received a visit, just before I set out, from the King. He came in alone, and made most gracious inquiries into my health, and whether I was sufficiently recovered for the journey.[23]

The four days of my confinement, from the fever after the pain, were days of meditation the most useful: I reflected upon all my mental sufferings in the last year; their cause seemed inadequate to their poignancy. In the hour of sickness and confinement, the world, in losing its attractions, forfeits its regrets:—a new train of thinking, a new set of ideas, took possession of all my faculties; a steady plan, calm, yet no longer sad, deliberately formed itself in my mind; my affliction was already subsided; I now banished, also, discontent. I found myself as well off, upon reflection, as I could possibly merit, and better, by comparison, than most of those around me. The beloved friends of my own heart had joined me unalterably, inviolably to theirs;—who, in number, who, in kindness, has more?

Now, therefore, I took shame to myself, and *Resolved to be happy....*

Friday, January 19

... I had two notes from Lady Rothes,[24] both very embarrassing to me. The first was an invitation to her own home, the second an offer to visit me in mine. I knew not at all what I might, or might not do, with respect to visits, either at home or abroad. Hitherto I had gone nowhere, and received nobody but a few of my relations, my dear Mr. and Mrs. Locke, Miss Cambridge, and Mrs. Ord. Spirits I had wanted, as much as knowledge and opportunity, for going further. Something, however, must be answered to this double proposition, and it compelled me to form some immediate plan. I determined, therefore, to speak openly to the Queen, upon the visiting subject, and to learn, if possible, my proper privileges, and her own desires concerning them. The next day we were to go to Windsor, and then I expected opportunity to open my suit. Meanwhile I sent no answer whatever to Lady Rothes.

Sunday, January 21

To-day I had the honour of a very long conference with Her Majesty, upon my own affairs and proceedings. She sent for me at noon, and with the greatest complacency desired me to explain what I had meant the preceding evening.

I came immediately to the point; I told her that there was nothing I more earnestly coveted than the high honour of her own personal directions, with regard to the acquaintance it might now be proper for me to keep or decline, and, for the time to come, to make or to refuse.

I saw instantly by her manner the importance she annexed to this subject: she treated it, at once, as a matter of serious concern, and entered upon it with the most ready concurrence to discuss it fully. My acquaintance, hitherto, I frankly told her, was not only very numerous, but very mixed, taking in not only most stations in life, but also most parties. . . .

I begged her permission to assure her that, for myself, I would form no connection, and make no acquaintance, but with her consent; nor even maintain those already made and formed, but by her knowledge: and I entreated her leave to constantly mention to her whomsoever I saw, or desired to see, that I might have the undoubted satisfaction of a security that I could run no risk, in the only way I feared it—that of ignorance.

She gave a pleased, though only tacit assent, but I saw that the proposal met with her entire approvance.

I told her of the two notes of Lady Rothes; and she cheerfully assured me her acquaintance was perfectly what she should approve my cultivating.

In the conclusion, with a high and just panegyric upon Mr. Smelt, she desired that whenever I had any perplexity with respect to this subject, I would consult with him, and abide by his counsel. . . .

January 22

We returned early to town, Mr. Turbulent, Miss Planta, and myself; and I had the gratification of a very long visit from Mr. Smelt, to whom I communicated, in full detail, my whole conference with Her Majesty. . . .

. . . [T]he general directions and counsel of Mr. Smelt, which I have scrupulously observed ever since, were, in abridgment, these:—

That I should see nobody at all but by appointment. This, as he well said, would obviate, not only numerous personal inconveniences to myself, but prevent alike surprises from those I had no leave to admit, and repetitions of visits from others who might inadvertently come too often. He advised me to tell this to my father, and beg it might be spread, as a settled part of my situation, among all who inquired for me.

That I should see no fresh person whatsoever without an immediate permission from the Queen, nor any party, even amongst those already authorised, without apprising her of such a plan.

That I should never go out without an immediate application to her, so that no possible inquiry for me might occasion surprise or disappointment.

These, and other similar ties, perhaps, had my spirits been better, I might have less readily acceded to: as it was, I would have bound myself to as many more.

At length, however, even then, I was startled when Mr. Smelt, with some earnestness, said, "And, with respect to your parties, such as you may occasionally have here, you have but one rule for keeping all things smooth, and all partisans unoffended, at a distance—which is, to have *no men—none!*"

I stared a little, and made no answer.

"Yes," cried he, "Mr. Locke may be admitted; but him singly. Your father, you know, is of course."

Still I was silent: after a pause of some length, he plumply, yet with an evidently affected unmeaningness, said, "Mr. Cambridge —as to Mr. Cambridge——"

I stopped him short at once; I dared not trust to what might follow, and eagerly called out "Mr. Cambridge, sir, I cannot exclude! So much friendship and kindness I owe, and have long owed him, that he would go about howling at my ingratitude, could I seem so suddenly to forget it!"

My impetuosity in uttering this surprised, but silenced him; he said not a word more, nor did I. . . .

Friday, [November] 27

I had a terrible journey indeed to town, Mrs. Schwellenberg finding it expedient to have the glass down on my side, whence there blew in a sharp wind, which so painfully attacked my eyes that they were inflamed even before we arrived in town.

Mr. de Luc and Miss Planta both looked uneasy, but no one durst speak; and for me, it was among the evils that I can always best bear: yet before the evening I grew so ill that I could not propose going to Chelsea, lest I should be utterly unfitted for Thursday's Drawing-room.

The next day, however, I received a consolation that has been some ease to my mind ever since. My dear father spent the evening with me, and was so incensed at the state of my eyes, which were now as piteous to behold as to feel, and at the relation of their usage, that he charged me, another time, to draw up my glass in defiance of all opposition, and to abide by all consequences, since my place was wholly immaterial when put in competition with my health. . . .

On the Thursday I was obliged to dress, just as if nothing was the matter.

The next day, when we assembled to return to Windsor, Mr. de Luc was in real consternation at sight of my eyes; and I saw an indignant glance at my coadjutrix, that could scarce content itself without being understood. Miss Planta ventured not at such a glance, but a whisper broke out, as we were descending the stairs, expressive of horror against the same poor person—*poor* person indeed—to exercise a power productive only of abhorrence, to those that view as well as to those that feel it!

Some business of Mrs. Schwellenberg's occasioned a delay of the journey, and we all retreated back; and when I returned to my room, Miller, the old head housemaid, came to me, with a little neat tin saucepan in her hand, saying, "Pray, ma'am, use this for your eyes; 'tis milk and butter, *such as I used to make for Madame Hoggerdorn* when she travelled in the winter with Mrs. Schwellenberg."

Good Heaven! I really shuddered when she added, that all that poor woman's misfortunes with her eyes, which, from inflammation after inflammation, grew nearly blind, were attributed by herself to these journeys, in which she was forced to have the glass down at her side in all weathers, and frequently the glasses behind her also!

Upon my word, this account of my predecessor was the least exhilarating intelligence I could receive! Goter[25] told me, afterwards, that all the servants in the house had remarked *I was going just the same way*! . . .

Soon after, however, we all assembled again, and got into the coach. Mr. de Luc, who was my *vis-à-vis*, instantly pulled up the glass.

"Put down that glass!" was the immediate order.

He affected not to hear her, and began conversing.

She enraged quite tremendously, calling aloud to be obeyed without delay. He looked compassionately at me, and shrugged his shoulders, and said, "But, ma'am——"

"Do it, Mr. de Luc, when I tell you! I will have it! When you been too cold, you might bear it!"

"It is not for me, ma'am, but poor Miss Burney."

"Oh, poor Miss Burney might bear it the same! put it down, Mr. de Luc! without, I will get out! put it down, when I tell you! It is my coach! I will have it selfs! I might go alone in it, or with one, or with what you call nobody, when I please!"

Frightened for good Mr. de Luc, and the more for being much obliged to him, I now interfered, and begged him to let down the glass. Very reluctantly he replied, and I leant back in the coach, and held up my muff to my eyes. . . .

When we were about half-way, we stopped to water the horses. He then again pulled up the glass, as if from absence. A voice of fury exclaimed, "Let it down! without I won't go!"

"I am sure," cried he, "all Mrs. de Luc's plants will be killed by this frost!"

For the frost was very severe indeed.

Then he proposed my changing places with Miss Planta, who sat opposite Mrs. Schwellenberg, and consequently on the sheltered side. "Yes!" cried Mrs. Schwellenberg, "Miss Burney might sit there, and so she ought!"

I told her, briefly, I was always sick in riding backwards.

"Oh, ver well! when you don't like it, don't do it. You might bear it when you like it! what did the poor Haggerdorn bear it! when the blood was all running down from her eyes!"

This was too much! "I must take, then," I cried, "the more warning!"

After that I spoke not a word. I ruminated all the rest of the way upon my dear father's recent charge and permission. I was upon the point continually of availing myself of both, but, alas! I felt the deep disappointment I should give him, and I felt the most cruel repugnance to owe a resignation to a quarrel. . . .

Mr. de Luc called upon me next morning, and openly avowed

his indignation, protesting it was an oppression he could not bear to see used, and reproving me for checking him when he would have run all risks. I thanked him most cordially; but assured him the worst of all inflammations to me was that of a quarrel, and I entreated him, therefore, not to interfere. But we have been cordial friends from that time forward.

Miss Planta also called, kindly bringing me some eye-water, and telling me she had "Never so longed to beat anybody in her life; and yet, I assure you," she added, "everybody remarks that she behaves, altogether, better to you than to anybody!"

O Heavens! . . .

Such was this month: in which, but for the sweet support of Mrs. Delany, I must almost wholly have sunk under the tyranny, whether opposed or endured, of my most extraordinary coadjutrix.

Saturday, December 1

'Tis strange that two feelings so very opposite as love and resentment should have nearly equal power in inspiring courage *for* or *against* the object that excites them; yet so it is. In former times I have often, on various occasions, felt it raised to anything possible, by affection, and now I have found it mount to the boldest height, by disdain. For, be it known, such gross and harsh usage I experienced in the end of last month, since the inflammation of the eyes, which I bore much more composedly than sundry personal indignities that followed, that I resolved upon a new mode of conduct—namely, to go out every evening, in order to show that I by no means considered myself as bound to stay at home after dinner, if treated very ill; and this most courageous plan I flattered myself must needs either procure me a liberty of absence, always so much wished, or occasion a change of behaviour to more decency and endurability.

I had received for to-day an invitation to meet Lady Bute and Lady Louisa Stuart[26] at my dearest Mrs. Delany's, and I should have wished it at all times, so much I like them both. I had no opportunity to speak first to my Royal Mistress, but I went to her at noon, rather more dressed than usual, and when I saw her look a little surprised, I explained my reason. She seemed very well satisfied with it, but my coadjutrix appeared in an astonishment unequalled; and at dinner, when we necessarily met again, new testimonies of conduct quite without example were exhibited: for when Mrs. Thackeray and Miss Planta were helped, she helped herself, and appeared publicly to send me to Coventry—though the sole provocation was intending to forgo her society this evening! . . .

So unpleasant were the sensations that filled me, that I could recover no gaiety, even at the house of my beloved friend, though received there by her dear self, her beautiful niece, and Lady Bute and Lady Louisa, in the most flattering manner. Yet I stayed till ten o'clock, though hitherto I had returned at nine. I was willing to make manifest that I did not make such sacrifice of my time equally to the extremest rudeness as to common civility; for more than common civility never, at best, repays it. . . .

My reception at home was not quite similar; and I observed, even in my Royal Mistress, a degree of gravity that seemed not pleased. I conjectured that *my absence had been lamented.* How hard, if so, not to make known, in my turn, how my *presence* is accepted! However, I will not complain of her; I will only continue to absent myself, while she behaves thus intolerably. . . .

The behaviour of my coadjutrix continued in the same strain —really shocking to endure. I always began, at our first meeting, some little small speech, and constantly received so harsh a rebuff at the second word, that I then regularly seated myself by a table, at work, and remained wholly silent the rest of the day. . . .

I know well, at a distance, you may think such conduct, in common with such a character, a mere subject for contempt, and be amazed at its effect: but were you here, and were you spending in one day a mere anticipation of every day—alas! my dearest friends, you would find, as I find, peace must be purchased by any sacrifice that can obtain it.

Mine was, indeed, a severe one: I gave up either going to my beloved solace, or receiving her here, and offered my service to play at piquet.—At first, this was disdainfully refused, and but very proudly accepted afterwards. I had no way to compose my own spirit to an endurance of this, but by considering myself as *married to her,* and therefore that all rebellion could but end in disturbance, and that concession was my sole chance for peace! Oh what reluctant nuptials!—how often did I say to myself—Were these chains voluntary, how could I bear them!—how forgive myself that I put them on! . . .

To finish, however, with respect to the *Présidente*,[27] I must now acquaint you that, as my eyes entirely grew well, her incivility entirely wore off, and I became a far greater favourite than I had ever presumed to think myself till that time! I was obliged to give up my short-lived privilege of retirement, and live on as before, making only my two precious little visits to my beloved comforter and supporter, and to devote the rest of my wearisome time to her presence—better satisfied, however, since I now saw that open war made me wretched, even when a victor, beyond what any subjection could do that had peace for its terms. . . .

My favour, now, was beyond the favour of all others; I was "My good Miss Berner," at every other word, and no one else was listened to if I would speak, and no one else was accepted for a partner if I would play! I found no cause to which I could attribute this change. I believe the whole mere matter of caprice. . . .

[1788]

Queen's Lodge, Windsor,
Tuesday, January 1

I began the new year, as I ended the old one, by seizing the first moment it presented to my own disposal, for flying to Mrs. Delany, and begging her annual benediction. She bestowed it with the sweetest affection, and I spent, as usual, all the time with her I had to spare. It seems always so short; yet we now meet almost regularly twice a day. . . .

Wednesday, January 9

To-day Mrs. Schwellenberg did me a real favour, and with real good-nature; for she sent me the letters of my poor lost friends, Dr. Johnson and Mrs. Thrale, which she knew me to be almost pining to procure.[28] . . .

With what a sadness have I been reading! what scenes has it revived!—what regrets renewed! These letters have not been more improperly published in the whole, than they are injudiciously displayed in their several parts. She has given all—every word—and thinks that, perhaps, a justice to Dr. Johnson, which, in fact, is the greatest injury to his memory.

The few she has selected of her own do her, indeed, much credit: she has discarded all that were trivial and merely local, and given only such as contain something instructive, amusing, or ingenious. . . .

Our name once occurs: how I started at its sight!—'Tis to mention the party that planned the first visit to our house: Miss Owen, Mr. Seward, Mrs. and Miss Thrale, and Dr. Johnson. How well shall we ever, my Susan, remember that morning! . . .

February 13

. . . The Trial, so long impending, of Mr. Hastings, opened to-day.[29] The Queen yesterday asked me if I wished to be present at the beginning, or had rather take another day. I was greatly obliged by her condescension, and preferred the opening. I thought it would give me a general view of the Court, and the manner of proceeding, and that I might read hereafter the speeches and evidence. . . .

Charles was not in time, but we all did well in the end. We got to Westminster Hall between nine and ten o'clock. . . .

The business did not begin till near twelve o'clock. The opening to the whole then took place, by the entrance of the *Managers of the Prosecution;* all the company were already long in their boxes or galleries.

I shuddered, and drew involuntarily back, when, as the doors were flung open, I saw Mr. Burke, as Head of the Committee, make his solemn entry. He held a scroll in his hand, and walked alone, his brow knit with corroding care and deep labouring thought,—a brow how different to that which had proved so alluring to my warmest admiration when first I met him! so highly as he had been my favourite, so captivating as I had found his

manners and conversation in our first acquaintance, and so much
as I had owed to his zeal and kindness to me and my affairs in its
progress! How did I grieve to behold him now the cruel Prose-
cutor (such to me he appeared) of an injured and innocent
man!

Mr. Fox followed next, Mr. Sheridan, Mr. Wyndham, Messrs.
Anstruther, Grey, Adam, Michael Angelo Taylor, Pelham, Colonel
North, Mr. Frederick Montagu, Sir Gilbert Elliot, General Bur-
goyne, Dudley Long, etc. They were all named over to me by
Lady Claremont, or I should not have recollected even those of my
acquaintance, from the shortness of my sight.

When the Committee Box was filled the House of Commons
at large took their seats on their green benches, which stretched,
as I have said, along the whole left side of the Hall, and, taking
in a third of the upper end, joined to the Great Chamberlain's
Box, from which nothing separated them but a partition of about
two feet in height.

Then began the procession, the Clerks entering first, then the
Lawyers according to their rank, and the Peers, Bishops, and
Officers, all in their coronation robes; concluding with the Princes
of the Blood,—Prince William, son to the Duke of Gloucester,
coming first, then the Dukes of Cumberland, Gloucester, and
York, then the Prince of Wales; and the whole ending by the
Chancellor, with his train borne.

They then all took their seats.

A Sergeant-at-Arms arose, and commanded silence in the Court,
on pain of imprisonment.

Then some other officer, in a loud voice, called out, as well as
I can recollect, words to this purpose:—"Warren Hastings, Esquire, come forth! Answer to the charges brought against you;
save your bail, or forfeit your recognizance!"

Indeed I trembled at these words, and hardly could keep my
place when I found Mr. Hastings was being brought to the bar.
He came forth from some place immediately under the Great
Chamberlain's Box, and was preceded by Sir Francis Molyneux,
Gentleman-Usher of the Black Rod; and at each side of him
walked his bail, Messrs. Sulivan and Sumner.

The moment he came in sight, which was not for full ten
minutes after his awful summons, he made a low bow to the
Chancellor and Court facing him. I saw not his face, as he was

directly under me. He moved on slowly, and, I think, supported between his two bails, to the opening of his own box; there, lower still, he bowed again; and then, advancing to the bar, he leant his hands upon it, and dropped on his knees; but a voice in the same moment proclaiming he had leave to rise, he stood up almost instantaneously, and a third time profoundly bowed to the Court.

What an awful moment this for such a man!—a man fallen from such height of power to a situation so humiliating—from the almost unlimited command of so large a part of the Eastern World to be cast at the feet of his enemies, of the great Tribunal of his Country, and of the Nation at large, assembled thus in a body to try and to judge him! Could even his Prosecutors at that moment look on—and not shudder at least, if they did not blush?

The Crier, I think it was, made, in a loud and hollow voice, a public proclamation, "That Warren Hastings, Esquire, late Governor-General of Bengal, was now on his trial for high crimes and misdemeanors, with which he was charged by the Commons of Great Britain; and that all persons whatsoever who had aught to allege against him were now to stand forth."

A general silence followed, and the Chancellor, Lord Thurlow, now made his speech. . . .

Again Mr. Hastings made the lowest reverence to the Court, and, leaning over the bar, answered, with much agitation, through evident efforts to suppress it, "My Lords—Impressed—deeply impressed—I come before your Lordships, equally confident in my own integrity, and in the justice of the Court before which I am to clear it."

"Impressed" and "deeply impressed," too, was my mind, by this short yet comprehensive speech, and all my best wishes for his clearance and redress rose warmer than ever in my heart.

A general silence again ensued, and then one of the Lawyers opened the cause. He began by reading from an immense roll of parchment the general charges against Mr. Hastings, but he read in so monotonous a chant that nothing more could I hear or understand than now and then the name of Warren Hastings. . . .

Another lawyer now arose, and read so exactly in the same manner, that it was utterly impossible to discover even whether it was a charge or an answer.

Such reading as this, you may well suppose, set everybody pretty much at their ease; and but for the interest I took in looking from time to time at Mr. Hastings, and watching his countenance, I might as well have been away. He seemed composed after the first half-hour, and calm; but he looked with a species of indignant contempt towards his accusers, that could not, I think, have been worn had his defence been doubtful. Many there are who fear for him; for me, I own myself wholly confident in his acquittal. . . .

April

I have scarce a memorandum of this fatal month, in which I was bereft of the most revered of friends, and, perhaps, the most perfect of women.[30] . . .

I believe I heard the last words she uttered; I cannot learn that she spoke after my reluctant departure. She finished with that cheerful resignation, that lively hope, which always broke forth when this last—awful—but, to her, most happy change seemed approaching.

Poor Miss P—— and myself were kneeling by her bedside. She had just given me her soft hand; without power to see either of us, she felt and knew us. Oh, never can I cease to cherish the remembrance of the sweet, benign, *holy* voice with which she pronounced a blessing upon us both! We kissed her; and, with a smile all beaming—I thought it so—of heaven, she seemed then to have taken leave of all earthly solicitudes. Yet then, even then, short as was her time on earth, the same soft human sensibility filled her for poor human objects. She would not bid us farewell—would not tell us she should speak with us no more —she only said, as she turned gently away from us, "And now—*I'll go to sleep!*"—But oh, in what a voice she said it! I felt what the sleep would be; so did poor Miss P——. . . .

She bid me—how often did she bid me—not grieve to lose her! Yet she said, in my absence, she knew I must, and sweetly regretted how much I must miss her. I teach myself to think of her felicity; and I never dwell upon that without faithfully feeling I would not desire her return. But, in every other channel in which my thoughts and feelings turn, I miss her with so sad a void! She was all that I dearly loved that remained within my reach;

she was become the bosom repository of all the livelong day's transactions, reflections, feelings, and wishes. . . .

I was much blamed here, universally, for my conduct at this time, in keeping alive all my sorrow, by going so continually to that scene of distress. They knew not it was my only balm! . . .

It was, however, a very fortunate circumstance that for the two or three first comings Mr. Fairly happened to be of the King's party.[31] Inured himself to sorrow, his soul was easily turned to pity; and far from censuring the affliction, or contemning the misfortunes, which were inferior to his own, his kind and feeling nature led him to no sensation but of compassion, which softened every feature of his face, and took place of all the hard traces of personal suffering which most severely had marked it. The tone of his voice was all in sympathy with this gentleness; and there was not an attention in his power to show me that he did not exert with the most benevolent and even flattering alacrity; interesting himself about my diet, my health, my exercise; proposing walks to me, and exhorting me to take them, and even intimating he should see that I did, were not his time occupied by royal attendance. . . .

July

Early in this month the King's indisposition occasioned the plan of his going to Cheltenham, to try the effect of the waters drunk upon the spot.[32] It was settled that the party should be the smallest that was possible, as His Majesty was to inhabit the house of Lord Fauconberg, vacated for that purpose, which was very small. . . .

Cheltenham, Sunday, July 13

. . . So now for yesterday, Saturday, July 12.

We were all up at five o'clock; and the noise and confusion reigning through the house, and resounding all around it, from the quantities of people stirring, boxes nailing, horses neighing, and dogs barking, was tremendous.

I must now tell you the party:—

Their Majesties; the Princesses Royal, Augusta and Elizabeth; Lady Weymouth, Mr. Fairly, Colonel Gwynn, Miss Planta, and a person you have sometimes met. Pages for King, Queen, and Princesses, wardrobe-women for ditto, and footmen for all.

A smaller party for a royal excursion cannot well be imagined. How we shall all manage Heaven knows. . . .

All the towns through which we passed were filled with people, as closely fastened one to another as they appear in the pit of the playhouse. Every town seemed all face; and all the way upon the road we rarely proceeded five miles without encountering a band of most horrid fiddlers, scraping "God Save the King" with all their might, out of tune, out of time, and all in the rain; for, most unfortunately, there were continual showers falling all the day. . . .

When we arrived at Cheltenham, which is almost all one street, extremely long, clean, and well paved, we had to turn out of the public way about a quarter of a mile, to proceed to Fauconberg Hall. . . .

After tea Mrs. Tracy went, and the King sent for Lord Courtown.

Mr. Fairly was going too, and I was preparing to return upstairs to my toils; but he presently changed his design, and asked leave to stay a little longer, if I was at leisure.

At leisure I certainly was not; but I was most content to work double tides for the pleasure of his company, especially where given thus voluntarily, and not accepted officially. What creatures are we all for liberty and freedom. . . .

From this circumstance we entered into discourse with no little spirit. I felt flattered, and he knew he had given me *de quoi;* so we were both in mighty good humour.

Our sociability, however, had very soon an interruption. The King re-entered; he started back at sight of our diminished party, and exclaimed, with a sort of arch surprise, "What! only you two?"

Mr. Fairly laughed a little, and I—smiled ditto! But I had rather His Majesty had made such a comment on any other of his establishment, if make it he must: since I am sure Mr. Fairly's aversion to that species of raillery is equal to my own.

The King gave some fresh orders about the letter, and instantly went away. As soon as he was gone, Mr. Fairly—perhaps to show himself superior to that little sally—asked me whether he might write his letter in my room?

"Oh yes!" cried I, with all the alacrity of the same superiority. . . .

He pretended to require my assistance in his letter, and consulted and read over all that he writ. So I gave my opinion as he went on, though I think it really possible he might have done without me!

Away then he went with it, to dispatch it by a royal footman; and I thought him gone, and was again going myself, when he returned,—surprising me not a little by saying, as he held the door in his hand, "Will there be any—impropriety—in my staying here a little longer?"

I must have said no, if I had thought yes; but it would not have been so plump and ready a no! and I should not, with quite so courteous a grace, have added that his stay could do me nothing but honour.

On, therefore, we sat, discoursing on various subjects, till the twilight made him rise to take leave. He was in much better spirits than I have yet seen him, and I know not when I have spent an hour more socially to my taste. . . .

Monday, July 14

. . . Our subject to-night—his subject, rather [33]—was, the necessity of participation, to every species of happiness. "His" subject, you may easily believe; for to him should I never have dared touch on one so near and so tender to him. . . . He seems born with the tenderest social affections; and, though religiously resigned to his loss—which, I have been told, the hopeless sufferings of Lady —— rendered, at last, even a release to be desired—he thinks life itself, single and unshared, a mere melancholy burthen, and the wish to have done with it appears the only wish he indulges.

I could not perceive this without the deepest commiseration, but I did what was possible to conceal it; as it is much more easy, both to the hearer and the speaker, to lead the discourse to matters more lively, under an appearance of being ignorant of the state of a sad heart, than with a betrayed consciousness. . . .

. . . While the Royals were upon the walks, Miss Planta and I strolled in the meadows, and who should I meet there but Mr. Seward! This was a great pleasure to me. I had never seen him since the first day of my coming to St. James's, when he handed me into my father's coach, in my sacque and long ruffles. You may think how much we had to talk over. He had a gentleman with him, fortunately, who was acquainted with Miss Planta's brother, so that we formed two parties without difficulty. All my aim was to inquire about Mrs. Piozzi,[34]—I must, at last, call her by her now real name!—and of her we conversed incessantly. . . .

We strolled so long, talking over this ever-interesting subject, that the Royals were returned before us, and we found Mr. Fairly waiting tea in my parlour. . . .

When Miss Planta went off for her exercise, he again proposed a little reading, which again I thankfully accepted. He took out the little poem, and read on the mournful tale of Anna,[35] with a sensibility that gave pathos to every word.

How unexpected an indulgence—a luxury, I may say, to me, are these evenings now becoming! While I listen to such reading, and such a reader, all my work goes on with an alacrity that renders it all pleasure to me. I have had no regale like this for many and many a grievous long evening! never since I left Norbury Park,—never since my dear Fredy there read Madame de Sévigné. And how little could I expect, in royal residence, a relief of this sort! Indeed, I much question if there is one other person, in the whole establishment, that, in an equal degree, could afford it. . . .

This whole evening I spent *tête-à-tête* with Mr. Fairly. There is something singular in the perfect trust he seems to have in my discretion, for he speaks to me when we are alone with a frankness unequalled; and something very flattering in the apparent relief he seems to find in dedicating what time he has to dispose of to my little parlour.

In the long conference of this evening I found him gifted with the justest way of thinking and the most classical taste. I speak that word only as I may presume to judge it by English literature.

"I have another little book," he said, "here, which I am sure you would like, but it has a title so very silly that nobody reads or names it: *Original Love-Letters*,[36]—from which you might expect mere nonsense and romance, though, on the contrary, you would find in them nothing but good sense, moral reflections, and refined ideas, clothed in the most expressive and elegant language."

How I longed to read a book that had such a character!—yet, laughable and prudish as it may seem to you, I could not bring myself to accept the half-offer, to make any other reply than to exclaim against the injudiciousness of the title-page.

Yet, whatever were our subjects, books, life, or persons, all concluded with the same melancholy burthen—speed to his existence here, and welcome to that he is awaiting! I fear he has been unfortunate from his first setting out. . . .

Thursday, July 24

"Pray, Miss Burney," cried Colonel Gwynn,[37] "do you think Mr. Fairly will ever marry again?"

"I think it very doubtful," I answered, "but I hope he will, for, whether he is happy or not in marrying, I am sure he will be wretched in singleness; the whole turn of his mind is so social and domestic. He is by no means formed for going always abroad for the relief of society; he requires it more at hand."

"And what do you think of Miss Fuzilier?" [38]

"That he is wholly disengaged with her and with everybody."

"Well, I think it will be, for I know they correspond; and what should he correspond with her for else?"

"Because, I suppose, he has done it long before this could be suggested as the motive. And, indeed, the very quickness of the report makes me discredit it; 'tis so utterly impossible for a man whose feelings are so delicate to have taken any steps towards a second connection at so early a period."

"Why, I know he's very romantic; but I should like to know your opinion."

"I have given it you," cried I, "very exactly." . . .

Saturday, July 26

. . . About twelve o'clock I was reading in my private loan book, when, hearing the step of Miss Planta on the stairs, I put it

back in my workbox, and was just taking thence some other
employment, when her voice struck my ear almost in a scream—
"Is it possible? Mr. Fairly!"

My own with difficulty refrained echoing it when I heard his
voice answer her; and in a few minutes they parted, and he rapped
at the door and entered my little parlour.

He came in hobbling, leaning on a stick, and with a large cloth
shoe over one of his feet, which was double the size of the other.

We sat down together, and he soon inquired what I had done
with his little book.

I had only, I answered, read two more letters.

"Have you read two?" he cried, in a voice rather disappointed;
and I found he was actually come to devote the morning, which
he knew to be unappropriated on my part, to reading it on to me
himself. Then he took up the book and read on from the fifth
letter. But he read at first with evident uneasiness, throwing down
the book at every noise, and stopping to listen at every sound.
At last he asked me if anybody was likely to come?

Not a soul, I said, that I knew or expected.

He laughed a little at his question and apparent anxiety; but
with an openness that singularly marks his character, he frankly
added, "I must put the book away, pure as it is, if any one comes;
or, without knowing a word of the contents, they will run away
with the title alone, exclaiming, 'Mr. Fairly reading love-letters
to Miss Burney!' A fine story that would make!"

'Pon honour, thought I, I would not hear such a tale for the
world. However, he now pursued his reading more at his ease. . . .

Columb [39] now soon came in to inquire what time I should
dine, but a ghost could not have made him stare more than
Mr. Fairly, whose confinement with the gout had been spread all
over the house by Colonel Gwynn.

I ordered an early dinner on account of the play.

"Will you invite me," cried Mr. Fairly, laughing, "to dine with
you?"

"Oh yes!" I cried, "with the greatest pleasure"; and he said
he would go to his home and dress, and return to my hour. . . .

I told [Miss Planta] she would have a beau at dinner. "Well,"
she exclaimed, " 'tis the oddest thing in the world he should
come so when the King and Queen are away! I am sure, if I was
you, I would not mention it."

"Oh yes, I shall," cried I; "I receive no visitors in private;

and I am sure if I did, Mr. Fairly is the last who would condescend to make one of them."

Such was my proud, but true speech, for him and for myself. . . .

When dinner and a very sociable dessert were over, we proposed going to the King's dining-parlour, while the servants removed the things, etc., against tea. But the weather was so very fine we were tempted by the open door to go out into the air. Miss Planta said she would take a walk; Mr. Fairly could not, but all without was so beautiful he would not go into the parlour, and rather risked the fatigue of standing, as he leant against the porch, to losing the lovely prospect or sweet air.

And here, for near two hours, on the steps of Fauconberg Hall, we remained; and they were two hours of such pure serenity, without and within, as I think, except in Norbury Park, with its loved inhabitants and my Susan, I scarce ever remember to have spent. . . .

Sunday, July 27

This morning in my first attendance I seized a moment to tell Her Majesty of yesterday's dinner. "So I hear!" she cried; and I was sorry any one had anticipated my information, nor can I imagine who it might be.

"But pray, ma'am," very gravely, "how did it happen? I understood Mr. Fairly was confined by the gout."

"He grew better, ma'am, and hoped by exercise to prevent a serious fit."

She said no more, but did not seem pleased. The fatigues of a Court attendance are so little comprehended, that persons known to be able to quit their room and their bed are instantly concluded to be qualified for all the duties of their office. . . .

Friday, August 1

. . . Hearing now the barking of the dogs, I knew the Royals must be going forth to their promenade; but I found Mr. Fairly either did not hear or did not heed them. . . .

While I expected him every moment to recollect himself, and

hasten to the walks, he quietly said, "They are all gone but me. I shall venture, to-night, to shirk;—though the King will soon miss me. But what will follow? He will say—'Fairly is tired! How shabby!' Well! let him say so; I *am* tired!"

Miss Planta went off, soon after, to her walk. . . .

He then began reading *The Pleasures of the Imagination,*[40] and I took some work, for which I was much in haste, and my imagination was amply gratified. . . .

After the first hour, however, he grew uneasy; he asked me when I expected the King and Queen from their walk, and whether they were likely to come into my room?

"All," I said, "was uncertain."

"Can nobody," he cried, "let you know when they are coming?"

"Nobody," I answered, "would know till they were actually arrived."

"But," cried he, "can you not bid somebody watch?"

'Twas rather an awkward commission, but I felt it would be an awkwardness still less pleasant to me to decline it, and therefore I called Columb, and desired he would let me know when the Queen returned.

He was then easier, and laughed a little, while he explained himself, "Should they come in and find me reading here before I could put away my book, they would say we were two blue stockings!" [41]

I am always ready enough to enter into any caution to save that pedantic charge, and therefore we were perfectly agreed. And perhaps he was a little the more anxious not to be surprised to-night, lest his being too tired for walking should be imputed to his literary preference of reading to *a blue.*

At tea Miss Planta again joined us, and instantly behind him went the book. He was very right; for nobody would have thought it more odd—or more blue. . . .

Saturday, August 9

. . . I sat down to make my solitary tea, and had just sent up a basin to Miss Planta when, to my equal surprise and pleasure, Mr. Fairly entered the room. "I come now," he said, "to take my leave." [42] . . .

"And I must not say," cried I, "that I am sorry you are going, because I know so well you wish to be gone that it makes me wish it for you myself."

"No," answered he, "you must not be sorry; when our friends are going to any joy we must think of them, and be glad to part with them."

Readily entering into the same tone, with similar plainness of truth I answered, "No, I will not be sorry you go, though miss you at Cheltenham I certainly must."

"Yes," was his unreserved assent, "you will miss me here, because I have spent my evenings with you; but you will not long remain at Cheltenham."

Oimè! thought I, you little think how much worse will be the quitting it. . . .

This drew him on into some reflections upon affection and upon happiness. "There is no happiness," he said, "without participation; no participation without affection. There is, indeed, in affection a charm that leaves all things behind it, and renders even every calamity that does not interfere with it inconsequential; and there is no difficulty, no toil, no labour, no exertion, that will not be endured where there is a view of reaping it."

My concurrence was too perfect to require many words.

"And affection there sometimes is," he continued, "even in this weak world, so pure, so free from alloy, that one is tempted to wonder, without deeply considering, why it should not be permanent, and why it should be vain."

Here I did not quite comprehend his conclusion; but it was a sort of subject I could not probe, for various reasons. Besides, he was altogether rather obscure. . . .

He then rose and took his hat, saying, "Well, so much for the day; what may come to-morrow I know not; but, be it what it may, I stand prepared." . . .

"We will say," cried he, "nothing of any regrets," and bowed, and was hastening off.

The "we," however, had an openness and simplicity that drew from me an equally open and simple reply. "No," I cried, "but I will say—for that you will have pleasure in hearing—that you have lightened my time here in a manner that no one else could have done, of this party." . . .

He said not a word of answer, but bowed, and went away,

leaving me firmly impressed with a belief that I shall find in him a true, an honourable, and even an affectionate friend, for life. . . .

Saturday, August 16

. . . And thus ends the Cheltenham episode. May I not justly call it so, different as it is to all the mode of life I have hitherto lived here, or alas! am in a way to live henceforward? . . .

September 2

. . . Mr. Turbulent was in high rage that I was utterly invisible since my return from Cheltenham; he protested he had called seven times at my door without gaining admission, and never was able to get in but when "Dr. Shepherd had led the way."

He next began a mysterious attack upon the proceedings of Cheltenham. He had heard, he said, strange stories of flirtations there.[43] I could not doubt what he meant, but I would not seem to understand him: first, because I know not from whom he has been picking up this food for his busy spirit, since no one there appeared collecting it for him; and secondly, because I would not degrade an acquaintance which I must hope will prove as permanent as it is honourable, by conceiving the word flirtation to be possibly connected with it. . . .

Friday, October 17

Our return to Windsor is postponed till to-morrow.[44] The King is not well; he has not been quite well some time, yet nothing I hope alarming, though there is an uncertainty as to his complaint not very satisfactory; so precious, too, is his health. . . .

Sunday, October 19

. . . We are to stay here some time longer, and so unprepared were we for more than a day or two, that our distresses are prodigious, even for clothes to wear; and as to books, there are not three amongst us; and for company, only Mr. de Luc and Miss Planta; and so, in mere desperation for employment, I have just begun a tragedy.[45] We are now in so spiritless a situation that my mind would bend to nothing less sad, even in fiction. But I am very glad something of this kind has occurred to me; it may while away the tediousness of this unsettled, unoccupied, unpleasant period.

Saturday, October 25

. . . The King was so much better that our Windsor journey at length took place, with permission of Sir George Baker, the only physician His Majesty will admit.[46] . . .

I had a sort of conference with His Majesty, or rather I was the object to whom he spoke, with a manner so uncommon, that a high fever alone could account for it; a rapidity, a hoarseness of voice, a volubility, an earnestness—a vehemence, rather—it startled me inexpressibly; yet with a graciousness exceeding even all I ever met with before—it was almost kindness! . . .

Saturday, November 1

Our King does not advance in amendment; he grows so weak that he walks like a gouty man, yet has such spirits that he has talked away his voice, and is so hoarse it is painful to hear him. The Queen is evidently in great uneasiness. God send him better! . . .

During the reading this morning, twice, at pathetic passages, my poor Queen shed tears. "How nervous I am!" she cried; "I am quite a fool! Don't you think so?"

"No, ma'am!" was all I dared answer. . . .

Nor can I ever forget him in what passed this night. When I came to the Queen's dressing-room he was still with her. He constantly conducts her to it before he retires to his own. He was begging her not to speak to him when he got to his room, that he might fall asleep, as he felt great want of that refreshment. He repeated this desire, I believe, at least a hundred times, though, far enough from needing it, the poor Queen never uttered one syllable! He then applied to me, saying he was really very well, except in that one particular, that he could not sleep. . . .

Wednesday, November 5

Oh, dreadful day! . . .

I found my poor Royal Mistress, in the morning, sad and sadder still; something horrible seemed impending, and I saw her whole resource was in religion. We had talked lately much upon solemn subjects, and she appeared already preparing herself to be resigned for whatever might happen. . . .

I had but just reached my own room, deeply musing on the state of things, when a chaise stopped at the rails; and I saw Mr. Fairly and his son Charles alight, and enter the house. He walked lamely, and seemed not yet recovered from his late attack.

Though most happy to see him at this alarming time when I knew he could be most useful, as there is no one to whom the Queen opens so confidentially upon her affairs, I had yet a fresh start to see, by his anticipated arrival, though still lame, that he must have been sent for, and hurried hither. . . .

Meanwhile, a stillness the most uncommon reigned over the whole house. Nobody stirred; not a voice was heard; not a step, not a motion. I could do nothing but watch, without knowing for what: there seemed a strangeness in the house most extraordinary.

At seven o'clock Columb came to tell me that the music was all forbid, and the musicians ordered away!

This was the last step to be expected, so fond as His Majesty is of his Concert, and I thought it might have rather soothed him: I could not understand the prohibition; all· seemed stranger and stranger. . . .

Oh, my dear friends, what a history! The King, at dinner, had broken forth into positive delirium, which long had been menacing all who saw him most closely; and the Queen was so overpowered as to fall into violent hysterics. All the Princesses were in misery, and the Prince of Wales had burst into tears.[47] No one knew what was to follow—no one could conjecture the event. . . .

If this beginning of the night was affecting, what did it not grow

afterwards! Two long hours I waited—alone, in silence, in ignorance, in dread! I thought they would never be over; at twelve
o'clock I seemed to have spent two whole days in waiting. I then
opened my door, to listen, in the passage, if anything seemed
stirring. Not a sound could I hear. My apartment seemed wholly
separated from life and motion. Whoever was in the house kept
at the other end, and not even a servant crossed the stairs or
passage by my rooms.

I would fain have crept on myself, anywhere in the world, for
some inquiry, or to see but a face, and hear a voice, but I did
not dare risk losing a sudden summons.

I re-entered my room and there passed another endless hour,
in conjectures too horrible to relate.

A little after one, I heard a step—my door opened—and a page
said I must come to the Queen.

I could hardly get along—hardly force myself into the room;
dizzy I felt, almost to falling. But, the first shock passed, I became
more collected. Useful, indeed, proved the previous lesson of the
evening: it had stilled, if not fortified my mind, which had else,
in a scene such as this, been all tumult and emotion.

My poor Royal Mistress! never can I forget her countenance
—pale, ghastly pale she looked; she was seated to be undressed,
and attended by Lady Elizabeth Waldegrave and Miss Goldsworthy; her whole frame was disordered, yet she was still and quiet.

These two ladies assisted me to undress her, or rather I assisted them, for they were firmer, from being longer present; my
shaking hands and blinded eyes could scarce be of any use.

I gave her some camphor julep, which had been ordered her
by Sir George Baker. "How cold I am!" she cried, and put her
hand on mine; marble it felt! and went to my heart's core! . . .

How reluctantly did I come away! how hardly to myself leave
her! Yet I went to bed, determined to preserve my strength to
the utmost of my ability, for the service of my unhappy mistress.
I could not,. however, sleep. I do not suppose an eye was closed in
the house all night.

Thursday, November 6

I rose at six, dressed in haste by candlelight, and unable
to wait for my summons in a suspense so awful, I stole along the

passage in the dark, a thick fog intercepting all faint light, to see if I could meet with Sandys,[48] or any one, to tell me how the night had passed. . . .

. . . I could not resist the opportunity to venture myself before her. I glided into the room, but stopped at the door: she was in bed, sitting up; Miss Goldsworthy was on a stool by her side!

I feared approaching without permission, yet could not prevail with myself to retreat. She was looking down, and did not see me. Miss Goldsworthy, turning round, said, " 'Tis Miss Burney, ma'am."

She leaned her head forward, and in a most soft manner, said, "Miss Burney, how are you?"

Deeply affected, I hastened up to her, but, in trying to speak, burst into an irresistible torrent of tears.

My dearest friends, I do it at this moment again, and can hardly write for them; yet I wish you to know all this piercing history right.

She looked like death—colourless and wan; but nature is infectious; the tears gushed from her own eyes, and a perfect agony of weeping ensued, which, once begun, she could not stop; she did not, indeed, try; for when it subsided, and she wiped her eyes, she said, "I thank you, Miss Burney—you have made me cry—it is a great relief to me—I had not been able to cry before, all this night long."

Oh what a scene followed! what a scene was related! The King, in the middle of the night, had insisted upon seeing if his Queen was not removed from the house; and he had come into her room, with a candle in his hand, opened the bed-curtains, and satisfied himself she was there, and Miss Goldsworthy by her side. This observance of his directions had much soothed him; but he stayed a full half hour, and the depth of terror during that time no words can paint. The fear of such another entrance was now so strongly upon the nerves of the poor Queen, that she could hardly support herself. . . .

. . . We all three stayed with her; she frequently bid me listen, to hear what the King was saying or doing. I did, and carried the best accounts I could manage, without deviating from truth, except by some omissions. Nothing could be so afflicting as this task; even now, it brings fresh to my ear his poor exhausted voice. "I am nervous," he cried; "I am not ill, but I am nervous: if you would know what is the matter with me, I am nervous. But I love you both very well; if you would tell me truth: I love Dr. Heberden best,[49] for he has not told me a lie: Sir George has told me a lie—a white lie, he says, but I hate a white lie! If you will tell me a lie, let it be a black lie!"

This was what he kept saying almost constantly, mixed in with other matter, but always returning, and in a voice that truly will never cease vibrating in my recollection. . . .

. . . Colonel Goldsworthy sent in to beg an audience. It was granted, a long cloak only being thrown over the Queen.

He now brought the opinion of all the physicians in consultation, "That Her Majesty would remove to a more distant apartment, since the King would undoubtedly be worse from the agitation of seeing her, and there could be no possibility to prevent it while she remained so near."

She instantly agreed, but with what bitter anguish! Lady Elizabeth, Miss Goldsworthy, and myself attended her; she went to an apartment in the same row, but to which there was no entrance except by its own door. . . .

At the entrance into this new habitation the poor wretched Queen once more gave way to a perfect agony of grief and affliction; while the words, "What will become of me! What will become of me!" uttered with the most piercing lamentation, struck deep and hard into all our hearts. . . .

Alone wholly, without seeing a human being, or gathering any, the smallest intelligence of what was going forwards, I remained till tea-time.

Impatient then for information, I planted myself in the eating-parlour; but no one came. Every minute seemed an hour. I grew as anxious for the tea society as heretofore I had been anxious to escape it; but so late it grew, and so hopeless, that Columb came to propose bringing the water.

No; for I could swallow nothing voluntarily.

In a few minutes he came again, and with the compliments of Mr. Fairly, who desired him to tell me he would wait upon me to tea whenever I pleased.

A little surprised at this single message, but most truly rejoiced, I returned my compliments, with an assurance that all time was the same to me.

He came directly, and indeed his very sight, at this season of still horror and silent suspense, was a repose to my poor aching eyes. . . .

Our tea was very sad. He gave me no hope of a short seizure; he saw it, in perspective, as long as it was dreadful: perhaps even worse than long, he thought it—but that he said not. He related to me the whole of the day's transactions, but my most dear and most honourable friends will be the first to forgive me when I promise that I shall commit nothing to paper on this terrible event that is told me in confidence. . . .

Friday, November 7

I was now arrived at a sort of settled regularity of life more melancholy than can possibly be described. I rose at six, dressed, and hastened to the Queen's apartments, uncalled, and there waited in silence and in the dark till I heard her move or speak with Miss Goldsworthy, and then presented myself to the sad bedside of the unhappy Queen. She sent Miss Goldsworthy early every morning, to make inquiry what sort of night His Majesty had passed; and in the middle of the night she commonly also sent for news by the wardrobe-woman, or Miss Macenton, whichever sat up. . . .

At noon now I never saw her, which I greatly regretted; but she kept on her dressing-gown all day, and the Princes were continually about the passages, so that no one unsummoned dared approach the Queen's apartments.

It was only therefore at night and morning I could see her; but my heart was with her the livelong day. And how long, good Heaven! how long that day became! Endless I used to think it, for nothing could I do—to wait and to watch—starting at every sound, yet revived by every noise. . . .

Saturday, November 8

. . . From this time, as the poor King grew worse, general hope seemed universally to abate; and the Prince of Wales now took the government of the house into his own hands.[50] Nothing was done but by his orders, and he was applied to in every difficulty. The Queen interfered not in anything; she lived entirely in her two new rooms, and spent the whole day in patient sorrow and retirement with her daughters. . . .

The next news that reached me, through Mr. de Luc, was, that the Prince had sent his commands to the porter, to admit only four persons into the house on any pretence whatever: these were Mr. Majendie, Mr. Turbulent, General Harcourt,[51] and Mr. de Luc himself; and these were ordered to repair immediately to the Equerry-room below-stairs, while no one whatsoever was to be allowed to go to any other apartment.

From this time commenced a total banishment from all intercourse out of the house, and an unremitting confinement within its walls. . . .

Sunday, November 9

No one went to church; not a creature now quits the house: but I believe devotion never less required the aid and influence of public worship. For me, I know, I spent almost my whole time between prayer and watching. Even my melancholy resource, my tragedy, was now thrown aside; misery so actual, living, and present, was knit too closely around me to allow my depressed imagination to fancy any woe beyond what my heart felt. . . .

Saturday, November 29

Shall I ever forget the varied emotions of this dreadful day!

I rose with the heaviest of hearts, and found my poor Royal Mistress in the deepest dejection: she told me now of our intended expedition to Kew. Lady Elizabeth hastened away to dress, and I was alone with her for some time.

Her mind, she said, quite misgave her about Kew: the King's dislike was terrible to think of, and she could not foresee in what it might end. She would have resisted the measure herself, but that she had determined not to have upon her own mind any opposition to the opinion of the physicians.

The account of the night was still more and more discouraging: it was related to me by one of the pages, Mr. Brawan; and though a little I softened or omitted particulars, I yet most sorrowfully conveyed it to the Queen.

Terrible was the morning!—uninterruptedly terrible! all spent in hasty packing up, preparing for we knew not what, nor for how long, nor with what circumstances, nor scarcely with what view! We seemed preparing for captivity, without having committed any offence; and for banishment, without the least conjecture when we might be recalled from it.

The poor Queen was to get off in private: the plan settled, between the Princes and the physicians, was that Her Majesty and the Princesses should go away quietly, and then that the King should be told that they were gone, which was the sole method they could devise to prevail with him to follow. He was then to be allured by a promise of seeing them at Kew; and, as they knew he would doubt their assertion, he was to go through the rooms and examine the house himself.

When we arrived at Kew, we found the suspense with which the King was awaited truly terrible. Her Majesty had determined to return to Windsor at night, if he came not. We were all to forbear unpacking in the meanwhile.

The house [52] was all now regulated by express order of the Prince of Wales, who rode over first, and arranged all the apartments, and writ, with chalk, the names of the destined inhabitants on each door. . . .

Dinner went on, and still no King. We now began to grow very anxious, when Miss Planta exclaimed that she thought she heard a carriage. We all listened. "I hope!" I cried. "I see you do!" cried he; "you have a very face of hope at this moment!"— and it was not disappointed. The sound came nearer, and presently a carriage drove into the front court. I could see nothing, it was so dark; but I presently heard the much-respected voice of the dear unhappy King, speaking rapidly to the porter, as he alighted from the coach. Mr. Fairly flew instantly upstairs, to acquaint the Queen with the welcome tidings.

The poor King had been prevailed upon to quit Windsor with the utmost difficulty: he was accompanied by General Harcourt, his aide-de-camp, and Colonels Goldsworthy and Welbred—no one else! He had passed all the rest with apparent composure, to come to his carriage, for they lined the passage, eager to see him once more! and almost all Windsor was collected round the rails, etc., to witness the mournful spectacle of his departure, which left them in the deepest despondence, with scarce a ray of hope ever to see him again.

The bribery, however, which brought, was denied him!—he was by no means to see the Queen! . . .

Sunday, November 30

Here, in all its dread colours, dark as its darkest prognostics, began the Kew campaign. I went to my poor Queen at seven o'clock: the Princess Augusta arose and went away to dress, and I received Her Majesty's commands to go down for inquiries. She had herself passed a wretched night and already lamented leaving Windsor.

I waited very long in the cold dark passages below, before I could find any one of whom to ask intelligence. The parlours were without fires, and washing. I gave directions afterwards to have a fire in one of them by seven o'clock every morning.

At length I procured the speech of one of the pages, and heard that the night had been the most violently bad of any yet passed! —and no wonder! [53]

I hardly knew how to creep upstairs, frozen both within and without, to tell such news; but it was not received as if unexpected, and I omitted whatever was not essential to be known.

Afterwards arrived Mrs. Schwellenberg, so oppressed between her spasms and the house's horrors, that the oppression she inflicted ought perhaps to be pardoned. It was, however, difficult enough to bear! Harshness, tyranny, dissension, and even insult, seemed personified. I cut short details upon this subject—they would but make you sick. . . .

Monday, December 15

This whole day was passed in great internal agitation throughout the house, as the great and important business of the Regency was to be discussed to-morrow in Parliament. All is now too painful and intricate for writing a word. I begin to confine my memorandums almost wholly to my own personal proceedings.

Wednesday, December 17

My account this morning was most afflictive once more: it was given by Mr. Hawkins,[54] and was cruelly subversive of all our rising hopes. I carried it to the Queen in trembling; but she bore it most mildly. What resignation is hers!

Miss Planta tells me the Queen has given her commands that no one shall bring her any account of the night but me. She has been teased, I fancy, with erroneous relations, or unnecessarily wounded with cruel particulars. Be this as it may, I can hardly, when my narration is bad, get out the words to tell it; and I come upon the worst parts, if of a nature to be indispensably told, with as much difficulty as if I had been author of them. But her patience in hearing and bearing them is truly edifying.

Mr. Hawkins to-day, after a recital of some particulars extremely shocking, said, "But you need not tell that to the Queen."

"I could not, sir," was my true, though dry answer. Yet I never omit anything essential to be known. Detail is rarely of that character.

Monday, December 22

With what joy did I carry, this morning, an exceeding good account of the King to my Royal Mistress! It was trebly welcome, as much might depend upon it in the resolutions of the House concerning the Regency, which was of to-day's discussion. . . .

The King went on now better, now worse, in a most fearful manner; but Sir Lucas Pepys never lost sight of hope, and the management of Dr. Willis and his two sons was most wonderfully acute and successful.[55] Yet so much were they perplexed and tormented by the interruptions given to their plans and methods, that they were frequently almost tempted to resign the undertaking from anger and confusion.

[1789]

Tuesday, January 13

. . . I took the opportunity to decamp to my own room, where I found Mr. Fairly in waiting.

In the course of conversation that followed, Mrs. Carter was named: Mr. Smelt is seriously of opinion her ode [56] is the best in our language. I spoke of her very highly, for indeed I reverence her.

Learning in women was then our theme: I rather wished to hear than to declaim upon this subject, yet I never seek to disguise that I think it has no recommendation of sufficient value to compensate its evil excitement of envy and satire.

He spoke with very uncommon liberality on the female powers and intellects, and protested he had never, in his commerce with the world, been able to discern any other inferiority in their parts than what resulted from their pursuits;—and yet, with all this, he doubted much whether he had ever seen any woman who might not have been rather better without than with the learned languages, one only excepted.

He was some time silent, and I could not but suppose he meant his correspondent, Miss Fuzilier; but, with a very tender sigh, he said, "And she was my mother,—who neglected nothing else, while she cultivated Latin, and who knew it very well, and would have known it very superiorly, but that her brother disliked her studying, and one day burnt all her books!"

This anecdote led to one in return, from myself. I told him briefly the history of Dr. Johnson's most kind condescension, in desiring to make me his pupil, and beginning to give me regular lessons of the Latin language, and I proceeded to the speedy conclusion—my great apprehension, *conviction* rather, that what I learnt of so great a man could never be *private,* and that he himself would contemn concealment, if any progress should be made; which to me was sufficient motive for relinquishing the scheme, and declining the honour, highly as I valued it, of obtaining such a master.[57]—"And this," I added, "though difficult to be done without offending, was yet the better effected, as my father himself likes and approves all accomplishments for women better than the dead languages."

He made afterwards many inquiries concerning my own present mode of going on.

"What a situation," he once cried, "it is, to live pent up thus, day after day, in this forlorn apartment!—confinement!—attendance!—seclusion!—uncertain, for months to come, how long it may last."

I could not command philosophy adequate for treating this subject as I felt upon it; I therefore had recourse to a letter I had

just received from my affectionate Charlotte, telling me she seriously feared I should be quite *killed* by living such a life, and
supplicating me most earnestly to give it up, and to let Mr.
Francis apply to my father to obtain his permission for me to
resign, and then to propose to me a constant residence in their
house, to be only broken in upon by my going to my father himself, and to another, to whom she would always yield—my Susanna.

'Tis a most sweetly kind intention, and urged with the most innocent artlessness of its impracticability.

He inquired her name and abode, etc., but most promptly
agreed her scheme, though truly sisterly, was out of all question. . . .

Tuesday, [January] 27

. . . Sir Lucas declared my confinement menaced my health,
and charged me to walk out, and take air and exercise very
sedulously, if I would avoid an illness.

Colonel Welbred instantly offered me a key of Richmond Gardens, which opened into them by a nearer door than what was
used in common.

I accepted his kindness, and took an hour's walk,—for the first
time since last October; ten minutes in Kew Gardens are all I
have spent without doors since the middle of that month.

Thursday, [January] 29

Still good news from the two good doctors. All else bad,—Cerbera dreadful! [58] more rough and harsh than I have words to
tell. She has done, palpably, what was possible to procure a censure from the Magnolia; [59] but the Magnolia cannot enjoin an
injustice—though she may wish me more subservient. But I will
not enter upon these matters here.

Friday, [January] 30

. . . Not long after came Mr. Fairly, looking harassed. "May
I," he cried, "come in?—and—for an hour? Can you allow me
entrance and room for that time?"

Much surprised, for already it was three o'clock, I assented: he then told me he had something to copy for Her Majesty, which was of the highest importance, and said he could find no quiet room in the house but mine for such a business.

I gave him every accommodation in my power.

When he had written a few lines, he asked if I was very busy, or could help him? Most readily I offered my services; and then I read to him the original, sentence by sentence, to facilitate his copying; receiving his assurances of my "great assistance" every two lines.

In the midst of this occupation, a tap at my door made me precipitately put down the paper to receive—Lady Charlotte Finch! [60]

"Can you," she cried, "have the goodness to tell me anything of Mr. Fairly?"

The screen had hidden him; but, gently,—though I believe ill enough pleased,—he called out himself, "Here is Mr. Fairly."

She flew up to him, crying, "Oh, Mr. Fairly, what a search has there been for you, by the Queen's orders! She has wanted you extremely, and no one knew where to find you. They have been to the waiting-room, to the equerries', all over the garden, to the Prince's House, in your own room, and could find you nowhere, and at last they thought you were gone back to town."

He calmly answered, while he still wrote on, he was sorry they had had so much trouble, for he had only been executing Her Majesty's commands.

She then hesitated a little, almost to stammering, in adding, "So—at last—I said—that perhaps—you might be here!"

He now raised his head from the paper, and bowing in towards me, "Yes," he cried, "Miss Burney is so good as to give me leave, and there is no other room in the house in which I can be at rest."

"So I told Her Majesty," answered Lady Charlotte, "though she said she was sure you could not be here; but I said there was really no room of quiet here for any business, and so then I came to see."

"Miss Burney," he rejoined, "has the goodness also to help me —she has taken the trouble to read as I go on, which forwards me very much."

Lady Charlotte stared, and I felt sorry at this confession of a confidence she could not but think too much, and I believe he half repented it, for he added, "This, however, you need not perhaps mention, though I know where I trust!" . . .

Kew Palace, Monday, February 2

What an adventure had I this morning! one that has occasioned me the severest personal terror I ever experienced in my life.

Sir Lucas Pepys still persisting that exercise and air were absolutely necessary to save me from illness, I have continued my walks, varying my gardens from Richmond to Kew, according to the accounts I received of the movements of the King. For this I had Her Majesty's permission on the representation of Sir Lucas.

This morning, when I received my intelligence of the King from Dr. John Willis, I begged to know where I might walk in safety. "In Kew Gardens," he said, "as the King would be in Richmond."

"Should any unfortunate circumstance," I cried, "at any time, occasion my being seen by His Majesty, do not mention my name, but let me run off without call or notice."

This he promised. Everybody, indeed, is ordered to keep out of sight.

Taking, therefore, the time I had most at command, I strolled into the gardens. I had proceeded, in my quick way, nearly half the round, when I suddenly perceived, through some trees, two or three figures. Relying on the instructions of Dr. John, I concluded them to be workmen and gardeners; yet tried to look sharp, and in so doing, as they were less shaded, I thought I saw the person of His Majesty!

Alarmed past all possible expression, I waited not to know more, but turning back, ran off with all my might. But what was my terror to hear myself pursued!—to hear the voice of the King himself loudly and hoarsely calling after me, "Miss Burney! Miss Burney!"

I protest I was ready to die. I knew not in what state he might be at the time; I only knew the orders to keep out of his way were universal; that the Queen would highly disapprove any unauthorised meeting, and that the very action of my running away might deeply, in his present irritable state, offend him. Nevertheless, on I ran, too terrified to stop, and in search of some short passage, for the garden is full of little labyrinths, by which I might escape.

The steps still pursued me, and still the poor hoarse and altered voice rang in my ears:—more and more footsteps resounded frightfully behind me,—the attendants all running, to catch their eager master, and the voices of the two Dr. Willises loudly exhorting him not to heat himself so unmercifully. . . .

Soon after, I heard other voices, shriller, though less nervous, call out, "Stop! stop! stop!"

I could by no means consent: I knew not what was purposed, but I recollected fully my agreement with Dr. John that very morning, that I should decamp if surprised, and not be named. . . .

. . . [S]uch was my speed, so almost incredible to relate or recollect, that I fairly believe no one of the whole party could have over-taken me, if these words, from one of the attendants, had not reached me, "Dr. Willis begs you to stop!"

"I cannot! I cannot!" I answered, still flying on, when he called out, "You must, ma'am; it hurts the King to run."

Then, indeed, I stopped—in a state of fear really amounting to agony. I turned round, I saw the two Doctors had got the King between them, and three attendants of Dr. Willis's were hovering about. They all slackened their pace, as they saw me stand still; but such was the excess of my alarm, that I was wholly insensible to the effects of a race which, at any other time, would have required an hour's recruit.

As they approached, some little presence of mind happily came to my command: it occurred to me that, to appease the wrath of my flight, I must now show some confidence: I therefore faced them as undauntedly as I was able, only charging the nearest of the attendants to stand by my side.

When they were within a few yards of me, the King called out, "Why did you run away?"

Shocked at a question impossible to answer, yet a little assured by the mild tone of his voice, I instantly forced myself forward, to meet him, though the internal sensation which satisfied me this was a step the most proper, to appease his suspicions and displeasure, was so violently combated by the tremor of my nerves, that I fairly think I may reckon it the greatest effort of personal courage I have ever made.

The effort answered: I looked up, and met all his wonted benignity of countenance, though something still of wildness in his eyes. Think, however, of my surprise, to feel him put both his hands round my two shoulders, and then kiss my cheek!

I wonder I did not really sink, so exquisite was my affright when I saw him spread out his arms! Involuntarily, I concluded he meant to crush me: but the Willises, who have never seen him till this fatal illness, not knowing how very extraordinary an action this was from him, simply smiled and looked pleased, supposing, perhaps, it was his customary salutation! . . .

He now spoke in such terms of his pleasure in seeing me, that I soon lost the whole of my terror; astonishment to find him so nearly well, and gratification to see him so pleased, removed every uneasy feeling, and the joy that succeeded, in my conviction of his recovery, made me ready to throw myself at his feet to express it.

What a conversation followed! When he saw me fearless, he grew more and more alive, and made me walk close by his side, away from the attendants, and even the Willises themselves, who, to indulge him, retreated. I own myself not completely composed, but alarm I could entertain no more.

Everything that came uppermost in his mind he mentioned; he seemed to have just such remains of his flightiness as heated his imagination without deranging his reason, and robbed him of all control over his speech, though nearly in his perfect state of mind as to his opinions.

What did he not say!—He opened his whole heart to me,— expounded all his sentiments, and acquainted me with all his intentions. . . .

He assured me he was quite well—as well as he had ever been in his life; and then inquired how I did, and how I went on? and whether I was more comfortable?

If these questions, in their implication, surprised me, imagine how that surprise must increase when he proceeded to explain them! He asked after the coadjutrix, laughing, and saying, "Never mind her!—don't be oppressed—I am your friend! don't let her cast you down!—I know you have a hard time of it—but don't mind her!"

Almost thunderstruck with astonishment, I merely curtsied to his kind "I am your friend," and said nothing.

Then presently he added, "Stick to your father—stick to your own family—let them be your objects."

How readily I assented!

Again he repeated all I have just written, nearly in the same words, but ended it more seriously: he suddenly stopped, and held me to stop too, and putting his hand on his breast, in the most solemn manner, he gravely and slowly said, "I will protect you!—I promise you that—and therefore depend upon me!"

I thanked him; and the Willises, thinking him rather too elevated, came to propose my walking on. "No, no, no!" he cried, a hundred times in a breath; and their good-humour prevailed, and they let him again walk on with his new companion.

He then gave me a history of his pages, animating almost into a rage, as he related his subjects of displeasure with them, particularly with Mr. Ernst, who he told me had been brought up by himself. I hope his ideas upon these men are the result of the mistakes of his malady.

Then he asked me some questions that very greatly distressed me, relating to information given him in his illness, from various motives, but which he suspected to be false, and which I knew he had reason to suspect: yet was it most dangerous to set anything right, as I was not aware what might be the views of their having been stated wrong. I was as discreet as I knew how to be, and I hope I did no mischief; but this was the worst part of the dialogue.

He next talked to me a great deal of my dear father, and made a thousand inquiries concerning his *History of Music.* [61] This brought him to his favourite theme, Handel; [62] and he told me innumerable anecdotes of him, and particularly that celebrated tale of Handel's saying of himself, when a boy, "While that boy lives, my music will never want a protector." And this, he said, I might relate to my father.

Then he ran over most of his oratorios, attempting to sing the subjects of several airs and choruses, but so dreadfully hoarse that the sound was terrible.

Dr. Willis, quite alarmed at this exertion, feared he would do himself harm, and again proposed a separation. "No! no! no!" he exclaimed, "not yet; I have something I must just mention first."

Dr. Willis, delighted to comply, even when uneasy at compliance, again gave way.

The good King then greatly affected me. He began upon my revered old friend, Mrs. Delany; and he spoke of her with such warmth—such kindness! "She was my friend!" he cried, "and I loved her as a friend! I have made a memorandum when I lost her—I will show it you."

He pulled out a pocket-book, and rummaged some time, but to no purpose.

The tears stood in his eyes—he wiped them, and Dr. Willis again became very anxious. "Come, sir," he cried, "now do you come in and let the lady go on her walk,—come, now you have talked a long while,—so we'll go in,—if your Majesty pleases."

"No, no!" he cried, "I want to ask her a few questions;—I have lived so long out of the world, I know nothing!"

This touched me to the heart. We walked on together, and he inquired after various persons, particularly Mrs. Boscawen,[63] because she was Mrs. Delany's friend! Then, for the same reason, after Mr. Frederick Montagu,[64] of whom he kindly said, "I know he has a great regard for me, for all he joined the opposition." Lord Grey de Wilton, Sir Watkin Wynn, the Duke of Beaufort, and various others, followed.

He then told me he was very much dissatisfied with several of his state officers, and meant to form an entire new establishment. He took a paper out of his pocket-book, and showed me his new list.

This was the wildest thing that passed; and Dr. John Willis now seriously urged our separating; but he would not consent; he had only three more words to say, he declared, and again he conquered.

He now spoke of my father, with still more kindness, and told me he ought to have had the post of Master of the Band, and not that little poor musician Parsons, who was not fit for it.[65] "But Lord Salisbury," he cried, "used your father very ill in that business, and so he did me! However, I have dashed out his name, and I shall put your father's in,—as soon as I get loose again!"

This again—how affecting was this!

"And what," cried he, "has your father got, at last? nothing but that thing at Chelsea? Oh fie! fie! fie! But never mind! I will take care of him! I will do it myself!"

Then presently he added, "As to Lord Salisbury, he is out already, as this memorandum will show you, and so are many more. I shall be much better served; and when once I get away, I shall rule with a rod of iron!"

This was very unlike himself, and startled the two good doctors, who could not bear to cross him, and were exulting at my seeing his great amendment, but yet grew quite uneasy at his earnestness and volubility.

Finding we now must part, he stopped to take leave, and renewed again his charges about the coadjutrix. "Never mind her!" he cried, "depend upon me! I will be your friend as long as I live! —I here pledge myself to be your friend!" And then he saluted me again just as at the meeting, and suffered me to go on.

What a scene! how variously was I affected by it! but, upon the whole, how inexpressibly thankful to see him so nearly himself— so little removed from recovery!

I went very soon after to the Queen, to whom I was most eager to avow the meeting, and how little I could help it. Her astonishment, and her earnestness to hear every particular, were very great. I told her almost all. Some few things relating to the distressing questions I could not repeat; nor many things said of Mrs. Schwellenberg, which would much, and very needlessly, have hurt her. . . .

Wednesday, [February] 18

I had this morning the highest gratification, the purest feeling of delight, I have been regaled with for many months: I saw, from the road, the King and Queen, accompanied by Dr. Willis, walking in Richmond Gardens, near the farm, arm-in-arm!—It was a pleasure that quite melted me, after a separation so bitter, scenes so distressful—to witness such harmony and security! Heaven bless and preserve them! was all I could incessantly say while I kept in their sight. . . .

Thursday, [February] 19

. . . This was a sweet, and will prove a most memorable day: the Regency was put off, in the House of Lords, by a motion from the Chancellor! [66]

Huzza! huzza!

And this evening, for the first time, the King came upstairs, to drink tea with the Queen and Princesses in the drawing-room!

My heart was so full of joy and thankfulness, I could hardly breathe! Heaven—Heaven be praised!

Monday, [February] 23

. . . The King I have seen again—in the Queen's dressing-room. On opening the door, there he stood! He smiled at my start, and saying he had waited on purpose to see me, added, "I am quite well now,—I was nearly so when I saw you before—but I could overtake you better now!" And then he left the room.

I was quite melted with joy and thankfulness at this so entire restoration.

End of February, 1789. *Dieu merci!*

Thursday, June 25

This morning I was called before five o'clock, though various packages and business had kept me up till near three.

The day was rainy, but the road was beautiful; Windsor Great Park, in particular, is charming.

The crowds increased as we advanced, and at Winchester the town was *one head*. I saw Dr. Warton,[67] but could not stop the carriage. The King was everywhere received with acclamation. His popularity is greater than ever. Compassion for his late sufferings seems to have endeared him now to all conditions of men.

At Romsey, on the steps of the Town-Hall, an orchestra was formed, and a band of musicians, in common brown coarse cloth and red neckcloths, and even in carters' loose gowns, made a chorus of "God save the King," in which the countless multitude joined, in such loud acclamation, that their loyalty and heartiness, and natural joy, almost surprised me into a sob before I knew myself at all affected by them.

The New Forest is all beauty, and when we approached Lyndhurst the crowds wore as picturesque an appearance as the landscapes; they were all in decent attire, and, the great space giving them full room, the cool beauty of the verdure between the groups took away all idea of inconvenience, and made their live gaiety a scene to joy beholders.

Carriages of all sorts lined the roadside:—chariots, chaises, landaus, carts, waggons, whiskies, gigs, phaëtons—mixed and intermixed, filled within and surrounded without by faces all glee and delight. . . .

Arrived at Lyndhurst, we drove to the Duke of Gloucester's.[68] The Royal Family were just before us, but the two colonels came and handed us through the crowd.

The house, intended for a mere hunting-seat, was built by Charles II., and seems quite unimproved and unrepaired from its first foundation. It is the King's, but lent to the Duke of Gloucester. It is a straggling, inconvenient, old house, but delightfully situated, in a village,—looking, indeed, at present, like a populous town, from the amazing concourse of people that have crowded into it. . . .

I have a small old bedchamber, but a large and commodious parlour, in which the gentlemen join Miss Planta and me to breakfast and to drink tea. They dine at the royal table. We are to remain here some days.

During the King's dinner, which was in a parlour looking into the garden, he permitted the people to come to the window; and their delight and rapture in seeing their monarch at table, with the evident hungry feeling it occasioned, made a contrast of admiration and deprivation, truly comic. They crowded, however, so excessively, that this can be permitted them no more. They broke down all the paling, and much of the hedges, and some of the windows, and all by eagerness and multitude, for they were perfectly civil and well-behaved. . . .

Tuesday, June 30

. . . The journey to Weymouth was one scene of festivity and rejoicing. The people were everywhere collected, and everywhere delighted. We passed through Salisbury,[69] where a magnificent arch was erected, of festoons of flowers, for the King's carriage to pass under, and mottoed with "The King restored," and "Long live the King," in three divisions. The green bowmen accompanied the train thus far; and the clothiers and manufacturers here met it, dressed out in white loose frocks, flowers, and ribbons, with sticks or caps emblematically decorated from their several manufactories. And the acclamations with which the King was received amongst them—it was a rapture past description.

At Blandford there was nearly the same ceremony.

At every gentleman's seat which we passed, the owners and their families stood at the gate, and their guests or neighbours were in carriages all round.

At Dorchester the crowd seemed still increased. The city had so antique an air, I longed to investigate its old buildings. The houses have the most ancient appearance of any that are inhabited that I have happened to see: and inhabited they were indeed! every window-sash was removed, for face above face to peep out, and every old balcony and all the leads of the houses seemed turned into booths for fairs. . . .

Gloucester House, which we now inhabit, at Weymouth, is situated in front of the sea, and the sands of the Bay before it are perfectly smooth and soft. . . .

I have here a very good parlour, but dull, from its aspect. Nothing but the sea at Weymouth affords any life or spirit. My bedroom is in the attics. Nothing like living at a court for exaltation. . . .

To Dr. Burney

Gloucester House, Weymouth, July 13

My dearest Padre's kind letter was most truly welcome to me. When I am so distant, the term of absence or of silence seems always doubly long to me.

The bay here is most beautiful; the sea never rough, generally calm and gentle, and the sands perfectly smooth and pleasant. I have not yet bathed, for I have had a cold in my head, which I caught at Lyndhurst, and which makes me fear beginning; but I have hopes to be well enough to-morrow, and thenceforward to ail nothing more. It is my intention to cast away all superfluous complaints into the main ocean, which I think quite sufficiently capacious to hold them; and really my little frame will find enough to carry and manage without them. . . .

His Majesty is in delightful health, and much-improved spirits.

All agree he never looked better. The loyalty of all this place is excessive; they have dressed out every street with labels of "God save the King": all the shops have it over the doors; all the children wear it in their caps, all the labourers in their hats, and all the sailors *in their voices,* for they never approach the house without shouting it aloud, nor see the King, or his shadow, without beginning to huzza, and going on to three cheers.

The bathing-machines make it their motto over all their windows; and those bathers that belong to the royal dippers wear it in bandeaus on their bonnets, to go into the sea; and have it again, in large letters, round their waists, to encounter the waves. Flannel dresses, tucked up, and no shoes nor stockings, with bandeaus and girdles, have a most singular appearance; and when first I surveyed these loyal nymphs it was with some difficulty I kept my features in order.

Nor is this all. Think but of the surprise of His Majesty when, the first time of his bathing, he had no sooner popped his royal head under water than a band of music, concealed in a neighboring machine, struck up "God save great George our King."

One thing, however, was a little unlucky;—when the Mayor and burgesses came with the address, they requested leave to kiss hands: this was graciously accorded; but, the Mayor advancing, in a common way, *to take the Queen's hand,* as he might that of any lady mayoress, Colonel Gwynn, who stood by, whispered, "You must kneel, sir!" He found, however, that he took no notice of this hint, but kissed the Queen's hand erect. As he passed him, in his way back, the Colonel said, "You should have knelt, sir!"

"Sir," answered the poor Mayor, "I cannot."

"Everybody does, sir."

"Sir,—I have a wooden leg!"

Poor man! 'twas such a surprise! and such an excuse as no one could dispute.

But the absurdity of the matter followed;—all the rest did the same; taking the same privilege, by the example, without the same or any cause! . . .

A thousand thanks for your home news.

I am, most dear sir,

Affectionately and dutifully, your

F. B.

To Dr. Burney

Queen's Lodge, Windsor, October 27

Most Dear Sir—We go on here amazingly well, though every day now presents some anniversary of such miseries as scarce any house ever knew before last year. They call back to my mind every circumstance, with daily accuracy, and a sort of recollective melancholy that I find always ready to mix with the joy and thanksgiving of the most blessed deliverance and change.

Nor is it possible to think more of our escape than of the sudden adversity of the French.[70] Truly terrible and tremendous are revolutions such as these. There is nothing in old history that I shall any longer think fabulous; the destruction of the most ancient empires on record has nothing more wonderful, nor of more sounding improbability, than the demolition of this great nation, which rises up all against itself for its own ruin—perhaps annihilation. . . .

Ever, dearest Sir,
Most lovingly and dutifully, your

F. B.

Wednesday, November 18

We were to go to town: but while I was taking my hasty breakfast Miss Planta flew into the room, eagerly exclaiming, "Have you heard the news?"

I saw, instantly, by her eyes and manner, what she meant; and therefore answered, "I believe so."

"Mr. Fairly is going to be married! I resolved I would tell you."

"I heard the rumour," I replied, "the other day, from Colonel Gwynn."

"Oh, it's true!" she cried; "he has written to ask leave; but for Heaven's sake don't say so!"

I gave her my ready promise, for I believed not a syllable of the matter; but I would not tell her that.

Friday, November 20

Some business sent me to speak with Miss Planta before our journey back to Windsor. When it was executed and I was coming away, she called out, "Oh! *à propos*—it's all declared, and the Princesses wished Miss Fuzilier joy yesterday in the drawing-room. She looked remarkably well; but said Mr. Fairly had still a little gout, and could not appear."

Now first my belief followed assertion;—but it was only because it was inevitable, since the Princesses could not have proceeded so far without certainty.[71] . . .

[1790]

And now, my dear sisters, to a subject and narration interesting to your kind affections, because important to my future life.

Friday, May 28

The Princess Augusta condescended to bring me a most gracious message from the King, desiring to know if I wished to go to Handel's Commemoration,[72] and if I should like the *Messiah*, or prefer any other day?

With my humble acknowledgments for his goodness, I fixed instantly on the *Messiah;* and the very amiable Princess came smiling back to me, bringing me my ticket from the King.

This would not, indeed, much have availed me, but that I fortunately knew my dear father meant to go to the Abbey. I despatched Columb to Chelsea,[73] and he promised to call for me the next morning. . . .

He was all himself; all his native self;—kind, gay, open, and full fraught with converse.

Chance favoured me: we found so little room, that we were fain to accept two vacant places at once, though they separated us from my uncle, Mr. Burney, and his brother James, who were all there, and all meant to be of the same party.

I might not, at another time, have rejoiced in this disunion, but it was now most opportune: it gave me three hours' conference with my dearest father—the only conference of that length I have had in four years.

Fortune again was kind; for my father began relating various anecdotes of attacks made upon him for procuring to sundry strangers some acquaintance with his daughter, particularly with the Duchesse de Biron, and the Mesdames de Boufflers; to whom he answered, he had no power; but was somewhat struck by a question of Madame de B. in return, who exclaimed, "Mais, monsieur, est-ce possible! Mademoiselle votre fille n'a-t-elle point de vacance?" [74]

This led to much interesting discussion, and to many confessions and explanations on my part, never made before; which induced him to enter more fully into the whole of the situation, and its circumstances, than he had ever yet had the leisure or the spirits to do; and he repeated sundry speeches of discontent at my seclusion from the world.

All this encouraged me to much detail: I spoke my high and constant veneration for my Royal Mistress, her merits, her virtues, her condescension, and her even peculiar kindness towards me. But I owned the species of life distasteful to me: I was lost to all private comfort, dead to all domestic endearment; I was worn with want of rest, and fatigued with laborious watchfulness and attendance. My time was devoted to official duties; and all that in life was dearest to me—my friends, my chosen society, my best affections—lived now in my mind only by recollection, and rested upon that with nothing but bitter regret. With relations the most deservedly dear, with friends of almost unequalled goodness, I lived like an orphan—like one who had no natural ties, and must make her way as she could by those that were factitious. . . .

The silence of my dearest father now silencing myself, I turned to look at him; but how was I struck to see his honoured head bowed down almost into his bosom with dejection and discomfort!—We were both perfectly still a few moments; but when he raised his head I could hardly keep my seat, to see his eyes filled with tears!—"I have long," he cried, "been uneasy, though I have not spoken; . . . but . . . if you wish to resign—my house, my purse, my arms, shall be open to receive you back!"

The emotion of my whole heart at this speech—this sweet, this generous speech—Oh my dear friends, I need not say it! . . .

He promised to drink tea with me before I left town, and settle
all our proceedings. I acknowledged my intention to have ventured to solicit this very permission of resigning.—"But I," cried
he, smiling with the sweetest kindness, "have spoken first myself."

What a joy to me, what a relief, this very circumstance! it will
always lighten any evil that may, unhappily, follow this proposed
step.

Queen's Lodge, Windsor, August

. . . Know then, fair ladies, about the middle of this August,
1790, the author finished the rough first draft and copy of her first
tragedy. What species of a composition it may prove she is very unable to tell; she only knows it was an almost spontaneous work,
and soothed the melancholy of imagination for a while, though
afterwards it impressed it with a secret sensation of horror, so like
real woe, that she believes it contributed to the injury her sleep
received about this period.

Nevertheless, whether well or ill, she is pleased to have done
something at last, she had so long lived in all ways as nothing.

You will smile, however, at my next trust; but scarce was this
completed,—as to design and scenery I mean, for the whole is in its
first rough state, and legible only to herself,—scarce, however, had
this done with imagination, to be consigned over to correction,
when imagination seized upon another subject for another
tragedy.[75]

The first therefore I have deposited in my strongbox, in all its
imperfections, to attend to the other; I well know correction may
always be summoned, imagination never will come but by choice.
I received her, therefore, a welcome guest,—the best adapted for
softening weary solitude, where only coveted to avoid irksome
exertion. . . .

October

. . . I was ill the whole of this month, though not once with
sufficient seriousness for confinement, yet with a difficulty of
proceeding as usual so great, that the day was a burthen—or rather,

myself a burthen to the day. A languor so prodigious, with so great
a failure of strength and spirit, augmented almost hourly, that I
several times thought I must be compelled to excuse my constancy of attendance; but there was no one to take my place, except
Miss Planta, whose health is insufficient for her own, and Mlle.
Montmollin,[76] to whom such an addition of duty is almost dis-
traction. I could not, therefore, but work on while to work at any
rate able.

I now drew up, however, my memorial,[77] or rather, showed it
now to my dearest father. He so much approved it, that he told
me he would not have a comma of it altered. I will copy it for you.
It is as respectful and as grateful as I had words at command to
make it, and expressive of strong devotion and attachment; but it
fairly and firmly states that my strength is inadequate to the duties
of my charge, and, therefore, that I humbly crave permission to resign it and retire into domestic life. It was written in my father's
name and my own.

I had now that dear father's desire to present it upon the first
auspicious moment: and oh! with what a mixture of impatience
and dread unspeakable did I look forward to such an
opportunity! . . .

November

This month will be very brief of annals; I was so ill, so unsettled, so unhappy during every day, that I kept not a memorandum.

All the short benefit I had received from the bark was now at
an end: languor, feverish nights, and restless days were incessant.
My memorial was always in my mind; my courage never rose to
bringing it from my letter-case. Yet the war was over,[78] the hope
of a ship for my brother demolished, and my health required a
change of life. . . .

December

. . . My loss of health was now so notorious, that no part of the
house could wholly avoid acknowledging it; yet was the terrible
picquet the catastrophe of every evening, though frequent pains

in my side forced me, three or four times in a game, to creep to my own room for hartshorn and for rest. And so weak and faint I was become, that I was compelled to put my head out into the air, at all hours, and in all weathers, from time to time, to recover the power of breathing, which seemed not seldom almost withdrawn.

Her Majesty was very kind during this time, and the Princesses interested themselves about me with a sweetness very grateful to me; indeed, the whole household showed compassion and regard, and a general opinion that I was falling into a decline ran through the establishment. ...

Thus there seemed about my little person a universal commotion; and it spread much further, amongst those I have never or slightly mentioned. ... There seemed, indeed, but one opinion, that resignation of place or of life was the only remaining alternative.

There seemed now no time to be lost; when I saw my dear father he recommended to me to be speedy, and my mother was very kind in urgency for immediate measures. I could not, however, summon courage to present my memorial; my heart always failed me, from seeing the Queen's entire freedom from such an expectation: for though I was frequently so ill in her presence that I could hardly stand, I saw she concluded me, while life remained, inevitably hers. ...

The next morning I was half dead with real illness, excessive nervousness, and the struggle of what I had to force myself to perform. The Queen again was struck with my appearance, which I believe indeed to have been shocking. ... I then tried to articulate that I had something of deep consequence to myself to lay before Her Majesty; but that I was so unequal in my weakened state to speak it, that I had ventured to commit it to writing, and entreated permission to produce it.

She could hardly hear me, yet understood enough to give immediate consent.

I then begged to know if I might present it myself, or whether I should give it to Mrs. Schwellenberg.

"Oh, to me! to me!" she cried, with kind eagerness.

She added, however, not then, as she was going to breakfast. ...

The next morning, Friday, when again I was alone with the Queen, she named the subject, and told me she would rather I should give the paper to the Schwellenberg, who had been lamenting to her my want of confidence in her, and saying I confided and told everything to the Queen. . . .

I now desired an audience of Mrs. Schwellenberg. With what trembling agitation did I deliver her my paper, requesting her to have the goodness to lay it at the feet of the Queen before Her Majesty left town! We were then to set out for Windsor before twelve o'clock. Mrs. Schwellenberg herself remained in town. . . .

Mrs. Schwellenberg took it, and promised me her services, but desired to know its contents. I begged vainly to be excused speaking them. She persisted, and I then was compelled to own they contained my resignation.

How aghast she looked!—how inflamed with wrath!—how petrified with astonishment! It was truly a dreadful moment to me.

She expostulated on such a step, as if it led to destruction: she offered to save me from it, as if the peace of my life depended on averting it; and she menaced me with its bad consequences, as if life itself, removed from these walls, would become an evil. . . .

I then frankly begged her to forbear so painful a discussion, and told her the memorial was from my father as well as myself—that I had no right or authority to hesitate in delivering it—that the Queen herself was prepared to expect it—and that I had promised my father not to go again to Windsor till it was presented. I entreated her, therefore, to have the goodness to show it at once.

This was unanswerable, and she left me with the paper in her hand, slowly conveying it to its place of destination.

Just as she was gone, I was called to Dr. Gisburne; [79] or, rather, without being called, I found him in my room, as I returned to it.

Think if my mind, now, wanted not medicine the most! I told him, however, my corporeal complaints; and he ordered me opium and three glasses of wine in the day, and recommended rest to me, and an application to retire to my friends for some weeks, as freedom from anxiety was as necessary to my restoration as freedom from attendance.

During this consultation I was called to Mrs. Schwellenberg. Do you think I breathed as I went along?—No!

She received me, nevertheless, with complacency and smiles; she began a laboured panegyric of her own friendly zeal and goodness, and then said she had a proposal to make me, which she considered as the most fortunate turn my affairs could take, and as a proof that I should find her the best friend I had in the world. She then premised that she had shown the paper,—that the Queen had read it, and said it was very modest, and nothing improper.

Her proposal was, that I should have leave of absence for six weeks, to go about and change the air, to Chelsea, and Norbury Park, and *Capitan* Phillips, and Mrs. Francis, and Mr. Cambrick, which would get me quite well; and, during that time, she would engage Mlle. Montmollin to perform my office.

I was much disturbed at this; and though rejoiced and relieved to understand that the Queen had read my memorial without displeasure, I was grieved to see it was not regarded as final. I only replied I would communicate her plan to my father.

Soon after this we set out for Windsor.

Here the first presenting myself before the Queen was a task the heaviest, if possible, of any. Yet I was ill enough, Heaven knows, to carry the apology of my retreat in my countenance. However, it was a terrible effort. I could hardly enter her room. She spoke at once, and with infinite softness, asking me how I did after my journey? "Not well, indeed," I simply answered. "But better?" she cried; "are you not a little better?"

I only shook my head; I believe the rest of my frame shook without my aid.

"What! not a little?—not a little bit better?" she cried, in the most soothing voice.

"To-day, ma'am," I said, "I did indeed not expect to be better."

I then muttered something, indistinctly enough, of the pain I had suffered in what I had done: she opened, however, upon another subject immediately, and no more was said upon this. . . .

I wrote the proposal to my poor father. I received, by return of post, the most truly tender letter he ever wrote me. He returns thanks for the clemency with which my melancholy memorial has been received, and is truly sensible of the high honour shown me in the new proposition; but he sees my health so impaired, my strength so decayed, my whole frame so nearly demolished, that he apprehends anything short of a permanent resignation, that would ensure lasting rest and recruit, might prove fatal. . . .

A scene almost horrible ensued, when I told Cerbera the offer was declined. She was too much enraged for disguise, and uttered the most furious expressions of indignant contempt at our proceedings. I am sure she would gladly have confined us both in the Bastille, had England such a misery, as a fit place to bring us to ourselves, from a daring so outrageous against imperial wishes. . . .

Adieu—undear December!

Adieu—and away for ever, most painful 1790!

[1791]

[*May*]

As no notice whatever was taken, all this time, of my successor, or my retirement, after very great harass of suspense, and sundry attempts to conquer it, I had at length again a conference with my Royal Mistress. She was evidently displeased at again being called upon, but I took the courage to openly remind her that the birthday was Her Majesty's own time, and that my father conceived it to be the period of my attendance by her especial appointment. And this was a truth which flashed its own conviction on her recollection. She paused, and then, assentingly, said, "Certainly." I then added, that as, after the birthday, their Majesties went to Windsor, and the early prayers began immediately, I must needs confess I felt myself wholly unequal to encountering the fatigue of rising for them in my present weakened state. She was now very gracious again, conscious all this was fair and true. She told me her own embarrassments concerning the successor, spoke confidentially of her reasons for not engaging an Englishwoman, and acknowledged a person was fixed upon, though something yet remained unarranged. She gave me, however, to understand that all would be expedited: and foreign letters were despatched, I know, immediately.

This painful task over, of thus frequently reminding my Royal Mistress that my services were ending, I grew easier. She renewed, in a short time, all her old confidence and social condescension, and appeared to treat me with no other alteration than a visible regret that I should quit her—shown rather than avowed, or much indeed it would have distressed me. . . .

Thursday, July 7

This, my last day of office, was big and busy,—joyful, yet affecting to me in a high degree.

In the morning, before I left Kew, I had my last interview with Mrs. Schwellenberg. She was very kind in it, desiring to see me whenever I could in town, during her residence at the Queen's house, and to hear from me by letter meanwhile.

She then much surprised me by an offer of succeeding to her own place, when it was vacated either by her retiring or her death. This was, indeed, a mark of favour and confidence I had not expected. I declined, however, to enter upon the subject, as the manner in which she opened it made it very solemn, and, to her, very affecting.

She would take no leave of me, but wished me better hastily, and, saying we should soon meet, she hurried suddenly out of the room. Poor woman! If her temper were not so irascible, I really believe her heart would be by no means wanting in kindness. . . .

I come now near the close of my Court career.

At St. James's all was graciousness; and my Royal Mistress gave me to understand she would have me stay to assist at her toilet after the drawing-room; and much delighted me by desiring my attendance on the Thursday fortnight, when she came again to town. This lightened the parting in the pleasantest manner possible.

When the Queen commanded me to follow her to her closet I was, indeed, in much emotion; but I told her that, as what had passed from Mrs. Schwellenberg in the morning had given me to understand Her Majesty was fixed in her munificent intention,[80] notwithstanding what I had most unaffectedly urged against it——

"Certainly," she interrupted, "I shall certainly do it." . . .

"Let me then humbly entreat," I cried, "still in some measure to be considered as a servant of your Majesty, either as reader, or to assist occasionally if Mlle. Jacobi [81] should be ill."

She looked most graciously pleased, and immediately closed in with the proposal, saying, "When your health is restored,—perhaps sometimes."

I then fervently poured forth my thanks for all her goodness, and my prayers for her felicity.

She had her handkerchief in her hand or at her eyes the whole time. I was so much moved by her condescending kindness, that as soon as I got out of the closet I nearly sobbed. I went to help Mlle. Jacobi to put up the jewels, that my emotion might the less be observed. The King then came into the room. He immediately advanced to the window, where I stood, to speak to me. I was not then able to comport myself steadily. I was forced to turn my head away from him. He stood still and silent for some minutes, waiting to see if I should turn about; but I could not recover myself sufficiently to face him, strange as it was to do otherwise; and perceiving me quite overcome he walked away, and I saw him no more.

His kindness, his goodness, his benignity, never shall I forget—never think of but with fresh gratitude and reverential affection.

They were now all going—I took, for the last time, the cloak of the Queen, and, putting it over her shoulders, slightly ventured to press them, earnestly, though in a low voice, saying, "God Almighty bless your Majesty!"

She turned round and, putting her hand upon my ungloved arm, pressed it with the greatest kindness, and said, "May you be happy!"

She left me overwhelmed with tender gratitude. The three eldest Princesses were in the next room: they ran in to me the moment the Queen went onward. Princess Augusta and Princess Elizabeth each took a hand, and the Princess Royal put hers over them. I could speak to none of them; but they repeated, "I wish you happy!—I wish you health!" again and again, with the sweetest eagerness.

They then set off for Kew.

Here, therefore, end my Court Annals; after having lived in the service of Her Majesty five years within ten days—from July 17, 1786, to July 7, 1791.

MARRIAGE

[1791-1840]

[1791]

Chelsea College, October

... I have lived altogether in the most quiet and retired manner possible. My health gains ground, gradually, but very perceptibly, and a weakness that makes me soon exhausted in whatever I undertake is all of illness now remaining.

I have never been so pleasantly situated at home since I lost the sister of my heart and my most affectionate Charlotte.[1] My father is almost constantly within. Indeed, I now live with him wholly; he has himself appropriated me a place, a seat, a desk, a table, and every convenience and comfort, and he never seemed yet so earnest to keep me about him. We read together, write together, chat, compare notes, communicate projects, and diversify each other's employments. He is all goodness, gaiety, and affection; and his society and kindness are more precious to me than ever.

Fortunately, in this season of leisure and comfort, the spirit of composition proves active. The day is never long enough, and I could employ two pens almost incessantly, in merely scribbling what will not be repressed. This is a delight to my dear father inexpressibly great: and though I have gone no further than to let him know, from time to time, the species of matter that occupies me, he is perfectly contented, and patiently waits till something is quite finished, before he insists upon reading a word. This "suits my humour well," as my own industry is all gone when once its intent is produced. ...

The library or study, in which we constantly sit, supplies such delightful variety of food, that I have nothing to wish. Thus, my beloved sisters and friends, you see me, at length, enjoying all that peace, ease, and chosen recreation and employment, for which so long I sighed in vain, and which, till very lately, I had reason to believe, even since attained, had been allowed me too late. ...

November

. . . Another evening, after visiting our Esther, my father took me to Sir Joshua Reynolds. I had long languished to see that kindly zealous friend, but his ill health had intimidated me from making the attempt; and now my dear father went upstairs alone, and inquired of Miss Palmer if her uncle was well enough to admit me. He returned for me immediately. I felt the utmost pleasure in again mounting his staircase.

Miss Palmer hastened forward and embraced me most cordially. I then shook hands with Sir Joshua. He had a bandage over one eye, and the other shaded with a green half-bonnet. He seemed serious even to sadness, though extremely kind. "I am very glad," he said, in a meek voice and dejected accent, "to see you again, and I wish I could see you better! but I have only one eye now,—and hardly that."

I was really quite touched. The expectation of total blindness depresses him inexpressibly; not, however, inconceivably. I hardly knew how to express, either my concern for his altered situation since our meeting, or my joy in again being with him: but my difficulty was short; Miss Palmer eagerly drew me to herself, and recommended to Sir Joshua to go on with his cards. He had no spirit to oppose; probably, indeed, no inclination. . . .

One other time we called again, in a morning. Sir Joshua and his niece were alone, and that invaluable man was even more dejected than before. How grievous to me it is to see him thus changed!

I called also one morning upon Mrs. Schwellenberg. She received me with much profession of regard, and with more than profession of esteem—since she evinced it by the confidential discourse into which she soon entered upon the Royal Family and herself. However, I easily read that she still has not forgiven my resignation, and still thinks I failed in loyalty of duty, by not staying, though to die, rather than retire, though to live.

This, however, is so much a part of her very limited knowledge, and very extensive prejudice, that I submit to it without either wonder or resentment. . . .

[1792]

Thursday, June 18

After many invitations and regulations, it was settled I was to accompany my father on a visit of three days to Mrs. Crewe at Hampstead.

The villa at Hampstead is small, but commodious. We were received by Mrs. Crewe with much kindness. The room was rather dark, and she had a veil to her bonnet, half down, and with this aid she looked still in a full blaze of beauty. I was wholly astonished. Her bloom, perfectly natural, is as high as that of Augusta Locke when in her best looks, and the form of her face is so exquisitely perfect that my eye never met it without fresh admiration. She is certainly, in my eyes, the most completely a beauty of any woman I ever saw. I know not, even now, any female in her first youth who could bear the comparison. She uglifies everything near her.

Her son was with her. He is just of age, and looks like her elder brother! he is a heavy, old-looking young man. He is going to China with Lord Macartney.[2]

My former friend, young Burke, was also there. I was glad to renew acquaintance with him; though I could see some little strangeness in him: this, however, completely wore off before the day was over.

Soon after entered Mrs. Burke, Miss F——, a niece, and Mr. Richard Burke the comic, humorous, bold, queer brother of *the* Mr. Burke, who, they said, was soon coming, with Mr. Elliot. The Burke family were invited by Mrs. Crewe to meet us.

Mrs. Burke was just what I have always seen her, soft, gentle, reasonable, and obliging; and we met, I think, upon as good terms as if so many years had not parted us.

At length Mr. Burke appeared, accompanied by Mr. Elliot. . . .

The moment I was named, to my great joy I found Mr. Burke had not recollected me. He is more near-sighted, considerably, than myself. "Miss Burney!" he now exclaimed, coming forward, and quite kindly taking my hand, "I did not see you"; and then he spoke very sweet words of the meeting, and of my looking far better than "while I was a courtier," and of how he rejoiced to see that I so little suited that station. "You look," cried he, "quite renewed, revived, disengaged; you seemed, when I conversed with you last, at the trial, quite altered; I never saw such a change for the better as quitting a Court has brought about!"

Ah! thought I, this is simply a mistake, from reasoning according to your own feelings. I only seemed altered for the worst at the trial, because I there looked coldly and distantly, from distaste and disaffection to your proceedings; and I here look changed for the better, only because I here meet you without the chill of disapprobation, and with the glow of my first admiration of you and your talents! [3] . . .

After this my father joined us, and politics took the lead. He spoke then with an eagerness and a vehemence that instantly banished the graces, though it redoubled the energies, of his discourse. "The French Revolution," he said, "which began by authorising and legalising injustice, and which by rapid steps had proceeded to every species of despotism except owning a despot, was now menacing all the universe and all mankind with the most violent concussion of principle and order." My father heartily joined, and I tacitly assented to his doctrines, though I feared not with his fears.

One speech I must repeat, for it is explanatory of his conduct, and nobly explanatory. When he had expatiated upon the present dangers, even to English liberty and property, from the contagion of havoc and novelty, he earnestly exclaimed, "This it is that has made ME an abettor and supporter of Kings! Kings are necessary, and, if we would preserve peace and prosperity, we must preserve THEM. We must all put our shoulders to the work! Ay, and stoutly, too!"

This subject lasted till dinner.

At dinner Mr. Burke sat next Mrs. Crewe, and I had the happiness to be seated next Mr. Burke; and my other neighbour was his amiable son.

The dinner, and the dessert when the servants were removed, were delightful. How I wish my dear Susanna and Fredy could meet this wonderful man when he is easy, happy, and with people he cordially likes! But politics, even on his own side, must always be excluded; his irritability is so terrible on that theme that it gives immediately to his face the expression of a man who is going to defend himself from murderers. . . .

FROM MRS. PHILLIPS

Mickleham, September

We shall shortly, I believe, have a little colony of unfortunate (or rather, fortunate, since here they are safe) French noblesse in our neighbourhood. Sunday evening Ravely informed Mr. Locke that two or three families had joined to take Jenkinson's house, Juniper Hall, and that another family had taken a small house at Westhumble, which the people very reluctantly let, upon the Christian-like supposition that, being nothing but French papishes, they would never pay.[4] Our dear Mr. Locke, while this was agitating, sent word to the landlord that he would be answerable for the rent; however, before this message arrived, the family were admitted. The man said they had pleaded very hard indeed, and said, if he did but know the distress they had been in, he would not hesitate.

This house is taken by Madame de Broglie, daughter of the Mareschal, who is in the army with the French Princes; or, rather, wife to his son, Victor Broglie, till very lately General of one of the French armies, and at present disgraced, and fled nobody knows where. This poor lady came over in an open boat, with a son younger than my Norbury,[5] and was fourteen hours at sea. She has other ladies with her, and gentlemen, and two little girls who had been sent to England some weeks ago; they are all to lodge in a sort of cottage, containing only a kitchen and parlour on the ground floor.

I long to offer them my house, and have been much gratified by finding Mr. Locke immediately determined to visit them; his taking this step will secure them the civilities, at least, of the other neighbours.

At Jenkinson's are—la Marquise de la Châtre, whose husband is with the emigrants; her son; M. de Narbonne,[6] lately Ministre de la Guerre; M. de Montmorency;[7] Charles or Theodore Lameth; Jaucourt; and one or two more, whose names I have forgotten, are either arrived to-day, or expected. I feel infinitely interested for all these persecuted persons. . . .

[1793]

To Dr. Burney

Norbury Park, Monday, January 28

My Dearest Padre—I have been wholly without spirit for writing, reading, working, or even walking or conversing, ever since the first day of my arrival. The dreadful tragedy acted in France has entirely absorbed me.[8] Except the period of the illness of our own inestimable King, I have never been so overcome with grief and dismay, for any but personal and family calamities. . . .

M. de Narbonne and M. d'Arblay [9] have been almost annihilated: they are for ever repining that they are French, and, though two of the most accomplished and elegant men I ever saw, they break our hearts with the humiliation they feel for their guiltless birth in that guilty country! . . . M. d'Arblay, from a very fine figure and good face, was changed, as if by magic, in one night, by the receipt of this inexpiable news, into an appearance as black, as meagre, and as miserable as M. de la Blancherie.[10]

We are all here expecting war every day. This dear family has deferred its town journey till next Wednesday. I have not been at all at Mickleham,[11] nor yet settled whether to return to town with the Lockes, or to pay my promised visit there first. All has been so dismal, so wretched, that I have scarce ceased to regret our living at such times, and not either sooner or later.

These immediate French sufferers here interest us, and these alone have been able to interest me at all. We hear of a very bad tumult in Ireland, and near Captain Phillips's property.[12] Mr. Brabazon writes word it is very serious. Heaven guard us from insurrections! What must be the feelings at the Queen's house? how acute, and how indignant!

Adieu, most dear sir; I am sure we sympathise but too completely on this subject,—

And am ever your

F. B.

To Dr. Burney

Mickleham, February 29 [13]

Have you not begun, dearest sir, to give me up as a lost sheep? Susanna's temporary widowhood, however, has tempted me on, and spelled me with a spell I know not how to break. It is long, long since we have passed any time so completely together; her three lovely children only knit us the closer. The widowhood, however, we expect now quickly to expire, and I had projected my return to my dearest father for Wednesday next, which would complete my fortnight here; but some circumstances are intervening that incline me to postpone it another week.

Madame de Staël, daughter of M. Necker, and wife of the Swedish Ambassador to France, is now head of the little French colony in this neighbourhood.[14] M. de Staël, her husband, is at present suspended in his embassy, but not recalled; and it is yet uncertain whether the Regent Duke of Sudermania will send him to Paris, during the present horrible Convention, or order him home. He is now in Holland, waiting for commands, Madame de Staël, however, was unsafe in Paris, though an ambassadress, from the resentment owed her by the Commune, for having received and protected in her house various destined victims of the 10th August and of the 2nd September. She was even once stopped in her carriage, which they called aristocratic, because of its arms and ornaments, and threatened to be murdered, and only saved by one of the worst wretches of the Convention, Tallien, who feared provoking a war with Sweden, from such an offence to the wife of its Ambassador. She was obliged to have this same Tallien to accompany her, to save her from massacre, for some miles from Paris, when compelled to quit it.

She is a woman of the first abilities, I think, I have ever seen; she is more in the style of Mrs. Thrale than of any other celebrated character, but she has infinitely more depth, and seems an even profound politician and metaphysician. She has suffered us to hear some of her works in MS., which are truly wonderful, for powers both of thinking and expression. She adores her father, but is much alarmed at having had no news from him since he has heard of the massacre of the martyred Louis;[15] and who can wonder it should have overpowered him?

Ever since her arrival she has been pressing me to spend some time with her before I return to town. She wanted Susan and me to pass a month with her, but, finding that impossible, she bestowed all her entreaties upon me alone, and they are grown so urgent, upon my preparation for departing, and acquainting her my furlough of absence was over, that she not only insisted upon my writing to you, and telling why I deferred my return, but declares she will also write herself, to ask your permission for the visit. She exactly resembles Mrs. Thrale in the ardour and warmth of her temper and partialities. I find her impossible to resist, and therefore, if your answer to her is such as I conclude it must be, I shall wait upon her for a week. She is only a short walk from hence, at Juniper Hall.

There can be nothing imagined more charming, more fascinating, than this colony; between their sufferings and their *agrémens* they occupy us almost wholly. . . .

M. d'Arblay is one of the most singularly interesting characters that can ever have been formed. He has a sincerity, a frankness, an ingenuous openness of nature, that I had been unjust enough to think could not belong to a Frenchman. With all this, which is his military portion, he is passionately fond of literature, a most delicate critic in his own language, well versed in both Italian and German, and a very elegant poet. He has just undertaken to become my French master for pronunciation, and he gives me long daily lessons in reading. Pray expect wonderful improvements! In return, I hear him in English; and for his theme this evening he has been writing an English address *à Mr. Burney* (*i.e.* M. le Docteur), joining in Madame de Staël's request. . . .

My dearest Father's

F. B.

FROM DR. BURNEY

Chelsea College, Tuesday Morning, February 19

Why, Fanny, what are you about, and where are you? I shall write *at* you, not knowing how to write *to* you, as Swift did to the flying and romantic Lord Peterborough.

I had written the above, after a yesterday's glimmering and a feverish night as usual, when behold! a letter of requisition for a further furlough! I had long histories ready for narration *de vive voix*, but my time is too short and my eyes and head too weak for much writing this morning. I am not at all surprised at your account of the captivating powers of Madame de Staël. It corresponds with all I had heard about her, and with the opinion I formed of her intellectual and literary powers, in reading her charming little *Apologie de Rousseau*. But as nothing human is allowed to be perfect, she has not escaped censure. Her house was the centre of revolutionists previous to the 10th of August, after her father's departure, and she has been accused of partiality to M. de N——. But perhaps all may be Jacobinical malignity. However, unfavourable stories of her have been brought hither, and the Burkes and Mrs. Ord have repeated them to me. But you know that M. Necker's administration, and the conduct of the nobles who first joined in the violent measures that subverted the ancient establishments by the abolition of nobility and the ruin of the church, during the first National Assembly, are held in greater horror by aristocrats than even the members of the present Convention. I know this will make you feel uncomfortable, but it seemed to me right to hint it to you. If you are not absolutely in the house of Madame de Staël when this arrives, it would perhaps be possible for you to waive the visit to her, by a compromise, of having something to do for Susy, and so make the addendum to your stay under her roof. . . .

Ever affectionately yours,

C. B.

To Dr. Burney

Mickleham, Friday, February 22

What a kind letter is my dearest father's, and how kindly speedy! yet it is too true it has given me very uncomfortable feelings. I am both hurt and astonished at the acrimony of malice; indeed, I believe all this party to merit nothing but honour, compassion, and praise. Madame de Staël, the daughter of M. Necker— the idolising daughter—of course, and even from the best principles, those of filial reverence, entered into the opening of the Revolution just as her father entered into it; but as to her house having become the centre of Revolutionists before the 10th of August, it was so only for the Constitutionalists, who, at that period, were not only members of the then established government, but the decided friends of the King. The aristocrats were then already banished, or wanderers from fear, or concealed and silent from cowardice; and the Jacobins——I need not, after what I have already related, mention how utterly abhorrent to her must be that fiend-like set. . . .

The intimation concerning M. de N. was, however, wholly new to us, and I do firmly believe it a gross calumny. M. de N. was of her society, which contained ten or twelve of the first people in Paris, and, occasionally, almost all Paris; she loves him even tenderly but so openly, so simply, so unaffectedly, and with such utter freedom from all coquetry, that, if they were two men, or two women, the affection could not, I think, be more obviously undesigning. She is very plain, he is very handsome; her intellectual endowments must be with him her sole attraction.[16]

M. de Talleyrand was another of her society, and she seems equally attached to him.[17] M. le Vicomte de Montmorenci she loves, she says, as her brother: he is another of this bright constellation, and esteemed of excellent capacity. She says, if she continues in England he will certainly come, for he loves her too well to stay away. In short, her whole côterie live together as brethren. . . .

I would, nevertheless, give the world to avoid being a guest under their roof, now I have heard even the shadow of such a rumour; and I will, if it be possible without hurting or offending them. I have waived and waived acceptance almost from the moment of Madame de Staël's arrival. I prevailed with her to let my letter go alone to you, and I have told her, with regard to your answer, that you were sensible of the honour her kindness did me, and could not refuse to her request the week's furlough; and then followed reasons for the compromise you pointed out, too diffuse for writing. As yet they have succeeded, though she is surprised and disappointed. She wants us to study French and English together, and nothing could to me be more desirable, but for this invidious report.

Susanna and her Captain intend going to town on Friday in next week, and I have fixed therefore on the same day for my return; thus, at all events, the time cannot be long. . . .

F. B.

The frequency and intimacy with which Miss Burney and M. d'Arblay now met, ripened into attachment the high esteem which each felt for the other; and, after many struggles and scruples, occasioned by his reduced circumstances and clouded prospects, M. d'Arblay wrote her an offer of his hand; candidly acknowledging, however, the slight hope he entertained of ever recovering the fortune he had lost by the Revolution.

At this time Miss Burney went to Chessington for a short period; probably hoping that the extreme quiet of that place would assist her deliberations, and tranquillise her mind during her present perplexities.[18]

To Mrs. Locke

Chessington

I have regretted excessively the finishing so miserably an acquaintance begun with so much spirit and pleasure, and the *dépit* I fear Madame de Staël must have experienced. I wish the world would take more care of itself, and less of its neighbours. I should have been very safe, I trust, without such flights, and distances, and breaches. But there seemed an absolute resolution formed to crush this acquaintance, and compel me to appear its wilful renouncer. All I did also to clear the matter, and soften to Madame de Staël any pique or displeasure, unfortunately serve only to increase both. Had I understood her disposition better, I should certainly have attempted no palliation, for I rather offended her pride than mollified her wrath. Yet I followed the golden rule, for how much should I prefer any acknowledgment of regret at such an apparent change, from any one I esteemed, to a seeming unconscious complacency in an unexplained caprice!

I am vexed, however, very much vexed, at the whole business. I hope she left Norbury Park with full satisfaction in its steady and more comfortable connection. I fear mine will pass for only a fashionable one.

Miss Kitty Cooke still amuses me very much by her incomparable dialect; and by her kindness and friendliness I am taken the best care of imaginable. . . .

F. B.

To Mrs. Phillips

Friday, May 31, Chessington

My heart so smites me this morning with making no answer to all I have been requested to weigh and decide, that I feel I cannot with any ease return to town without at least complying with one demand, which first, at parting yesterday, brought me to write fully to you, my Susan, if I could not elsewhere to my satisfaction.[19]

Much indeed in the course of last night and this morning has occurred to me, that now renders my longer silence as to prospects and proceedings unjustifiable to myself. I will therefore now address myself to both my beloved confidants, and open to them all my thoughts, and entreat their own with equal plainness in return.

M. d'Arblay's last three letters convince me he is desperately dejected when alone, and when perfectly natural. It is not that he wants patience, but he wants rational expectation of better times; expectation founded on something more than mere aërial hope, that builds one day upon what the next blasts; and then has to build again, and again to be blasted.

What affects me the most in this situation is, that his time may as completely be lost as another's peace, by waiting for the effects of distant events, vague, bewildering, and remote, and quite as likely to lead to ill as to good. The very waiting, indeed, with the mind in such a state, is in itself an evil scarce to be recompensed. . . .

My dearest Fredy, in the beginning of her knowledge of this transaction, told me that Mr. Locke was of opinion that the £100 per annum might do, as it does for many a curate. M. d'A. also most solemnly and affectingly declares that *le simple nécessaire* is all he requires, and here, in your vicinity, would unhesitatingly be preferred by him to the most brilliant fortune in another *séjour.*

If *he* can say that, what must *I* be not to echo it? I, who in the bosom of my own most chosen, most darling friends——

I need not enter more upon this; you all must know that to me a crust of bread, with a little roof for shelter, and a fire for warmth, near you, would bring me to peace, to happiness, to all that my heart holds dear, or even in any situation could prize. I cannot picture such a fate with dry eyes; all else but kindness and society has to me so always been nothing.

With regard to my dear father, he has always left me to myself; I will not therefore speak to him while thus uncertain what to decide.

It is certain, however, that, with peace of mind and retirement, I have resources that I could bring forward to amend the little situation; as well as that, once thus undoubtedly established and naturalised, M. d'A. would have claims for employment.

These reflections, with a mutual freedom from ambition, might lead to a quiet road, unbroken by the tortures of applications, expectations, attendance, disappointment, and time-wasting hopes and fears; if there were not apprehensions the £100 might be withdrawn. I do not think it likely, but it is a risk too serious in its consequences to be run. M. d'A. protests he could not answer to himself the hazard.

How to ascertain this, to clear the doubt, or to know the fatal certainty before it should be too late, exceeds my powers of suggestion. His own idea, to write to the Queen, much as it has startled me, and wild as it seemed to me, is certainly less wild than to take the chance of such a blow in the dark.

Yet such a letter could not even reach her. His very name is probably only known to her through myself.

In short, my dearest friends, you will think for me, and let me know what occurs to you, and I will defer any answer till I hear your opinions.

Heaven ever bless you! And pray for me at this moment.

F. B.

FROM DR. BURNEY

May

DEAR FANNY—I have for some time seen very plainly that you are *éprise,* and have been extremely uneasy at the discovery. You must have observed my silent gravity, surpassing that of mere illness and its consequent low spirits. I had some thoughts of writing to Susan about it, and intended begging her to do what I must now do for myself—that is, beg, warn, and admonish you not to entangle yourself in a wild and romantic attachment, which offers nothing in prospect but poverty and distress, with future inconvenience and unhappiness. M. d'Arblay is certainly a very amiable and accomplished man, and of great military ability I take for granted; but what employment has he for them of which the success is not extremely hazardous? His property, whatever it was, has been confiscated—*décrété*—by the Convention; and if a counter-revolution takes place, unless it be exactly such a one as suits the particular political sect in which he enlisted, it does not seem likely to secure to him an establishment in France. And as to an establishment in England, I know the difficulty which very deserving natives find in procuring one, with every appearance of interest, friends and probability; and, to a foreigner, I fear the difficulty will be more than doubled.

As M. d'Arblay is at present circumstanced, an alliance with anything but a fortune sufficient for the support of himself and partner would be very imprudent. He is a mere soldier of fortune, under great disadvantages. Your income, if it was as certain as a freehold estate, is insufficient for the purpose; and if the Queen should be displeased and withdraw her allowance, what could you do?

I own that, if M. d'Arblay had an establishment in France sufficient for him to marry a wife with little or no fortune, much as I am inclined to honour and esteem him, I should wish to prevent you from fixing your residence there; not merely from selfishness but for your own sake. I know your love for your family, and know that it is reciprocal; I therefore cannot help thinking that you would mutually be a loss to each other. The friends, too, which you have here, are of the highest and most desirable class. To quit them, in order to make new friendships in a strange land, in which the generality of its inhabitants at present seem incapable of such virtues as friendship is built upon, seems wild and visionary.

If M. d'Arblay had a sufficient establishment here for the purposes of credit and comfort, and determined to settle here for life, I should certainly think ourselves honoured by his alliance; but his situation is at present so very remote from all that can satisfy prudence, or reconcile to an affectionate father the idea of a serious attachment, that I tremble for your heart and future happiness. M. d'Arblay must have lived too long in the great world to accommodate himself contentedly to the little; his fate seems so intimately connected with that of his miserable country, and that country seems at a greater distance from peace, order, and tranquillity now than it has done at any time since the revolution.

These considerations, and the uncertainty of what party will finally prevail, make me tremble for you both. You see, by what I have said, that my objections are not personal, but wholly prudential. For Heaven's sake, my dear Fanny, do not part with your heart too rapidly, or involve yourself in deep engagements which it will be difficult to dissolve; and to the last degree imprudent, as things are at present circumstanced, to fulfil.

As far as character, merit, and misfortune demand esteem and regard, you may be sure that M. d'Arblay will be always received by me with the utmost attention and respect; but, in the present situation of things, I can by no means think I ought to encourage (blind and ignorant as I am of all but his misfortunes) a serious and solemn union with one whose unhappiness would be a reproach to the facility and inconsiderateness of a most affectionate father.

MEMORANDUM, THIS 7TH OF MAY 1825

In answer to these apparently most just, and, undoubtedly, most parental and tender apprehensions, Susanna, the darling child of Dr. Burney, as well as first chosen friend of M. d'Arblay, wrote a statement of the plans, and means, and purposes of M. d'A. and F. B.—so clearly demonstrating their power of happiness, with willing economy, congenial tastes, and mutual love of the country, that Dr. B. gave way, and sent, though reluctantly, a consent; by which the union took place the 31st of July, 1793, in Mickleham Church, in presence of Mr. and Mrs. Locke, Captain and Mrs. Phillips, M. de Narbonne, and Captain Burney, who was father to his sister, as Mr. Locke was to M. d'A.; and on the 1st of August the ceremony was re-performed in the Sardinian chapel, according to the rites of the Romish Church; [20] and never, never was union more blessed and felicitous; though, after the first eight years of unmingled happiness, it was assailed by many calamities, chiefly of separation or illness, yet still mentally unbroken.

F. d'ARBLAY.

To Mrs. [WADDINGTON] [21]

August 2

. . . Many, indeed, have been the miserable circumstances that have, from time to time, alarmed and afflicted in turn, and seemed to render a renunciation indispensable. Those difficulties, however, have been conquered; and last Sunday Mr. and Mrs. Locke, my sister and Captain Phillips, and my brother Captain Burney, accompanied us to the altar, in Mickleham Church; since which the ceremony has been repeated in the chapel of the Sardinian Ambassador, that if, by a counter-revolution in France, M. d'Arblay recovers any of his rights, his wife may not be excluded from their participation.

You may be amazed not to see the name of my dear father upon this solemn occasion; but his apprehensions from the smallness of our income have made him cold and averse; and though he granted his consent, I could not even solicit his presence. I feel satisfied, however, that time will convince him I have not been so imprudent as he now thinks me. Happiness is the great end of all our worldly views and proceedings, and no one can judge for another in what will produce it. To me, wealth and ambition would always be unavailing; I have lived in their most centrical possessions, and I have always seen that the happiness of the richest and the greatest has been the moment of retiring from riches and from power. Domestic comfort and social affection have invariably been the sole as well as ultimate objects of my choice, and I have always been a stranger to any other species of felicity.

M. d'Arblay has a taste for literature, and a passion for reading and writing, as marked as my own; this is a sympathy to rob retirement of all superfluous leisure, and insure to us both occupation constantly edifying or entertaining. He has seen so much of life, and has suffered so severely from its disappointments, that retreat, with a chosen companion, is become his final desire.

Mr. Locke has given M. d'Arblay a piece of ground in his beautiful park, upon which we shall build a little neat and plain habitation. We shall continue, meanwhile, in his neighbourhood, to superintend the little edifice, and enjoy the society of his exquisite house, and that of my beloved sister Phillips. We are now within two miles of both, at a farm-house,[22] where we have what apartments we require, and no more, in a most beautiful and healthy situation, a mile and a half from any town. The nearest is Bookham; but I beg that my letters may be directed to me at Captain Phillips's, Mickleham, as the post does not come this way, and I may else miss them for a week....

F. D'A.

To Mrs. [Waddington]

The account of your surprise, my sweet friend, was the last thing to create mine: I was well aware of the general astonishment, and of yours in particular. My own, however, at my very extraordinary fate, is singly greater than that of all my friends united. I had never made any vow against marriage, but I had long, long been firmly persuaded it was for me a state of too much hazard and too little promise to draw me from my individual plans and purposes. I remember, in playing at questions and commands, when I was thirteen, being asked when I intended to marry? and surprising my playmates by solemnly replying, "When I think I shall be happier that I am in being single." It is true, I imagined that time would never arrive; and I have pertinaciously adhered to trying no experiment upon any other hope; for, many and mixed as are the ingredients which form what is generally considered as happiness, I was always fully convinced that social sympathy of character and taste could alone have any chance with me; all else I always thought, and now know, to be immaterial. I have only this peculiar,—that what many contentedly assert or adopt in theory, I have had the courage to be guided by in practice.

We are now removed to a very small house in the suburbs of a very small village called Bookham. We found it rather inconvenient to reside in another person's dwelling, though our own apartments were to ourselves. Our views are not so beautiful as from Phenice Farm, but our situation is totally free from neighbours and intrusion. We are about a mile and a half from Norbury Park, and two miles from Mickleham. . . .

My dearest father, whose fears and drawbacks have been my sole subject of regret, begins now to see I have not judged rashly, or with romance, in seeing my own road to my own felicity. And his restored cheerful concurrence in my constant principles, though new station, leaves me, for myself, without a wish. *L'ennui*, which could alone infest our retreat, I have ever been a stranger to, except in tiresome company, and my companion has every possible resource against either feeling or inspiring it.

As my partner is a Frenchman, I conclude the wonder raised by the connection may spread beyond my own private circle; but no wonder upon earth can ever arrive near my own in having found such a character from that nation. This is a prejudice certainly, impertinent, and very John Bullish, and very arrogant; but I only share it with all my countrymen, and therefore must needs forgive both them and myself. I am convinced, however, from your tender solicitude for me in all ways, that you will be glad to hear that the Queen and all the Royal Family have deigned to send me wishes for my happiness through Mrs. Schwellenberg, who has written me "what you call" a very kind congratulation.

F. D'A.

[1794]

*In the year 1794, the happiness of the "Hermitage" was in-
creased by the birth of a son, who was christened Alexander
Charles Louis Piochard d'Arblay; receiving the names of his father, with those of his two godfathers, the Comte de Narbonne
and Dr. Charles Burney.*[23]

To Dr. Burney

Bookham, March 22

My Dear Father— . . . Can life, he often says, be more innocent than ours, or happiness more inoffensive? He works in his
garden, or studies English and mathematics, while I write. When I
work at my needle, he reads to me; and we enjoy the beautiful
country around us in long and romantic strolls, during which he
carries under his arm a portable garden-chair, lent us by Mrs.
Locke, that I may rest as I proceed. He is extremely fond, too, of
writing, and makes, from time to time, memorandums of such
memoirs, poems, and anecdotes as he recollects, and I wish to have
preserved. These resources for sedentary life are certainly the
first blessings that can be given to man, for they enable him to be
happy in the extremest obscurity, even after tasting the dangerous
draughts of glory and ambition. . . .

M. d'Arblay, to my infinite satisfaction, gives up all thoughts of
building, in the present awful state of public affairs.[24] To show
you, however, how much he is "of your advice" as to *son jardin*,
he has been drawing a plan for it, which I intend to beg, borrow,
or steal (all one), to give you some idea how seriously he studies to
make his manual labours of some real utility.

This sort of work, however, is so totally new to him, that he
receives every now and then some of poor Merlin's "disagreeable compliments";[25] for, when Mr. Locke's or the Captain's gar-

deners favour our grounds with a visit, they commonly make known that all has been done wrong. Seeds are sowing in some parts when plants ought to be reaping, and plants are running to seed while they are thought not yet at maturity. Our garden, therefore, is not yet quite the most profitable thing in the world; but M. d'A. assures me it is to be the staff of our table and existence.

A little, too, he has been unfortunate; for, after immense toil in planting and transplanting strawberries round our hedge, here at Bookham, he has just been informed they will bear no fruit the first year, and the second we may be "over the hills and far away!"

Another time, too, with great labour, he cleared a considerable compartment of weeds, and, when it looked clean and well, and he showed his work to the gardener, the man said he had demolished an asparagus-bed! M. d'A. protested, however, nothing could look more like *des mauvaises herbes.*

His greatest passion is for transplanting. Everything we possess he moves from one end of the garden to another, to produce better effects. Roses take place of jessamines, jessamines of honeysuckles, and honeysuckles of lilacs, till they have all danced round as far as the space allows; but whether the effect may not be a general mortality, summer only can determine.

Such is our horticultural history. But I must not omit that we have had for one week cabbages from our own cultivation every day! Oh, you have no idea how sweet they tasted! We agreed they had a freshness and a *goût* we had never met with before. We had them for too short a time to grow tired of them, because, as I have already hinted, they were beginning to run to seed before we knew they were eatable.

F. D'A.

To Dr. Burney

Bookham, August

It is just a week since I had the greatest gratification of its kind I ever, I think, experienced:—so kind a thought, so sweet a surprise as was my dearest father's visit! How softly and soothingly it has rested upon my mind ever since!

"Abdolomine" [26] has no regret but that his garden was not in better order; he was a little *piqué,* he confesses, that you said it was not *very neat*—and, *to be shor!*—but his passion is to do great works: he undertakes with pleasure, pursues with energy, and finishes with spirit; but, then, all is over! He thinks the business once done always done; and to repair, and amend, and weed, and cleanse,—Oh, these are drudgeries insupportable to him!

However, you should have seen the place before he began his operations, to do him justice; there was then nothing else but *mauvaises herbes;* now, you must at least allow there is a mixture of flowers and grain! I wish you had seen him yesterday, mowing down our hedge—with his sabre, and with an air and attitudes so military, that, if he had been hewing down other legions than those he encountered—*i.e.* of spiders—he could scarcely have had a mien more tremendous, or have demanded an arm more mighty. Heaven knows, I am "the most *contente personne* in the world" to see his sabre so employed!

You spirited me on in all ways; for this week past I have taken tightly to the *grand ouvrage.*[27] If I go on so a little longer, I doubt not but M. d'Arblay will begin settling where to have a new shelf for arranging it! . . .

F. D'A.

[1795]

TO MRS. [WADDINGTON]

Bookham, April 15

So dry a reproof from so dear a friend! And do you, then, measure my regard of heart by my remissness of hand? Let me give you the short history of my tragedy,[28] fairly and frankly.

I wrote it not, as your acquaintance imagined, for the stage, nor yet for the press. I began it at Kew Palace, and, at odd moments, I finished it at Windsor, without the least idea of any species of publication.

Since I left the Royal household, I ventured to let it be read by my father, Mr. and Mrs. Locke, my sister Phillips, and, of course, M. d'Arblay, and not another human being. Their opinions led to what followed, and my brother, Dr. Charles, showed it to Mr. Kemble while I was on my visit to my father last October. He instantly and warmly pronounced for its acceptance, but I knew not when Mr. Sheridan would see it, and had not the smallest expectation of its appearing this year. However, just three days before my beloved little infant came into the world, an express arrived from my brother, that Mr. Kemble wanted the tragedy immediately, in order to show it to Mr. Sheridan, who had just heard of it, and had spoken in the most flattering terms of his goodwill for its reception.

Still, however, I was in doubt of its actual acceptance till three weeks after my confinement, when I had a visit from my brother, who told me he was, the next morning, to read the piece in the green-room.

This was a precipitance for which I was every way unprepared, as I had never made but one copy of the play, and had intended divers corrections and alterations. Absorbed, however, by my new charge, and then growing ill, I had a sort of indifference about the matter, which, in fact, has lasted ever since.

The moment I was then able to hold a pen I wrote two short letters, to acknowledge the state of the affair to my sisters; and to one of these epistles I had an immediate laughing answer, informing me my confidence was somewhat of the latest, as the subject of it was already in all the newspapers! I was extremely chagrined at this intelligence; but, from that time, thought it all too late to be the herald of my own designs. And this, added to my natural and incurable dislike to enter upon these egotistical details unasked, has caused my silence to my dear M——, and to every friend I possess. Indeed, speedily after, I had an illness so severe and so dangerous, that for full seven weeks the tragedy was neither named nor thought of by M. d'Arblay or myself.

The piece was represented to the utmost disadvantage, save only Mrs. Siddons and Mr. Kemble; for it was not written with any idea of the stage, and my illness and weakness, and constant absorbment, at the time of its preparation, occasioned it to appear with so many undramatic effects, from my inexperience of theatrical requisites and demands, that, when I saw it, I myself perceived a thousand things I wished to change. The performers,

too, were cruelly imperfect, and made blunders I blush to have
pass for mine,—added to what belong to me. The most important
character after the hero and heroine had but two lines of his part
by heart! He made all the rest at random, and such nonsense as
put all the other actors out as much as himself; so that a more
wretched performance, except Mrs. Siddons, Mr. Kemble, and Mr.
Bensley, could not be exhibited in a barn.

All this concurred to make it very desirable to withdraw the
piece for alterations, which I have done.

And now you have the whole history—and now—are you ap-
peased?

F. D'A.

To Mrs. [Waddington]

Bookham, June 15

. . . I have a long work, which a long time has been in hand,
that I mean to publish soon—in about a year.[29] Should it succeed, like *Evelina* and *Cecilia,* it may be a little portion to our
Bambino. We wish, therefore, to print it for ourselves in this
hope; but the expenses of the press are so enormous, so raised by
these late Acts, that it is out of all question for us to afford it. We
have, therefore, been led by degrees to listen to counsel of some
friends, and to print it by subscription. This is in many—many
ways unpleasant and unpalatable to us both; but the real chance
of real use and benefit to our little darling overcomes all scruples,
and, therefore, to work we go!

You will feel, I dare believe, all I could write on this subject;
I once rejected such a plan, formed for me by Mr. Burke, where
books were to be kept by ladies, not booksellers,—the Duchess of
Devonshire, Mrs. Boscawen, and Mrs. Crewe; but I was an individual then, and had no cares of times to come: now, thank
Heaven! this is not the case;—and when I look at my little boy's
dear, innocent, yet intelligent face, I defy any pursuit to be painful that may lead to his good.

Adieu, my ever dear friend!

F. D'A.

During the years 1794 and 1795, Madame d'Arblay finished and prepared for the press her third novel, Camilla, *which was published partly by subscription in 1796; the Dowager Duchess of Leinster, the Hon. Mrs. Boscawen, Mrs. Crewe, and Mrs. Locke, kindly keeping lists, and receiving the names of subscribers.*[30]

This work having been dedicated by permission to the Queen, the authoress was desirous of presenting the first copy to Her Majesty, and made a journey to Windsor for that honour.

[1796]

To Dr. Burney

Bookham, Friday, October

How well I know and feel the pang of this cruel day to my beloved father![31] My heart seems visiting him almost every minute in grief and participation; yet I was happy to see it open with a smiling aspect, and encourage a superstition of hoping it portentous of a good conclusion. . . .

But I meant to have begun with our thanks for my dear kind father's indulgence of our extreme curiosity and interest in the sight of the reviews. I am quite happy in what I have escaped of greater severity, though my mate cannot bear that the palm should be contested by *Evelina* and *Cecilia;*[32] his partiality rates the last as so much the highest; so does the newspaper I have mentioned, of which I long to send you a copy. But those immense men, whose single praise was fame and security—who established, by a word, the two elder sisters—are now silent. Dr. Johnson and Sir Joshua are no more, and Mr. Burke is ill, or otherwise engrossed; yet, even without their powerful influence, to which I owe such unspeakable obligation, the essential success of *Camilla* exceeds that of the elders. The sale is truly astonishing. Charles has just sent to me that five hundred only remain of four thousand, and it has appeared scarcely three months.[33]

The first edition of *Evelina* was of eight hundred,[34] the second of five hundred, and the third of a thousand. What the following have been I have never heard. The sale from that period became more flourishing than the publisher cared to announce. Of *Cecilia* the first edition was reckoned enormous at two thousand; and as a part of payment was reserved for it, I remember our dear Daddy Crisp thought it very unfair. It was printed, like this, in July, and sold in October, to every one's wonder. Here, however, the sale is increased in rapidity more than a third. Charles says,—

> Now heed no more what critics thought 'em,
> Since this you know, all people bought 'em.

We have resumed our original plan, and are going immediately to build a little cottage for ourselves.[35] We shall make it as small and as cheap as will accord with its being warm and comfortable. We have relinquished, however, the very kind offer of Mr. Locke, which he has renewed, for his park. We mean to make this a property saleable or letable for our Alex, and in Mr. Locke's park we could not encroach any tenant, if the youth's circumstances, profession, or inclination should make him not choose the spot for his own residence. M. d'Arblay, therefore, has fixed upon a field of Mr. Locke's, which he will rent, and of which Mr. Locke will grant him a lease of ninety years. By this means, we shall leave the little Alex a little property, besides what will be in the funds, and a property likely to rise in value, as the situation of the field is remarkably beautiful. It is in the valley, between Mr. Locke's park and Dorking, and where land is so scarce, that there is not another possessor within many miles who would part, upon any terms, with half an acre. . . .

Alex has made no progress in phrases, but pronounces single words a few more. Adieu, most dear Sir.

F. D'A.

To Mrs. Phillips

Bookham, November 7

. . . The minute I received, from Sally, by our dearest father's desire, the last tidings, I set out for Chelsea.[36] I was much shocked by the news, long as it has been but natural to look forward to it. My better part spoke even before myself upon the propriety of my instant journey, and promised me a faithful nursing attendance during my absence. I went in a chaise, to lose no time; but the uncertainty how I might find my poor father made me arrive with a nervous seizure upon my voice that rendered it as husky as Mr. Rishton's.[37]

While I settled with the postillion, Sally, James, Charlotte, and Marianne, came to me. Esther and Charles had been there the preceding day; they were sent to as soon as the event had happened. My dearest father received me with extreme kindness, but though far, far more calm and quiet than I could expect, he was much shaken, and often very faint. However, in the course of the evening, he suffered me to read to him various passages from various books, such as conversation introduced, and, as his nature is as pure from affectation as from falsehood, encouraged in himself, as well as permitted in us, whatever could lead to cheerfulness.

Let me not forget to record one thing that was truly generous in my poor mother's last voluntary exertions. She charged Sally and her maid both not to call my father when she appeared to be dying; and not disturb him if her death should happen in the night, nor to let him hear it till he arose at his usual time. I feel sensibly the kindness of this sparing consideration and true feeling.

Yet, not so would I be served! Oh never should I forgive the misjudged prudence that should rob me of one little instant of remaining life in one who was truly dear to me! Nevertheless, I shall not be surprised to have his first shock succeeded by a sorrow it did not excite, and I fear he will require much watching and vigilance to be kept as well as I have quitted him.

F. d'A.

To Dr. Burney

Bookham, December 16

. . . My little man waits for your lessons to get on in elocution: he has made no further advance but that of calling out, as he saw our two watches hung on two opposite hooks over the chamber chimney-piece, "Watch, papa,—watch, mamma"; so, though his first speech is English, the idiom is French. We agree this is to avoid any heartburning in his parents. He is at this moment so exquisitely enchanted with a little penny trumpet, and finding he can produce such harmony his own self, that he is blowing and laughing till he can hardly stand. If you could see his little swelling cheeks, you would not accuse yourself of a misnomer in calling him cherub. I try to impress him with an idea of pleasure in going to see grandpapa, but the short visit to Bookham is forgotten, and the permanent engraving remains, and all his concurrence consists in pointing up to the print over the chimney-piece, and giving it one of his concise little bows. . . .

Our building is to be resumed the 1st of March; it will then soon be done, as it is only of lath and plaster, and the roof and wood-work are already prepared. My indefatigable superintendent goes every morning for two, three, or four hours to his field, to work at a sunk fence that is to protect his garden from our cow. I have sent Mrs. Boscawen, through Miss Cambridge, a history of our plan. The dwelling is destined by M. d'Arblay to be called the Camilla Cottage.

F. D'A.

[1797]

To Mrs. Phillips

West Humble, December

. . . We languished for the moment of removal [38] with almost infantine fretfulness at every delay that distanced it; and when at last the grand day came, our final packings, with all their toil and difficulties and labour and expense, were mere acts of pleasantry: so bewitched were we with the impending change, that, though from six o'clock to three we were hard at work, without a kettle to boil the breakfast, or a knife to cut bread for a luncheon, we missed nothing, wanted nothing, and were as insensible to fatigue as to hunger.

M. d'Arblay set out on foot, loaded with remaining relics of things, to us precious, and Betty afterwards with a remnant glass or two; the other maid had been sent two days before. I was forced to have a chaise for my Alex and me, and a few looking-glasses, a few folios, and not a few other oddments; and then, with dearest Mr. Locke, our founder's portrait, and my little boy, off I set, and I would my dearest Susan could relate to me as delicious a journey.

My mate, striding over hedge and ditch, arrived first, though he set out after, to welcome me to our new dwelling; and we entered our new best room, in which I found a glorious fire of wood, and a little bench, borrowed of one of the departing carpenters: nothing else. We contrived to make room for each other, and Alex disdained all rest. His spirits were so high upon finding two or three rooms totally free for his horse (alias any stick he can pick up) and himself, unincumbered by chairs and tables and such-like lumber, that he was as merry as a little Andrew and as wild as twenty colts. Here we unpacked a small basket containing three or four loaves, and, with a garden-knife, fell to work; some eggs had been procured from a neighbouring farm, and one saucepan had been brought. We dined, therefore, exquisitely, and drank to our new possession from a glass of clear water out of our new well.

At about eight o'clock our goods arrived. We had our bed put up in the middle of our room, to avoid risk of damp walls, and our Alex had his dear Willy's crib at our feet.[39]

We none of us caught cold. We had fire night and day in the maids' room, as well as our own—or rather in my Susan's room; for we lent them that, their own having a little inconvenience against a fire, because it is built without a chimney.

We continued making fires all around us the first fortnight, and then found wood would be as bad as an apothecary's bill, so desisted; but we did not stop short so soon as to want the latter to succeed the former, or put our calculation to the proof.

Our first week was devoted to unpacking, and exulting in our completed plan. To have no one thing at hand, nothing to eat, nowhere to sit—all were trifles, rather, I think, amusing than incommodious. The house looked so clean, the distribution of the rooms and closets is so convenient, the prospect everywhere around is so gay and so lovely, and the park of dear Norbury is so close at hand, that we hardly knew how to require anything else for existence than the enjoyment of our own situation. . . .

[1799]

To Mrs. Phillips

West Humble, December 10

Oh my Susan, my heart's dear sister! with what bitter sorrow have I read this last account! [40] With us, with yourself, your children,—all,—you have trifled in respect to health though in all things else you are honour and veracity personified; but nothing had prepared me to think you in such a state as I now find you. Would to God I could get to you! If Mr. Keirnan thinks you had best pass the winter in Dublin, stay, and let me come to you. Venture nothing against his opinion, for mercy's sake! Fears for your health take place of all impatience to expedite your return; only go not back to Belcotton, where you cannot be under his direction, and are away from the physician he thinks of so highly.

I shall write immediately to Charles about the carriage. [41] I am sure of his answer beforehand,—so must you be. Act, therefore, with regard to the carriage, as if already it were arranged. But I am well aware it must not set out till you are well enough to nearly fix your day of sailing. I say nearly, for we must always allow for accidents. I shall write to our dear father, and Etty, and James, and send to Norbury Park; but I shall wait till to-morrow, not to infect them with what I am infected. . . .

Oh my Susan! that I could come to you! But all must depend on Mr. Keirnan's decision. If you can come to us with perfect safety, however slowly, I shall not dare add to your embarrassment of persons and package. Else, Charles's carriage—Oh, what a temptation to air it for you all the way! Take no more large paper, that you may write with less fatigue, and, if possible, oftener;—to any one will suffice for all.

Yours affectionately,
F. d'A.

[1800]

To Dr. Burney

January 9

My most dear Padre—My mate will say all say,—so I can only offer up my earnest prayers I may soon be allowed the blessing —the only one I sigh for—of embracing my dearest Susan in your arms and under your roof. Amen.

F. d'A.

These were the last written lines of the last period—unsuspected as such—of my perfect happiness on earth; for they were stopped on the road by news that my heart's beloved sister, Susanna Elizabeth Phillips, had ceased to breathe.[42] The tenderest of husbands—the most feeling of human beings—had only reached Norbury Park, on his way to a believed meeting with that angel, when the fatal blow was struck; and he came back to West Humble—to the dreadful task of revealing the irreparable loss which his own goodness, sweetness, patience, and sympathy could alone have made supported.

To Dr. Burney

West Humble, March 22

Day after day I have meant to write to my dearest father; but I have been unwell ever since our return, and that has not added to my being sprightly.[43] I have not once crossed the threshold since I re-entered the house till to-day, when Mr. and Mrs. Locke almost insisted upon taking me an airing. I am glad of it, for it has done me good, and broken a kind of spell that made me unwilling to stir.

M. d'Arblay has worked most laboriously in his garden; but his misfortunes there, during our absence, might melt a heart of stone. The horses of our next neighboring farmer broke through our hedges, and have made a kind of bog of our meadow, by scampering in it during the wet; the sheep followed, who have eaten up all our greens, every sprout and cabbage and lettuce, destined for the winter; while the horses dug up our turnips and carrots; and the swine, pursuing such examples, have trod down all the young plants, besides devouring whatever the others left of vegetables. Our potatoes, left, from our abrupt departure, in the ground, are all rotten or frost-bitten, and utterly spoilt; and not a single thing has our whole ground produced us since we came home. A few dried carrots, which remain from the indoor's collection, are all we have to temper our viands. . . .

My Alex, I am sure you will be kindly glad to hear, is entirely well; and looks so blooming—no rose can be fresher. I am encouraging back his *spouting* propensity, to fit him for his royal interview with the sweet and gay young princess who has demanded him, who will, I know, be diverted with his speeches and gestures. We must present ourselves before Easter, as the Court then adjourns to Windsor for ten days. My gardener will not again leave his grounds to the four-footed marauders; and our stay, therefore, will be the *very* shortest we can possibly make it; for though we love retirement, we do not like solitude. . . .

F. D'A.

To Dr. Burney

West Humble, April 27

My Alex improves in all that I can teach, and my gardener is laboriously recovering from his winter misfortunes. He is now raising a hillock by the gate, for a view of Norbury Park from our grounds, and he has planted potatoes upon almost every spot where they can grow. The dreadful price of provisions makes this our first attention. The poor people about us complain they are

nearly starved, and the children of the journeymen of the trades-
men at Dorking come to our door to beg halfpence for a little
bread. What the occasion of such universal dearth can be we can
form no notion, and have no information. The price of *bread* we
can conceive from the bad harvest; but meat, butter, and *shoes!*—
nay, all sorts of nourriture or clothing seem to rise in the same
proportion, and without any adequate cause. The imputed one of
the war does not appear to me sufficient, though the drawback
from all by the income-tax is severely an underminer of comfort. . . .

F. D'A.

*Towards the close of the preceding year Dr. Charles Burney
had placed in the hands of Mr. Harris, the manager of Covent
Garden Theatre, a comedy by Madame d'Arblay, called* Love and
Fashion. *Mr. Harris highly approved the piece, and early in the
spring put it into rehearsal; but Dr. Burney was seized with a
panic concerning its success, and, to oblige him, his daughter and
her husband withdrew it. The following letter announced their
generous compliance with his wishes.*

To Dr. Burney

Monday

I hasten to tell you, dearest Sir, Mr. H. has at length listened
to our petitions, and has returned me my poor ill-fated [com-
edy], wholly relinquishing all claim to it for this season. He has
promised also to do his utmost, as far as his influence extends,
to keep the newspapers totally silent in future. We demand,
therefore, no contradictory paragraph, as the report must needs
die when the *reality* no more exists. Nobody has believed it from
the beginning, on account of the premature moment when it
was advertised. This release gives me present repose, which, indeed, I much wanted; for to combat your, to me, unaccountable
but most afflicting displeasure, in the midst of my own panics and
disturbance, would have been ample punishment to me had I

been guilty of a crime, in doing what I have all my life been urged to, and all my life intended,—writing a comedy. Your goodness, your kindness, your regard for my fame, I know have caused both your trepidation, which doomed me to *certain* failure, and your displeasure that I ran, what you thought, a wanton risk. But it is *not* wanton, my dearest father. My imagination is not at my own control, or I would always have continued in the walk you approved. The combinations for another long work did not occur to me; incidents and effects for a drama did. I thought the field more than open—inviting to me. The chance held out golden dreams.[44]—The risk could be only our own; for, permit me to say, appear when it will, you will find nothing in the principles, the moral, or the language that will make you blush for me. *A failure* upon those points only, can bring *disgrace;* upon mere cabal or want of dramatic powers, it can only cause *disappointment.*

I hope, therefore, my dearest father, in thinking this over you will cease to nourish such terrors and disgust at an essay so natural and rather say to yourself, with an internal smile, "After all, 'tis but *like father like child;* for to what walk do I confine myself? She took my example in writing—she takes it in ranging. Why then, after all, should I lock her up in one paddock, well as she has fed there, if she says she finds nothing more to nibble; while *I* find all the earth unequal to my ambition, and mount the skies to content it? Come on, then, poor Fan! the world has acknowledged you my offspring, and I will *disencourage* you no more. Leap the pales of your paddock—let us pursue our career; and, while you frisk from novel to comedy, I, quitting Music and Prose, will try a race with Poetry and the Stars."

I am sure my dear father will not infer, from this appeal, I mean to parallel our works. No one more truly measures her own inferiority, which, with respect to yours, has always been my pride. I only mean to show, that if my muse loves a little variety, she has an hereditary claim to try it.

F. D'A.

[1801]

To Dr. Burney

West Humble, October 3, 1810 [1801].

God avert mischief from this peace,[45] my dearest father! For in our hermitage you may imagine, more readily than I can express, the hopes and happiness it excites. M. d'Arblay now feels paid for his long forbearance, his kind patience, and compliance with my earnest wishes not to revisit his native land while we were at war with it. . . . He will now have his heart's desire granted, in again seeing his loved and respectable uncle,—and many relations, and more friends, and his own native town, as well as soil; and he will have the delight of presenting to that uncle, and those friends, his little pet Alex.

With all this gratification to one whose endurance of such a length of suspense, and repetition of disappointment, I have observed with gratitude, and felt with sympathy—must not I, too, find pleasure? Though, on my side, many are the drawbacks; but I ought not, and must not, listen to them. . . . *Fêtes*, joy, and pleasure, will probably for some months occupy the public in France; and it will not be till those rejoicings are past, that they will set about weighing causes of new commotion, the rights of their governors, or the means, or desirability of changing them. I would far rather go immediately, than six months hence.

I hope, too, this so long wished view of friends and country gratified, my life's partner will feel a tranquillity without which, even our little Hermitage and Great Book Room cannot make him completely happy.

F. d'A.

The projected journey of Madame d'Arblay with her husband did not take place this year; the season being already advanced, and their little boy not strong enough to bear the fatigue of such an expedition. Monsieur d'Arblay went alone to France.[46]

To Monsieur d'Arblay

West Humble, December 15

The relief, the consolation of your frequent letters I can never express, nor my grateful sense of your finding time for them, situated as you now are; and yet that I have this moment read, of the 15 *Frimaire*,[47] has made my heart ache heavily. Our hermitage is so dear to me—our book-room so precious, and in its retirement, its beauty of prospect, form, convenience and comforts, so impossible to replace, that I sigh, and deeply, in thinking of relinquishing it.[48]

Your happiness, however, is now *all* mine; if deliberately, therefore, you wish to try a new system, I will surely try it with you, be it what it may. I will try *anything* but what I try *now*—absence! Think, however, well, mon très cher ami, before you decide upon any occupation that robs you of being master of your own *time, leisure, hours, gardening, scribbling,* and *reading.* . . .

Should you find the sum total preponderate in favour of your new scheme, I will say no more. All schemes will to me be preferable to seeing you again here, without the same fondness for the place, and way of life, that has made it to me what it has been. With regard to the necessity or urgency of the measure, I could say much that I cannot write. You know *now*, I can live with *you*, and you know I am not without views, as well as hopes, of ameliorating our condition. . . .

. . . I put the whole consideration into your own hands; what, upon mature deliberation, you judge to be best, I will abide by. Heaven guide and speed your determination!

[1802]

The beginning of this year was attended with much anxiety to Madame d'Arblay. Her husband, disappointed in the hopes suggested by his friends, of his receiving employment as French

Commercial Consul in London, directed his efforts to obtaining his half-pay on the retired list of French officers. This was promised, on condition that he should previously serve at St. Domingo, where General Leclerc was then endeavouring to put down Toussaint's insurrection.[49] *He accepted the appointment conditionally on his being allowed to retire as soon as that expedition should be ended. This, he was told, was impossible, and he therefore hastened back to his family towards the end of January.*

In February, a despatch followed him from General Berthier, then Minister at War, announcing that his appointment was made out, and on his own terms. To this M. d'Arblay wrote his acceptance, but repeated a stipulation he had before made, that while he was ready to fight against the enemies of the Republic, yet, should future events disturb the peace lately established between France and England, it was his unalterable determination never to take up arms against the British Government. As this determination had already been signified by M. d'Arblay, he waited not to hear the result of its repetition, but set off again for Paris to receive orders, and proceed thence to St. Domingo.

After a short time he was informed that his stipulation of never taking up arms against England could not be accepted, and that his military appointment was, in consequence, annulled. Having been required at the Alien Office, on quitting England, to engage that he would not return for the space of one year, he now proposed that Madame d'Arblay, with her little boy, should join him in France. . . .

To Miss Planta

Paris, April 27

A week have I been here, my dear Miss Planta, so astonishingly engaged, so indispensably occupied, or so suffering from fatigue, that I have not been able till now to take up my pen, except to satisfy my dear father of our safe arrival. To give you some idea of these *engagements, occupations,* and *fatigues,* I must begin with the last.

We were a whole long, languid day, a whole restless, painful night upon the sea; my little Alex sick as death, suffering if possible yet more than myself, though I had not a moment of ease and comfort. . . .

At Calais we spent a day, and half a night to refit; and pray try to imagine my pleased emotion and surprise, when, as soon as we were seated to dinner at the hotel, a band of musicians came to the window, with French horns and other instruments, and struck up *"God save the King."* So unexpected a sound in a foreign country, and a country so lately hostile, affected me with uncommon pleasure. . . .

As to my *occupations;*—my little apartment to arrange, my trunks and baggage to unpack and place, my poor Adrienne [50] to consign to her friends, my Alex to nurse from a threatening malady; letters to deliver, necessaries to buy; a femme de chambre to engage; and, most important of all! my own sumptuous wardrobe to refit, and my own poor exterior to reorganise! I see you smile, methinks, at this hint; but what smiles would brighten the countenance of a certain young lady called Miss Rose, who amused herself by anticipation, when I had last the honour of seeing her, with the changes I might have to undergo, could she have heard the exclamations which followed the examination of my attire! *"This* won't do! *That* you can never wear! *This* you can never be seen in! *That* would make you stared at as a curiosity!—*Three* petticoats! no one wears more than one!— Stays? everybody has left off even corsets!—Shift-sleeves? not a soul now wears even a chemise!" etc. etc. In short, I found all that I possessed seemed so hideously old-fashioned, or so comically rustic, that as soon as it was decreed I must make my appearance in the *grand monde,* hopeless of success in exhibiting myself in the *costume Français,* I gave over the attempt, and ventured to come forth as a Gothic *Anglaise,* who had never heard of, or never heeded, the reigning *metamorphoses.* . . .

As to my *engagements;*—when should I finish, should I tell of all that have been made or proposed, even in the short space of a single week? The civilities I have met with, contrary to all my expectations, have not more amazed me for myself, than gratified me for M. d'Arblay, who is keenly alive to the kind, I might say distinguished, reception I have been favoured with by those to whom my arrival is known.

Your favourite hero is excessively popular at this moment from three successive grand events, all occurring within the short time of my arrival,—the Ratification of the Treaty of Peace—the Restoration of Sunday, and Catholic Worship—and the amnesty of the Emigrants. At the Opera Buffa, the *loge* in which I sat was exactly opposite to that of the First Consul; [51] but he and his family are all at Malmaison.

Adieu,

My dear Miss P., and believe me ever,

Your affectionate friend and servant,

F. D'ARBLAY

To Dr. Burney

May 5

Again a full day. M. d'Arblay had procured us three tickets for entering the apartments at the Tuileries to see the parade of General Hulin,[52] now high in actual rank and service, but who had been a *sous-officier* under M. d'Arblay's command; our third ticket was for Madame d'Henin.[53] . . .

The scene now, with regard to all that was present, was splendidly gay and highly animating. The room was full, but not crowded, with officers of rank in sumptuous rather than rich uniforms, and exhibiting a martial air that became their attire, which, however, generally speaking, was too gorgeous to be noble.

Our window was that next to the consular apartment, in which Bonaparte was holding a levee, and it was close to the steps ascending to it; by which means we saw all the forms of the various exits and entrances, and had opportunity to examine every dress and every countenance that passed and repassed. This was highly amusing, I might say historic, where the past history and the present office were known.

Sundry footmen of the First Consul, in very fine liveries, were attending to bring or arrange chairs for whoever required them; various peace-officers, superbly begilt, paraded occasionally up and down the chamber, to keep the ladies to their windows and the gentlemen to their ranks, so as to preserve the passage or lane through which the First Consul was to walk upon his entrance, clear and open; and several gentlemanlike-looking persons, whom in former times I should have supposed pages of the back stairs, dressed in black, with gold chains hanging round their necks, and medallions pending from them, seemed to have the charge of the door itself, leading immediately to the audience chamber of the First Consul.

But what was most prominent in commanding notice, was the array of the aides-de-camp of Bonaparte, which was so almost furiously striking, that all other vestments, even the most gaudy, appeared suddenly under a gloomy cloud when contrasted with its brightness. . . .

While this variety of attire, of carriage, and of physiognomy amused us in facing the passage prepared for the First Consul, we were occupied, whenever we turned round, by seeing from the window the garden of the Tuileries filling with troops. . . .

At length the two human hedges were finally formed, the door of the audience chamber was thrown wide open with a commanding crash, and a vivacious officer—sentinel—or I know not what, nimbly descended the three steps into our apartment, and placing himself at the side of the door, with one hand spread as high as possible above his head, and the other extended horizontally; called out in a loud and authoritative voice, "Le Premier Consul!"

You will easily believe nothing more was necessary to obtain attention; not a soul either spoke or stirred as he and his suite passed along, which was so quickly that, had I not been placed so near the door, and had not all about me facilitated my standing foremost, and being least crowd-obstructed, I could hardly have seen him. As it was, I had a view so near, though so brief, of his face as to be very much struck by it. It is of a deeply impressive cast, pale even to sallowness, while not only in the eye but in every feature—care, thought, melancholy, and meditation are strongly marked, with so much of character, nay, genius, and so penetrating a seriousness, or rather sadness, as powerfully to sink into an observer's mind.

Yet, though the busts and medallions I have seen are, in general, such good resemblances that I think I should have known him untold, he has by no means the look to be expected from Bonaparte, but rather that of a profoundly studious and contemplative man. . . . The plainness, also, of his dress, so conspicuously contrasted by the finery of all around him, conspires forcibly with his countenance, so "sicklied o'er with the pale hue of thought," to give him far more the air of a student than a warrior. . . .

The review I shall attempt no description of. I have no knowledge of the subject, and no fondness for its object. It was far more superb than anything I had ever beheld; but while all the pomp and circumstance of war animated others, it only saddened me; and all of past reflection, all of future dread, made the whole grandeur of the martial scene, and all the delusive seduction of martial music, fill my eyes frequently with tears, but not regale my poor muscles with one single smile.

Bonaparte, mounting a beautiful and spirited white horse, closely encircled by his glittering aides-de-camp, and accompanied by his generals, rode round the ranks, holding his bridle indifferently in either hand, and seeming utterly careless of the prancing, rearing, or other freaks of his horse, insomuch as to strike some who were near me with a notion of his being a bad horseman. I am the last to be a *judge* upon this subject; but as a *remarker*, he only appeared to me a man who knew so well he could manage the animal when he pleased, that he did not deem it worth his while to keep constantly in order what he knew, if urged or provoked, he could subdue in a moment.

Precisely opposite to the window at which I was placed, the Chief Consul stationed himself after making his round; and thence he presented some swords of honour, spreading out one arm with an air and mien which changed his look from that of scholastic severity to one that was highly military and commanding. . . .

The review over, the Chief Consul returned to the palace. The lines were again formed, and he re-entered our apartment with his suite. . . .

The moment the Chief Consul had ascended the steps leading to the inner apartment, the gentlemen in black with gold chains gave a general hint that all the company must depart, as the ambassadors and the ministers were now summoned to their monthly public audience with the Chief Consul. The crowd, however, was so great, and Madame d'Henin was so much incommoded, and half ill, I fear, by internal suffering, that M. d'Arblay procured a pass for us by a private door down to a terrace leading to a quiet exit from the palace into the Tuileries garden.

F. D'A.

To Mrs. Burney

Paris

With the nearest relatives now existing of M. d'Arblay I am myself more pleased than I can tell you. We have spent a fortnight at *Joigny*,[54] and found them all awaiting us with the most enthusiastic determination to receive with open arms and open heart the choice and the offspring of their returned exile. Their kindness has truly penetrated me; and the heads of the family, the uncle and the aunt, are so charming as well as so worthy, that I could have remained with them for months had not the way of life which their residence in a country town has forced them to adopt, been utterly at war with all that, to me, makes peace, and happiness, and cheerfulness, namely, the real domestic life of living with my own small but all-sufficient family. . . . M. d'Arblay has so many friends, and an acquaintance so extensive, that the mere common decencies of established etiquettes demand, as yet, nearly all my time; and this has been a true fatigue both to my body and my spirits. . . .

F. D'A.

[1803]

To Dr. Burney

Passy, May 6

If my dearest father has the smallest idea of the suspense and terror in which I have spent this last fortnight, from the daily menace of war,[55] he will be glad, I am sure, of the respite allowed me—if no more—from a visit I have just received from Mrs. Huber, who assures me the Ambassador has postponed his setting off, and consented to send another courier. To say how I pray for his success would indeed be needless. I have hardly closed my eyes many nights past. My dearest father will easily conceive the varying conflicts of our minds, and how mutual are our sufferings. We have everywhere announced our intention to embrace you next October, the state of M. d'Arblay's affairs makes it impossible for him to indulge me sooner; but if the war takes place, the difficulties of procuring licence, passports, passage, and the ruinous length of travelling through Hamburgh, as well as the deadly sickness of so long a voyage—all these thoughts torment me night and day, and rest will, I fear, be a stranger to my eyes till the conflict is terminated; and then, whether it will bring me back rest, or added rest-robbing materials for destroying it, who can tell? At all events, let me intreat to hear from you, my beloved padre, as speedily as possible. . . .

[1805]

To Dr. Burney

Passy, May 29

Before I expected it, my promised opportunity for again writing to my most dear father is arrived. I entirely forget whether, before the breaking out of the war stopt our correspondence, M. d'Arblay had already obtained his *retraite;*[56] and, consequently, whether that is an event I have mentioned or not. Be that as it may, he now has it—it is 1500 livres, or £62:10s. per annum. But all our resources from England ceasing with the peace,[57] we had so little left from what we had brought over, and M. d'Arblay has found so nearly nothing remaining of his natural and hereditary claims in his own province, that he determined upon applying for some employment that might enable him to live with independence, however parsimoniously. This he has, with infinite difficulty, etc., at length obtained, and he is now a *redacteur* in the civil department of *les Batimens,* etc.[58] This is no sinecure. He attends at his bureau from half-past nine to half-past four o'clock every day; and as we live so far off as Passy he is obliged to set off for his office between eight and nine, and does not return to his hermitage till past five. However, what necessity has urged us to desire, and made him solicit, we must not, now acquired, name or think of with murmuring or regret. He has the happiness to be placed amongst extremely worthy people; and those who are his *chefs* in office treat him with every possible mark of consideration and feeling.

We continue steady to our little cell at Passy, which is retired, quiet, and quite to ourselves, with a magnificent view of Paris from one side, and a beautiful one of the country on the other. It is unfurnished—indeed, unpapered, and every way unfinished; for our workmen, in the indispensable repairs which preceded our entering it, ran us up bills that compelled us to turn them adrift, and leave everything at a stand, when three rooms only were made just habitable.

[1807]

To Dr. Burney, Chelsea

ce 16 Septembre

My Most Dear Father—I have just received a kind offer to send a few lines to the spot whence my most ardent wishes are to receive many, but whence the handwriting that most of all I sigh to behold has not blessed my sight since the return of Madame de Cadignan. Nor have I ever heard whether the last six letters I have written have as yet been received. Two of them were antiques that had waited three or four years some opportunity; a third was concerning the Institute, and M. le Breton's [59] wish to see you installed one of the foreign members and correspondents; the two last were to reach you through a voyage by America, and therefore may not yet be arrived. . . .

[1808]

21 Août

The expected opportunity for which I had strung this la-
mentable list of unacknowledged claims, nearly a twelvemonth
since, failed; another at this moment offers—may it prove more
propitious! . . . My paper is so stinted, and my time so limited,
that I can begin no regular account of our proceedings, which, indeed, have but little varied since we lost Maria.⁶⁰ Oh that any
one could give me here the history of yours! I am in such terrible
arrears of all such knowledge that I know not who will ever
undertake to pay me. My last intelligence was that you were
well, my dearest father, and that the family at large, in that at
least, imitated you. But details—none, none reach me! I have a
bitter anxiety of suspense upon some subjects very near my
heart. Not even the loved names of any of my family now reach
me; Esther, James, Charles, Charlotte, Sally, with all their younger
selves, and Richard and his boys, all are sounds strange to my
ears, and my beloved friends of Norbury are banished thence
with the same rigour! I am sad, sad indeed, at this deprivation;
though in all else I am still and constantly happy, for in my
two faithful companions I find sympathy in all my feelings, and
food, sweet food for all my hopes.

F. D'A.

[1810]

To Mrs. Locke

No. 13 Rue d'Anjou, Paris, September 16

. . . When, when, may I embrace you again! I think of late of
nothing else. I form projects, and dream dreams. Oh, dearest
friends, give me your prayers I may not dream only always!

My excellent mate, toujours the same, has not less desire, but is still wider from probability. His health is not all I could wish—it is preserved with watchfulness, but cannot bear neglect. Alex is thin and pale, but strong and without complaint. He is terribly singular, and more what they here call *sauvage* than any creature I ever beheld. He is untameably wild, and averse to all the forms of society. Where he can have got such a rebel humour we conceive not; but it costs him more to make a bow than to resolve six difficult problems of algebra, or to repeat twelve pages from Euripides; and as to making a civil speech, he would sooner renounce the world.

. . . But why have I not my dear Augusta's letter? [61] I beseech that it may be sent to Chelsea; occasions there present themselves sometimes; rarely, indeed, but yet sometimes. How kind of her to have written! No matter for the date; all will still, alas! to me be new; for I hear so seldom, and after such chasms, that a letter of six years ago will stand a chance to give me as much intelligence as one written last week.

F. D'A.

[1812]

JOURNAL FROM PARIS TO LONDON

Dunkirk

. . . In the year 1810, when I had been separated from my dear father, and country, and native friends, for eight years, my desire to again see them became so anxiously impatient that my tender companion proposed my passing over to England alone, to spend a month or two at Chelsea. Many females at that period, and amongst them the young Duchesse de Duras, had contrived to procure passports for a short similar excursion; though no male was permitted, under any pretence, to quit France, save with the army.[62]

Reluctantly—with all my wishes in favour of the scheme—yet most reluctantly, I accepted the generous offer; for never did I know happiness away from that companion, no, not even out of his sight! but still, I was consuming with solicitude to see my revered father—to be again in his kind arms, and receive his kind benediction.

For this all was settled, and I had obtained my passport, which was brought to me without my even going to the police office, by the especial favour of M. le Breton, the Secrétaire Perpétuel *à l'Institut*. The ever active services of M. de Narbonne aided this peculiar grant; though, had not Bonaparte been abroad with his army at the time, neither the one nor the other would have ventured at so hardy a measure of assistance. But whenever Bonaparte left Paris, there was always an immediate abatement of severity in the police. . . .

Thus armed, and thus authorised, I prepared, quietly and secretly, for my expedition, while my generous mate employed all his little leisure in discovering where and how I might embark; when, one morning, when I was bending over my trunk to press in its contents, I was abruptly broken in upon by M. de Boinville, who was in my secret, and who called upon me to stop! He had received certain, he said, though as yet unpublished information, that a universal embargo was laid upon every vessel, and that not a fishing-boat was permitted to quit the coast.

Confounded, affrighted, disappointed, and yet relieved, I submitted to the blow and obeyed the injunction. . . .

I pass on to my second attempt in the year 1812. Disastrous was that interval! All correspondence with England was prohibited under pain of death! One letter only reached me, most unhappily, written with unreflecting abruptness, announcing, without preface, the death of the Princess Amelia, the new and total derangement of the King,[63] and the death of Mr. Locke.[64] Three such calamities overwhelmed me, overwhelmed us both, for Mr. Locke, my revered Mr. Locke, was as dear to my beloved partner as to myself. . . .

When I was sufficiently recovered for travelling, after a dreadful operation,[65] my plan was resumed; but with an alteration which added infinitely to its interest, as well as to its importance. Bonaparte was now engaging in a new war, of which the aim and intention was no less than—the conquest of the world. This menaced a severity of conscription to which Alexander, who had now spent ten years in France, and was seventeen years of age, would soon become liable. His noble father had relinquished all his own hopes and emoluments in the military career, from the epoch that his king was separated from his country. . . .

. . . To see, therefore, his son bear arms in the very cause that had been his ruin—bear arms against the country which had given himself as well as his mother, birth, would indeed have been heart-breaking. We agreed, therefore, that Alexander should accompany me to England, where, I flattered myself, I might safely deposit him, while I returned to await, by the side of my husband, the issue of the war, in the fervent hope that it would prove our restoration to liberty and reunion.

My second passport was procured with much less facility than the first. . . .

Now, as before, the critical moment was seized by my friends to act for me when Bonaparte had left Paris to proceed towards the scene of his next destined enterprise, and he was, I believe, already at Dresden when my application was made. . . . For what place, nominally, my passport was assigned, I do not recollect; I think, for Newfoundland, but certainly for some part of the coast of America. Yet everybody at the police office saw and knew that England was my object. They connived, nevertheless, at the accomplishment of my wishes, with significant though taciturn consciousness. . . .

Our journey—Alexander's and mine—from Paris to Dunkirk was sad, from the cruel separation which it exacted, and the fearful uncertainty of impending events; though I was animated at times into the liveliest sensations, in the prospect of again beholding my father, my friends, and my country.

General d'Arblay, through his assiduous researches, aided by those of M. de Boinville and some others, found that a vessel was preparing to sail from Dunkirk to Dover, under American colours, and with American passports and licence; and, after privately landing such of its passengers as meant but to cross the Channel, to proceed to the western continents. M. d'Arblay found, at the same time, six or seven persons of his acquaintance who were to embark in this vessel. . . .

We all met, and severally visited at Dunkirk, where I was compelled, through the mismanagement and misconduct of the captain of the vessel, to spend the most painfully wearisome six weeks of my life, for they kept me alike from all that was dearest to me, either in France or in England, save my Alexander. I was twenty times on the point of returning to Paris; but whenever I made known that design, the captain promised to sail the next morning. The truth is, he postponed the voyage from day to day and from week to week, in the hope of obtaining more passengers; and, as the clandestine visit he meant to make to Dover, *in his way to America,* was whispered about, reinforcements very frequently encouraged his cupidity. . . .

When I found our stay indefinitely protracted, it occurred to me that if I had the papers of a work which I had then in hand, they might afford me an occupation to while away my truly vapid and uninteresting leisure. I wrote this idea to my *partner in all*—as M. de Talleyrand had called M. d'Arblay; and, with a spirit that was always in its first youth where any service was to be performed, he waited on M. de Saulnier at the police office, and made a request that my manuscripts might be sent after me. . . .

This work was *The Wanderer; or, Female Difficulties,* of which nearly three volumes were finished.[66] They arrived, nevertheless, vainly for any purpose at Dunkirk; the disturbance of my suspensive state incapacitating me for any composition, save of letters to my best friend, to whom I wrote, or dictated by Alexander, every day; and every day was only supported by the same kind diurnal return. . . .

Six weeks completely we consumed in wasteful weariness at Dunkirk; and our passage, when at last we set sail, was equally, in its proportion, toilsome and tedious. Involved in a sickening calm, we could make no way, but lingered two days and two nights in this long-short passage. The second night, indeed, might have been spared me, as it was spared to all my fellow-voyagers. But when we cast anchor, I was so exhausted by the unremitting sufferings I had endured, that I was literally unable to rise from my hammock. . . .

I now found we were rowing to Deal, not Dover, to which town we had been destined by our engagement: but we had been captured, it seems, *chemin faisant,* though so gently, and with such utter helplessness of opposition, that I had become a prisoner without any suspicion of my captivity.

We had anchored about half a mile, I imagine, from the shore; which I no sooner touched than, drawing away my arm from Mr. Hartford,[67] I took up on one knee, with irrepressible transport, the nearest bright pebble, to press to my lips in grateful joy at touching again the land of my nativity, after an absence, nearly hopeless, of more than twelve years. . . .

TO MRS. BROOME[68]

August 15

. . . We set off for Canterbury, where we slept, and on the 20th proceeded towards Chelsea. While, upon some common, we stopped to water the horses, a gentleman on horseback passed us twice, and then, looking in, pronounced my name; and I saw it was Charles, dear Charles! who had been watching for us several hours and *three nights* following, through a mistake. Thence we proceeded to Chelsea, where we arrived at nine o'clock at night. I was in a state almost breathless. I could only demand to see my dear father alone: fortunately, he had had the same feeling, and had charged all the family to stay away, and all the world to be denied. I found him, therefore, in his library, by himself—but oh! my dearest, very much altered indeed—weak, weak and changed—his head almost always hanging down, and his hearing most cruelly impaired. I was terribly affected, but most grateful to God for my arrival. Our meeting, you may be sure, was very tender, though I roused myself as quickly as possible to be gay and cheering. He was extremely kind to Alex, and said, in a tone the most impressive, "I should have been very glad to have seen M. d'Arblay!" In discourse, however, he reanimated, and was, at times, all himself. But he now admits scarcely a creature but of his family, and will only see for a short time even his children. He likes quietly reading, and lies almost constantly upon the sofa, and will never eat but alone! What a change!

[1813]

To Dr. Burney

Richmond Hill, October 12

My most dear Padre will, I am sure, congratulate me that I have just had the heartfelt delight of a few lines from M. d'Arblay, dated September 5th. I had not had any news since the 17th of August, and I had the melancholy apprehension upon my spirits that no more letters would be allowed to pass till the campaign was over.[69] It has been therefore one of the most welcome surprises I ever experienced.

He tells me, also, that he is perfectly well, and quite *accablé* with business. This, for the instant, gives me nothing but joy; for, were he not essentially necessary in some department of civil labour and use, he would surely be included in some *levée en masse*. Every way, therefore, this letter gives me relief and pleasure.

I have had, also, this morning, the great comfort to hear that my Alexander is "stout and well" at Cambridge, where his kind uncle Charles still remains.[70]

I am indescribably occupied, and have been so ever since my return from Ramsgate, in giving more and more last touches to my work, about which I begin to grow very anxious.[71] I am to receive merely £500 upon delivery of the MS.; the two following £500 by instalments from nine months to nine months, that is, in a year and a half from the day of *publication*.

If all goes well, the whole will be £3000, but only at the end of the sale of eight thousand copies.[72] Oh, my Padre, if *you* approve the work, I shall have good hope. . . .

Most affectionately yours,
F. B. d'A.

[1814]

*In the beginning of this year Madame d'Arblay published
her fourth work,* The Wanderer, *and nearly at the same time
Peace was declared between France and England. Her satisfaction at an event so long wished for, was deeply saddened by the
death of her father, Dr. Burney, whom she nursed and attended
to the last moment with dutiful tenderness.*[73]

*Soon after the Restoration of the French Royal Family, Mon-
sieur d'Arblay was placed by the Duke de Luxembourg in the
French "Gardes du Corps." He obtained leave of absence towards
the close of the year, and came to England for a few weeks; after
which Madame d'Arblay returned with him to Paris, leaving their
son to pursue his studies at Cambridge.*

Soon after the publication of The Wanderer, *Madame d'Arblay
wrote as follows to a friend:—*

I beseech you not to let your too ardent friendship disturb you
about the reviews and critiques, and I quite supplicate you to
leave their authors to their own severities or indulgence. I have
ever steadily refused all interference with public opinion or private criticism. I am told I have been very harshly treated;[74] but I
attribute it not to what alone would affect me, but which I trust
I have not excited, personal enmity. I attribute it to the false
expectation, universally spread, that the book would be a picture
of France, as well as to the astonishing *éclat* of a work in five volumes being all bespoken before it was published. The booksellers, erroneously and injudiciously concluding the sale would so
go on, fixed the rapacious price of two guineas, which again
damped the sale. But why say *damped*, when it is only their un-
reasonable expectations that are disappointed? for they acknowledge that 3600 copies are positively sold and paid for in the first
half year. What must I be, if not far more than contented? I have
not read or heard one of the criticisms; my mind has been wholly
occupied by grief for the loss of my dearest father, or the inspection of his MSS. and my harassing situation relative to my own
proceedings. Why, then, make myself *black bile* to disturb me

further? No; I will not look at a word till my spirits and time are calmed and quiet, and I can set about preparing a corrected edition. . . .

[1815]

To Alex d'Arblay, Esq.

April 26

At length, my long expecting eyes meet again your handwriting, after a breach of correspondence that I can never recollect without pain. Revive it not in my mind by any repetition, and I will dismiss it from all future power of tormenting me, by considering it only as a dream of other times.[75] Cry "Done!" my Alex, and I will skip over the subject, not perhaps as lightly, but as swiftly as you skip over the hills of Norbury Park. I delight to think of the good and pleasure that sojourn may do you; though easily, too easily, I conceive the melancholy reflections that were awakened by the sight of our dear, dear cottage; yet your expressions upon its view lose much of their effect by being overstrained, *recherchés,* and designing to be pathetic. We never touch others, my dear Alex, where we study to show we are touched ourselves. I beg you, when you write to me, to let your pen paint your thoughts as they rise, not as you seek or labour to embellish them. I remember you once wrote me a letter so very fine from Cambridge, that, if it had not made me laugh, it would certainly have made me sick. Be natural, my dear boy, and you will be sure to please your mother without wasting your time. Let us know what you have received, what you have spent, what you may have still unpaid, and what you yet want. But for this last article, we both desire you will not wait our permission to draw upon your aunt,[76] whom we shall empower to draw upon Mr. Hoare in our names. We know you to have no wanton extravagances, and no idle vanity; we give you, therefore, dear Alex, *carte blanche* to apply to your aunt, only consulting with her, and begging her kind, maternal advice to help your inexperience in regulating your expenses. She knows the difference that must be made between our fortune and that of Clement,[77] but she knows our affection for our boy, and our confidence in his honour and probity, and will treat him with as much kindness, though not with equal luxury. Your father charges you never to be without your purse, and never to let it be empty. Your aunt will counsel you about your clothes. About your books we trust to yourself. And pray don't forget, when you make sleeping visits, to recompense the trouble you must unavoidably give to servants. And if you join any party to any public place, make a point to pay for yourself. It will be far better to go seldom, and with that gentlemanly spirit, than often, with the air of a hanger-on. How infinitely hospitable has been your uncle James![78] But hospitality is his characteristic. We had only insisted upon your regularity at chapel and at lectures, and we hear of your attention to them comparatively, and we are fixed to be contented *en attendant*. Don't lose courage, dear, dear Alex; the second place is the nearest to the first. I love you with all my heart and soul! . . .

To Mrs. Locke and Mrs. Angerstein[79]

Dover, October 18

Last night, my ever dear friends, we arrived once more in Old England.

I write this to send the moment I land in London. I cannot boast of our health, our looks, our strength; but I hope we may recover a part of all when our direful fatigues, mental and corporeal, cease to utterly weigh upon and wear us.

We shall winter in Bath. The waters of Plombières have been recommended to my poor *boiteux*, but he has obtained a *congé* that allows this change. Besides his present utter incapacity for military service,[80] he is now unavoidably on the *retraite* list, and the King of France permits his coming over, not alone without difficulty, but with wishing him a good journey, through the Duc de Luxembourg, his captain in the *Gardes du Corps*. . . .

[1816]

To Mrs. Locke

Bath, February 15

. . We have had our Alexander for six weeks; he left us three
days ago, and I won't tell my dear friend whether or not we miss
him. He is precisely such as he was—as inartificial in his character,
as irregular in his studies. He cannot bring himself to conquer
his disgust of the routine of labour at Cambridge; and while he
energetically argues upon the innocence of a preference to his
own early practice, which he vindicates, I believe unanswerably,
with regard to its real superiority, he is insensible, at least forget-
ful, of all that can be urged of the mischiefs to his prospects in
life that must result from his not conquering his inclinations. I
have nearly lost all hope of his taking the high degree adjudged
to him by general expectation at the University, from the promise
of his opening. . . .

Of old friends here, I have found stationary, Mrs. Holroyd, and
Mrs. Frances and Harriet Bowdler.[81] Mrs. Holroyd still gives parties, and tempted me to hear a little *medley music,* as she called
it. Mrs. F. Bowdler lives on Lansdowne Crescent, and scarcely
ever comes down the hill; Mrs. Harriet I have missed, though we
have repeatedly sought a meeting on both sides; but she left
Bath for some excursion soon after my arrival. Another new resident here will excite, I am sure, a more animated interest—Mrs.
Piozzi.[82] . . .

F. B. d'A.

To a Friend

Bath, August 17

. . . General d'Arblay is gone to France, and here at Bath
rest *sa femme et son fils.* There was no adjusting the excursion
but by separation. Alexander would have been wilder than ever

for his French mathematics in revisiting Paris; and, till his degree
is taken, we must not contribute to lowering it by feasting his
opposing pursuits with fresh nourishment. M. d'Arblay nevertheless could by no means forego his intention, which a thousand
circumstances led him to consider as right. . . . He hopes also to
arrange for receiving here his half-pay, when sickness or affairs
or accident may prevent his crossing the Channel. Choice and
happiness will, to his last breath, carry him annually to France;
for, not to separate us from his son, or, in the bud of life, to force
that son's inclination in fixing his place or mode of residence,
alone decides his not fixing there his own last staff. But Alexander, young as he left that country, has seen enough of it to be
aware that no line is open there to ambition or importance, but
the military, most especially for the son of an officer so known
and marked for his military character: and I need not tell you
that, with my feelings and sentiments, to see him wield a sword
that could only lead him to renown by being drawn against the
country of *his* birth and of *mine,* would demolish my heart, and
probably my head; and, to believe in any war in which England
and France will not be rivals, is to entertain Arcadian hopes, fit
only for shepherds and shepherdesses of the drama.

Equally, I fear, would be romantic all expectation of a really
permanent peace, though I am persuaded we shall certainly enjoy a long one.

Enjoy, did I say? What do we enjoy? Every seeming and coveted good only arrives, only is granted, to be transformed into
evil.

[1817-1819]

To Her Son

Bath, Friday, April 25

Why, what a rogue you are! four days in town! As there
can be no scholarship[33]—hélas! it matters not; but who knew
that circumstance when they played truant? Can you tell me that,

hey! Mr. Cantab.? Why you *dish* me as if I were no more worth than Paley or Newton, or such like worthies!

Your dear Padre is very considerably better, *surtout* in his looks, but by no means re-established;[84] for cold air—too much exertion—too little—and all sorts of nourishment or beverage that are not precisely adapted to the present state of the poor shattered frame, produce instant pain, uneasiness, restlessness, and suffering. Such, however, is the common condition of convalescence, and therefore I observe it with much more concern than surprise; and Mr. Hay[85] assures me all is as well as can possibly be expected after so long and irksome an illness.

> The scholarship is at an end—
> So much for that!

Pretty cool, my friend!

Will it make you double your diligence for what is *not* at an end? hey, mon petit monsieur?

But I am sorry for your disappointment in the affair you mention, my dear Alex: though your affections were not so far engaged, methinks, but that your *amour propre* is still more *blessé* than your heart! hey? However, 'tis a real loss, though little more than of an ideal friend, at present. But no idea is so flattering and so sweet, as that which opens to expectation a treasure of such a sort. I am really, therefore, sorry for you, my dear Alex.[86]

Your determination to give way to no *sudden* impulse in future is quite right. Nothing is so pleasant as giving way to impulse; nothing so hazardous. . . .

To Mrs. Broome

Ilfracombe, Post Office, July 23[87]

I have letters very frequently from Paris, all assuring me M. d'A. is re-establishing upon the whole; yet all letting me see, by collateral accounts, anecdotes, or expressions, that he is constantly in the hands of his physician, and that a difficulty of breathing attacks him from time to time, as it did before his journey; with a lassitude, a weakness, and a restlessness which make him *there,* as *here* they made him since his illness, unfit for company, and incapable, but by starts and for moments, to have any enjoyment of mixed society! I do not therefore feel comfortable about him, though, thank Heaven, not alarmed. And at all events I am glad he tries the change of air. Change of scene also was advised for him by all; but he is too kind to find that beneficial when we are separated; and he writes me frequent avowals of seizures of dejection and sadness that reduce him to a state of great suffering. The parting, while he was in a situation so discouraging, was very cruel; but Alexander had, and has, no chance of taking a tolerable degree without a friend constantly at hand to remind him of the passage of Time. He never thinks of it: every day seems a day by itself, which he may fill up at pleasure, but which opens to him no prospect of the day that will succeed! So little reflection on the future, with so good capacity for judging the present, were never before united. We are very well lodged for pleasantness, and for excellent people. We have a constant view of the sea from our drawing-room, which is large and handsome; our bedrooms also are good; but our minor accommodations, our attendance, dinner equipage, cooking, etc., would very ill have contented my General had he been here. The best *men,* the most moderate and temperate, are difficult, nay, dainty, compared with *women.* When he comes, if I am so happy as to see him return while we are here, I must endeavour to ameliorate these matters. . . .

NARRATIVE OF THE ILLNESS AND DEATH OF GENERAL D'ARBLAY

. . . On the opening of October, 1817, Alex and I returned from Ilfracombe to Bath to meet our best friend. He arrived soon after, attended by his favourite medical man, Mr. Hay, whom he had met in Paris. We found him extremely altered—not in mind, temper, faculties—oh, no!—but in looks and strength: thin and weakened so as to be fatigued by the smallest exertion. He tried, however, to revive; we sought to renew our walks, but his strength was insufficient. He purchased a garden in the Crescent Fields, and worked in it, but came home always the worse for the effort. His spirits were no longer in their state of native, genial cheerfulness: he could still be awakened to gaiety, but gaiety was no longer innate, instinctive with him.

In this month, October, 1817, I had a letter from the Princess Elizabeth, to inform me that Her Majesty and herself were coming to pass four weeks in Bath. . . .

He had always purposed being presented to Her Majesty in the pump-room, and the Queen herself deigned to say "she should be very glad to see the General." Ill he was! suffering, emaciated, enfeebled! But he had always spirit awake to every call; and just before Christmas, 1817, we went together, between seven and eight o'clock in the morning, in chairs, to the pump-room.

I thought I had never seen him look to such advantage. His fine brow so open, his noble countenance so expressive, his features so formed for a painter's pencil! This, too, was the last time he ever wore his military honours—his three orders of "St. Louis," "the Legion of Honour," and "Du Lys," or "De la Fidélité"; decorations which singularly became him, from his strikingly martial port and character. . . .

. . . Highly sensible to the honour of her distinction, he forgot his pains in his desire to manifest his gratitude;—and his own smiles—how winning they became! Her Majesty spoke of Bath, of Windsor, of the Continent; and while addressing him, her eyes turned to meet mine with a look that said, "Now I know I am making you happy!" . . .

. . . Alas! the Queen no sooner ceased to address him than the pains he had suppressed became intolerable, and he retreated from the circle and sunk upon a bench near the wall; he could stand no longer, and we returned home to spend the rest of the day in bodily misery.

Very soon after the opening of this fatal year 1818, expressions dropped from my beloved of his belief of his approaching end: they would have broken my heart, had not an incredulity—now my eternal wonder!—kept me in a constant persuasion that he was hypochondriac, and tormented with false apprehensions. . . .

At this critical period in April I was called down one day to Madame la Marquise de S——, who urged me to summon a priest of the Roman Catholic persuasion to my precious sufferer. I was greatly disturbed every way; I felt in shuddering the danger she apprehended, and resisted its belief; yet I trembled lest I should be doing wrong. . . . I was a Protestant, and had no faith in *confession to man*. I had long had reason to believe that my beloved partner was a Protestant, also, in his heart; but he had a horror of *apostasy*, and *therefore*, as he told me, would not investigate the differences of the two religions. . . . All this made me personally easy for him, yet, as this was not known, and as nothing definitive had ever passed between us upon this delicate subject, I felt that he apparently belonged still to the Roman Catholic Church; and after many painful struggles I thought it my absolute duty to let him judge for himself. . . .

Never shall I forget the heavenly composure with which my beloved partner heard me announce that the priest, Dr. Elloi, was come. Cheerfully as I urged myself to name him, still he could but regard the visit as an invitation to make his last preparations for quitting mortal life. With a calm the most gentle and genuine, he said he had better be left alone with him, and they remained together, I believe, three hours. . . .

Thenceforth he talked openly, and almost solely, of his approaching dissolution, and prepared for it by much silent mental prayer. He also poured forth his soul in counsel for Alexander and myself. I now dared no longer oppose to him my hopes of his recovery; the season was too awful. I heard him only with deluges of long-restrained tears, and his generous spirit seemed better satisfied in thinking me now awakened to a sense of his danger, as preparatory for supporting its consequence. . . .

He then asked for Alexander, embraced him warmly, and half raising himself with a strength that had seemed extinct but the day before, he took a hand of Alexander and one of mine, and putting them together between both his own, he tenderly pressed them, exclaiming, "How happy I am! . . . I fear I am too happy!" . . .

. . . On Sunday, the fatal 3rd of May, my patient was still cheerful, and slept often, but not long. This circumstance was delightful to my observation, and kept off the least suspicion that my misery could be so near.

My pen lingers now!—reluctant to finish the little that remains.

About noon, gently awaking from a slumber, he called to me for some beverage, but was weaker than usual, and could not hold the cup. I moistened his lips with a spoon several times. He looked at me with sweetness inexpressible, and pathetically said, *"Qui . . . ?"* He stopped, but I saw he meant *"Who shall return this for you?"* I instantly answered to his obvious and most touching meaning, by a cheerful exclamation of *"You!* my dearest Ami! *You* yourself! You shall recover, and take your revenge." He smiled, but shut his eyes in silence. . . .

After this, he bent forward, as he was supported nearly upright by pillows in his bed . . . and taking my hand, and holding it between both his own, he impressively said, "Je ne sais si ce sera le dernier mot . . . mais ce sera la dernière pensée—*Notre réunion!"*[88] . . . How little knew I then that he should speak to me no more!

Towards evening I sat watching in my armchair, and Alex remained constantly with me. His sleep was so calm, that an hour passed in which I indulged the hope that a favourable crisis was arriving; that a turn would take place by which his vital powers would be restored . . . but . . . when the hour was succeeded by another hour, when I saw a universal stillness in the whole frame, such as seemed to stagnate all around, I began to be strangely moved. "Alex!" I whispered, "this sleep is critical! a crisis arrives! Pray God—Almighty God!—that it be fav——" I could not proceed. . . .

His face had still its unruffled serenity, but methought the hands were turning cold; I covered them; I watched over the head of my beloved; I took new flannel to roll over his feet; the stillness grew more awful; the skin became colder.

Alex, my dear Alex, proposed calling in Mr. Tudor, and ran off for him.

I leant over him now with sal volatile to his temple, his forehead, the palms of his hands, but I had no courage to feel his pulse, to touch his lips.

Mr. Tudor came; he put his hand upon the heart, the noblest of hearts, and pronounced that all was over! . . .

I suffered certainly a partial derangement, for I cannot to this moment recollect anything that now succeeded, with truth or consistency. . . .

Even to this instant I always see the room itself charged with a medley of silent and strange figures grouped against the wall just opposite me. Mr. Tudor, methought, was come to drag me by force away; and in this persuasion, which was false, I remember supplicating him to grant me but one hour, telling him I had solemnly engaged myself to pass it in watching. . . .

But why go back to my grief? Even yet, at times, it seems as fresh as ever, and at *all* times weighs on me with a feeling that seems stagnating the springs of life. But for Alexander—*our* Alexander!—I think I could hardly have survived. . . .

EXTRACTS FROM POCKET-BOOK DIARY

Tuesday, June 23

To-day I have written my first letter since my annihilated happiness—to my tenderly sympathising Charlotte. I covet a junction with that dear and partial sister for ending together our latter days. I hope we shall bring it to bear.

With Alex read part of St. Luke.

Wednesday, July 8

. . . I have given to Alex the decision of where we shall dwell. Unhappy myself everywhere, why not leave unshackled his dawning life? To quit Bath—unhappy Bath!—he had long desired: and, finally, he has fixed his choice in the very capital itself. I cannot hesitate to oblige him.

August 28

My admirable old friend, Mrs. Frances Bowdler, spent the afternoon with me. Probably we shall meet no more; but judiciously, as suits her enlightened understanding, and kindly, as accords with her long partiality, she forbore any hint on that point. Yet her eyes swam in tears, not ordinary to her, when she bade me adieu.

Wednesday, September 30

This morning I left Bath with feelings of profound affliction; yet, reflecting that hope was ever open—that future union may repay this laceration. . . .

My dear James received me with tender pity; so did his good wife, son, and daughter.

Tuesday, October 6

My dear Alexander left me this morning for Cambridge. How shall I do, thus parted from both! My kind brother, and his worthy house, have softened off the day much; yet I sigh for seclusion—my mind labours under the weight of assumed sociability.

Thursday, October 8

I came this evening to my new and probably last dwelling, No. 11 Bolton Street, Piccadilly. My kind James conducted me.[89] Oh, how heavy is my forlorn heart! I have made myself very busy all day; so only could I have supported this first opening to my baleful desolation! No adored husband! No beloved son! But the latter is only at Cambridge. Ah! let me struggle to think more of the other, the first, the chief, as also only removed from my sight by a transitory journey!

Wednesday, October 14

Wrote to my—erst—dearest friend, Mrs. Piozzi. I can never forget my long love for her, and many obligations to her friendship, strangely as she had been estranged since her marriage.

Tuesday, November 17

This day, at one o'clock, breathed her last the inestimable QUEEN OF ENGLAND! Heaven rest and bless her soul!

[1819]

Sunday, April 11

This morning my dearest Alexander was ordained a priest by the Bishop of Chester in St. James's Church. I went thither with my good Eliz. Ramsay,[90] and from the gallery witnessed the ceremony. Fifty-two were ordained at the same time. I fervently pray to God that my son may meet this his decided calling with a disposition and conduct to sanction its choice! and with virtues to merit his noble father's name and exemplary character! Amen! Amen!

[1820]

FROM MRS. PIOZZI

Bath, October 20

It was very gratifying, dear Madam, to find myself so kindly remembered, and with all my heart I thank you for your letter. My family are gone to Sandgate for the purpose of bathing in the sea, this wonderfully beautiful October; and were you not detained in London by such a son as I hear you are happy in, I should wish you there too. . . .

How changed is the taste of verse, prose, and painting! since *le bon vieux temps*, dear Madam! Nothing attracts us but what terrifies, and is within—*if* within—a hair's-breadth of positive disgust. The picture of Death on his Pale Horse,[91] however, is very grand certainly—and some of the strange things they *write* remind me of Squire Richard's visit to the Tower Menagerie, when he says "They are *pure* grim devils,"—particularly a wild and hideous tale called Frankenstein.[92] Do you ever see any of the friends we used to live among? . . .

Old Jacob and his red night-cap are the only live creatures, as an Irishman would say, that come about *me* of those you remember, and death alone will part us,—he and I both lived longer with Mr. Piozzi than we had done with Mr. Thrale. . . .

Adieu! *Leisure for men of business,* you know, *and business for men of leisure,* would cure many complaints.

Once more, Farewell! and accept my thanks for your good-natured recollection of poor

H. L. P.

To Mrs. Piozzi

Bolton Street, December 15

Now at last, dear Madam, with a real pen I venture to answer your kind acceptance of my Bath leave-taking address, of a date I would wish you to forget—but the letter is before me, and has no other word I should like to relinquish. But more of grief at the consequence of my silence, namely your own, hangs upon the circumstance than shame, for I have been so every way unwell,—unhinged, shattered, and unfitted for any correspondence that could have a chance of reciprocating pleasure, that perhaps I ought rather to demand your thanks than your pardon for this delay. . . .

You inquire if I ever see any of the friends we used to live amongst:—almost none; but I may resume some of those old ties this winter, from the ardent desire of my son. I have, till very lately, been so utterly incapable to enjoy society, that I have held it as much kindness to others as to myself, to keep wholly out of its way. I am now, in health, much better, and consequently more able to control the murmuring propensities that were alienating me from the purposes of life while yet living. . . .

But Time,—"uncalled, unheeded, unawares,"—works as secretly upon our spirits as upon our years, and gives us as little foresight into what we can endure, as into how long we shall exist. . . .

Your obliged and affectionate

F. d'Arblay

My son is at Cambridge, far, alas, from robust; but free from complaint.

[1821]

To Mrs. Piozzi

Bolton Street, Berkeley Square, February 6

You would be repaid, dear Madam, if I still, as I believe, know you, for the great kindness of your prompt answer, had you witnessed the satisfaction with which it was received; even at a time of new and dreadful solicitude; for my son returned from Cambridge unwell, and in a few days after his arrival at home was seized with a feverish cold which threatened to fasten upon the whole system of his existence, not with immediate danger, but with a perspective to leave but small openings to any future view of health, strength, or longevity. I will not dwell upon this period, but briefly say, it seems passed over. He is now, I thank Heaven, daily reviving, and from looking like—not a walking, but a creeping spectre, he is gaining force, spirit, and flesh visibly, and almost hour by hour; still, however, he requires the utmost attention, and the more from the extreme *insouciance,* from being always absorbed in some mental combinations, with which he utterly neglects himself. I am therefore wholly devoted to watching him. . . . However, I do not yet despair, for in the multitude of MSS. that have fallen to my mournfully surviving lot to select, or destroy, etc., chaos seems come again; and though I have worked at them during the last year so as to obtain a little light, it is scarcely more than darkness visible.[93] To all the vast mass left to my direction by my dear father, who burnt nothing, not even an invitation to dinner, are added not merely those that devolved to me by fatal necessity in 1818, but also all the papers possessed from her childhood to her decease of that sister you so well, dear Madam, know to have been my heart's earliest darling.[94] When on this pile are heaped the countless hoards which my own now long life has gathered together, of my personal property, such as it is, and the correspondence of my family and my friends, and innumerable incidental windfalls, the whole forms a body that might make a bonfire to illuminate me nearly from hence to Penzance. And such a bonfire might perhaps be not only the shortest, but the wisest way to dispose of such materials. This enormous accumulation has been chiefly owing to a long unsettled home, joined to a mind too deeply occupied by immediate affairs and feelings to have the intellect at liberty for retrospective investigations.

What a long detail! I know not what has urged me to write it—yet I feel as if you would take in it some interest; and an instinct of that flattering sort is always pleasant, though far from always infallible. . . .

Your obliged, affectionate, and
obedient servant,
F. D'A.

May

I have lost now, just lost, my once most dear, intimate, and admired friend, Mrs. Thrale Piozzi,[95] who preserved her fine faculties, her imagination, her intelligence, her powers of allusion and citation, her extraordinary memory, and her almost unexampled vivacity, to the last of her existence. She was in her eighty-second year, and yet owed not her death to age nor to natural decay, but to the effects of a fall in a journey from Penzance to Clifton. On her eightieth birthday she gave a great ball, concert, and supper, in the public rooms at Bath, to upwards of two hundred persons, and the ball she opened herself. She was, in truth, a most wonderful character for talents and eccentricity, for wit, genius, generosity, spirit, and powers of entertainment. She had a great deal both of good and not good, in common with Madame de Staël Holstein. . . . Both were kind, charitable, and munificent, and therefore beloved; both were sarcastic, careless, and daring, and therefore feared. The morality of Madame de Staël was by far the most faulty, but so was the society to which she belonged; so were the general manners of those by whom she was encircled.

[1823]

To Mrs. [Esther] Burney

February 29

. . . You still ask about my health, etc. I thought the good result would have sufficed; but thus stands the detail: I was packing up a hoard of papers to carry with me to Richmond, many months now ago, and employed above an hour, bending my head over the trunk, and on my knees;—when, upon meaning to rise, I was seized with a giddiness, a glare of sparks before my eyes, and a torturing pain on one side of my head, that nearly disabled me from quitting my posture, and that was followed, when at last I rose, by an inability to stand or walk. My second threat of seizure was at Eliot Vale,[96] while Alex was at Tunbridge. I have been suddenly taken a third time, in the middle of the night, with a seizure as if a hundred windmills were turning round in my head: in short,—I had now recourse to serious medical help, . . . and, to come to the sum total, I am now so much better that I believe myself to be merely in the common road of such gentle, gradual decay as, I humbly trust, I have been prepared to meet with highest hope, though with deepest awe—for now many years back.

The chief changes, or reforms, from which I reap benefit are, 1st. Totally renouncing for the evenings all revision or indulgence in poring over those letters and papers whose contents come nearest to my heart, and work upon its bleeding regrets. Next, transferring to the evening, as far as is in my power, all of sociality, with Alex, or my few remaining friends, or the few he will present to me of new ones. 3rd. Constantly going out every day—either in brisk walks in the morning, or in brisk jumbles in the carriage of one of my three friends who send for me, to a *"tête-à-tête"* tea-converse. 4th. Strict attention to diet. . . .

The worst of all is, that I have lost, totally lost, my pleasure in reading! except when Alex is my lecturer, for whose sake my faculties are still alive to what—erst! gave them their greatest delight. But alone; I have no longer that resource! I have scarcely looked over a single sentence, but some word of it brings to my mind some mournful recollection, or acute regret, and takes from one all attention—my eyes thence glance vainly over pages that awaken no ideas.—This is melancholy in the extreme; yet I have tried every species of writing and writer—but all pass by me mechanically, instead of instructing or entertaining me intellectually. But for this sad deprivation of my original taste, my evenings might always be pleasing and reviving—but alas! . . .

. . . Sir William and Sir Lucas Pepys, who alone, of all the Streatham set, have lived, and found me out in Bolton Street, except the three daughters of the house,[97] now and then give me the pleasure of an hour's social recollection of old time, that is interesting to us all.

Adieu, my dearest Esther—remember me kindly to all who kindly remember me—if such, after this long absence, be found.

God bless you ever, prays your ever affectionate and faithful,

F. D'A.

Although Madame d'Arblay's intercourse with society was now usually confined to that of her relations and of old and established friends,[98] she yet greeted with admiration and pleasure Sir Walter Scott, who was brought to her by Mr. Rogers. Sir Walter, in his Diary for Nov. 18th, 1826, thus describes the visit:—"Was introduced by Rogers to Mad. d'Arblay, the celebrated authoress of Evelina *and* Cecilia—*an elderly lady, with no remains of personal beauty, but with a simple and gentle manner, a pleasing expression of countenance, and apparently quick feelings. She told me she had wished to see two persons—myself, of course, being one, the other, George Canning.[99] This was really a compliment to be pleased with—a nice little handsome pat of butter made up by a neat-handed Phillis of a dairy-maid, instead of the grease, fit only for cartwheels, which one is dosed with by the pound.*

"I trust I shall see this lady again."

From the year 1828 to 1832 Madame d'Arblay was chiefly occupied in preparing for the press the Memoirs of her father. . . .

[1835-1838]

Madame d'Arblay's letters were now very few. A complaint in one of her eyes, which was expected to terminate in a cataract, made both reading and writing difficult to her. The number of her correspondents had also been painfully lessened by the death of her eldest sister, Mrs. Burney, and that of her beloved friend, Mrs. Locke; and she had sympathised with other branches of her family in many similar afflictions, for she retained in a peculiar degree not only her intellectual powers, but the warm and generous affections of her youth.

"Though now her eightieth year was past," *she took her wonted and vivid interest in the concerns, the joys, and sorrows of those she loved.*

At this time her son formed an attachment which promised to secure his happiness, and to gild his mother's remaining days with affection and peace; and at the close of the year 1836 he was nominated minister of Ely Chapel, which afforded her considerable satisfaction. But her joy was mournfully short-lived. That building, having been shut up for some years, was damp and ill-aired. The Rev. Mr. d'Arblay began officiating there in winter, and during the first days of his ministry he caught the influenza, which became so serious an illness as to require the attendance of two physicians. Dr. Holland and Dr. Kingston exerted their united skill with the kindest interest; but their patient, never robust, was unable to cope with the malady, and on the 19th of January 1837, in three weeks from his first seizure, the death of this beloved son threw Madame d'Arblay again into the depths of affliction....

. . . [O]ne more such sorrow remained in her cup of life. Her gentle and tender sister Charlotte, many years younger than herself, was to precede her in that eternal world for which they were both preparing; and in the autumn of the year 1838, a short illness terminated in the removal of that beloved sister.

[1839]

In November 1839, Madame d'Arblay was attacked by an illness which showed itself at first in sleepless nights and nervous imaginations. Spectral illusions . . . formed part of her disorder; and though after a time Dr. Holland's skill removed these nervous impressions, yet her debility and cough increased, accompanied by constant fever. For several weeks hopes of her recovery were entertained; her patience assisted the remedies of her kind physician; and the amiable young friend, "who was to her as a daughter," watched over her with unremitting care and attention;[100] but she became more and more feeble, and her mind wandered; though at times every day she was composed and collected, and then given up to silent prayer, with her hands clasped and eyes uplifted.

During the earlier part of her illness she had listened with comfort to some portions of St. John's Gospel, but she now said to her niece, "I would ask you to read to me, but I could not understand one word—not a syllable! but I thank God my mind has not waited till this time."

At another moment she charged the same person with affectionate farewells and blessings to several friends, and with thanks for all their kindness to her. Soon after she said, "I have had some sleep." "That is well," was the reply; "you wanted rest." "I shall have it soon, my dear," she answered emphatically: and thus, aware that death was approaching, in peace with all the world, and in holy trust and reliance on her Redeemer, she breathed her last on the 6th of January 1840; the anniversary of that day she had long consecrated to prayer, and to the memory of her beloved sister Susanna.

NOTES

YOUTH [1768-1778]

1. Fanny is referring to her younger sister Susanna Burney (1755–1800), to whom much of her Diary was addressed.
2. Lynn Regis, a small port on the Norfolk coast, was Fanny's birthplace and the home of the Burneys from 1750 until 1760. It was there that Dr. Burney met his second wife, Elizabeth Allen, whom he married in 1767. The second Mrs. Burney owned a house at Lynn Regis where Fanny stayed.
3. *The History of Rasselas, Prince of Abyssinia,* by Samuel Johnson, published in 1759, was a pessimistic morality tale.
4. Samuel ("Daddy") Crisp (1707–1783), an old friend of Dr. Burney's. The two met between 1745 and 1747. Their friendship lapsed, however, and was not resumed until 1761. Fanny became close to Crisp at about this time (1768).
5. Esther ("Hetty" or "Etty") Burney (1749–1832), Fanny's eldest sister.
6. Chessington, the remote, secluded home of "Daddy" Crisp. Fanny was to spend considerable time there, particularly during the years 1778 to 1783, and much of her first two novels were written there.
7. The three are herself, her father, and her sister Esther.
8. Isabella Strange, wife of the famous Jacobite engraver Robert Strange (1721–1792). Fanny elsewhere noted her wit and conversational powers, and her happiness. The Stranges had a daughter, Mary Bruce Strange, and were longtime friends of the Burneys.
9. The "Masquerade Dutchman" was an otherwise unidentified Mr. Tomkin. This was a rather more serious case of love at

first sight on Tomkin's part than this diary entry indicates.

10. Charlotte Ann Burney (1761–1838), Fanny's youngest sister. Charlotte married Clement Francis (c.1744–1792) in 1786, and in 1798 Ralph Broome (1742–1805).

11. Charles Rousseau Burney (1747–1819), her first cousin, a musician. They had eight children, one of whom died in infancy, during their long and apparently happy marriage.

12. Dr. Burney lived on Poland Street, London, from 1760 to 1770, when he moved to a house in Queen Square. The Poland Street house was not large enough to accommodate Dr. Burney's six children as well as his wife's three children by her previous marriage. After the move, all the children were under one roof for the first time.

13. *The Present State of Music in France & Italy* (1771), the second of Dr. Burney's published works, and his first on music. He had written a pamphlet on comets in 1769.

14. Dr. John Hawkesworth (c.1715–1773), a playwright, editor, and miscellaneous writer most famous for his chronicle of Captain Cook's first Pacific voyage. Dr. Burney had assisted him in obtaining an Admiralty commission to write the official chronicle of that voyage.

15. William Mason (1724–1797), a minor poet, divine, and musician. He was also an old friend of Dr. Burney's.

16. David Garrick (1717–1779), the great eighteenth-century actor. He had been a very close friend of Dr. Burney since Burney's bachelor days.

17. Maria Allen (1751–1820), the eldest of the second Mrs. Burney's three children by her previous marriage; hence, Fanny's step sister.

18. Catherine ("Kitty") Cooke, niece of Mrs. Hamilton who owned Chessington Hall and who with her managed it.

19. Jenny Barsanti, a singer whose career Dr. Burney promoted. She was the daughter of the Italian instrumentalist and composer Francesco Barsanti (c.1690–c.1776). When she lost her singing voice a few years later, she became a distinguished actress.

20. Charles Burney, Jr. (1757–1817), Fanny's younger brother. He was to become a schoolmaster, classical scholar, and Chaplain to King George III. In 1777 he caused a family scandal by stealing books from the Cambridge University Library, for which he was expelled. In 1783 he married Sarah Rose (1759–1821) and had one son, Charles, the noted classical scholar.

21. Richard Burney (1768–1808), Fanny's half brother.

22. Giuseppi Millico (1730–1802), a male soprano and composer

who had come to England one year earlier; Antonio Sacchini (1734–1786), a prolific composer of operas, including *Il Cid* which had had its London premiere a few days before; Eligio Celestino (c.1739–1812), a noted Italian violinist.

23. James ("Jem") Burney (1750–1821), Fanny's eldest brother. He had been in the navy since 1761, having joined at the age of eleven. In 1772 he had joined Captain Cook's second Pacific voyage. Lord Sandwich, First Lord of the Admiralty, had promised Dr. Burney early advancement for James. In 1785 James married Sarah ("Sally") Payne, the daughter of the London bookseller and publisher who published Fanny's second novel, *Cecilia.*

24. Mrs. Rishton was Maria Allen, Fanny's step sister. In 1772 she eloped with Martin Rishton (c.1747–1820), who was heir to a considerable fortune. The Rishtons had no children.

25. Dr. Burney's *The Present State of Music in Germany, the Netherlands, and the United Provinces,* 2 volumes, London, 1773.

26. Tingmouth (Teignmouth), a seaside town in Devon on the Channel coast, where Fanny spent the summer of 1773 visiting the Rishtons.

27. Miss Frances Bowdler was one of three sisters of Thomas Bowdler (1754–1825), now remembered only as editor of an expurgated "family" edition of Shakespeare, which gave the word "bowdlerize" to the English language.

28. Torbay, a seaside town a few miles south of Teignmouth.

29. Garrick played the part of Abel Drugger in Ben Jonson's *The Alchemist.*

30. John Shebbeare (1709–1778), a physician and a Jacobite, who in 1757 was imprisoned and pilloried for his anti-Hanoverian *Letters to the People of England.* He was also a prolific, now-forgotten novelist, with thirty-four novels to his name.

31. James Burney had returned with Captain Cook in July 1775, after a voyage of over three years. Fanny, reacting to the horror of the episode, omits the fact that when the ten men from the *Adventure,* Cook's companion ship, were sent ashore to gather fresh vegetables, they were eaten by New Zealand cannibals.

32. Omai was a young Tahitian who had insisted on joining Cook's company when the ships called at Tahiti and the adjoining islands in 1773. He came with Cook to England in 1775 where he remained for a year, returning to Tahiti with Cook on his third Pacific voyage. Despite Fanny's praise of Omai's refinement and manners, Captain Cook had a rather low opinion of his intelligence.

33. James Bruce (1730–1794), the first great English explorer of

Africa. He did not publish the story of his explorations, *Travels to Discover the Source of the Nile*, until 1790, because of his fear of criticism. He was related to Sir Robert Strange, the engraver.

34. Mr. Hayes, an old, intimate friend of Dr. Burney, was reputed to be a natural son of Sir Robert Walpole. When he died he left his rare coin collection to Dr. Burney, and his London house to James Burney.

35. Joseph Banks (1743–1820), a landed proprietor, a Fellow, and later President, of the Royal Society, whose passion was botany. He had accompanied Captain Cook on his first Pacific voyage as one of the Royal Society's scientific representatives. He was created a baronet in 1781. Daniel Solander (1736–1782), a pupil of the Swedish botanist Linnaeus. He also accompanied Banks on Cook's first voyage as a representative of the Royal Society, of which he was a Fellow.

36. Lucrezia Agujari (1743–1783), an Italian singer whose execution surpassed all her rivals. Her patron was the Duke of Parma.

37. Giuseppe Colla (1731–1806), court conductor to the Duke of Parma. At this time he was Agujari's teacher, not her husband; they married in 1780.

38. A famous theater, also used as a concert hall and for masquerades and assemblies, in Oxford Street, London. It had been built in 1770, and Dr. Burney was an investor in it.

39. Sir John Turner and his wife. In 1750, Turner had obtained the organist's post at Lynn Regis for Dr. Burney, when he had to leave London for his health.

40. Thomas Barlow, whose only fame is his inclusion in Fanny's diary.

41. Martha Young (d. 1815), the sister of Dr. Burney's second wife. Noted for her shrewishness, she was the wife of Arthur Young (1741–1820), an agriculturalist and writer on agriculture.

42. Mrs. Hamilton was the owner of Chessington Hall where Mr. Crisp boarded.

43. Fanny's sister Susan.

44. Prince Alexis Orloff, an admiral in the Russian navy, and the brother of Gregory Orloff, then Empress Catherine II's minister to England. Alexis is reputed to have murdered Peter III of Russia. His brother Gregory sent him off on foreign travels when Alexis tried to supplant him as Catherine's "favorite."

45. Dr. John King (1731–1787), a friend of the Burneys from Lynn Regis. He had been chaplain to the British colony at St.

Petersburg, Russia, and afterwards held various minor ecclesi-
astical offices. Fanny characterized him as an affected man of
"half understanding."

46. James Burney sailed with Captain Cook on Cook's third and last
Pacific voyage in June 1776. The expedition did not return to
England until August 1780.

47. Hester Lynch Thrale (1741–1821), a celebrated and somewhat
controversial hostess of the period, a close friend and benefactor
of Samuel Johnson, a diarist, and, at a later period, herself
a writer. After the publication of Fanny's first novel, *Evelina*,
Mrs. Thrale became her patron, close friend, and an important
influence in her life. At this time Mrs. Thrale was married to
Henry Thrale, a wealthy Southwark brewer. Miss Thrale was
probably her eldest child, Hester Maria ("Queeney"), one of Dr.
Burney's pupils.

48. Margaret Owen (1743–1816), a distant cousin of Mrs. Thrale's.

49. William Seward (1747–1799), the only son of a wealthy brewer,
and a friend of the Thrales. Mrs. Thrale once characterized
him as an hypochondriac and as "not quite right" in the head.

50. Samuel Johnson (1709–1784), the famous poet, essayist, lexicog-
rapher (hence the name Lexiphanes), and literary dictator.
Johnson was the preeminent literary figure of his time and
probably did more than any other person to make writing a
profitable and socially acceptable profession. Dr. Burney first
met Johnson in 1758.

51. A series of periodical essays edited and largely written by Samuel
Johnson between 1758 and 1760.

52. Elizabeth Montagu (1720–1800), a famous letter writer, author
(*Essay on the Writings and Genius of Shakespeare*, 1769), and
founder of the formidable Bluestocking Club, an informal and
socially influential group of women with a great interest in
literature and wit.

53. *Lethe* was a farce which Garrick had written and in which he
customarily acted more than one part.

54. From April to July 1777, Fanny was visiting her uncle Richard
Burney (1723–1792) and his family, who lived near Worcester.
The diary she kept during this period is known as her Worcester
Journal.

55. The "new Essay" was her novel, *Evelina*.

56. Thomas Lowndes, the London bookseller and publisher with
whom Fanny was negotiating for the publication of *Evelina*.
The negotiations were carried on through her brother Charles
so that Fanny could hide her identity.

FAME [1778-1786]

1. *Evelina,* Fanny's first novel, was published anonymously in January 1778 in three volumes. By June it had been favorably reviewed and was a success. By the end of 1779 it had gone through four editions. Lowndes, the publisher, paid her a mere £20 for the novel, although later when he realized its success he voluntarily paid her another £10.

2. Fanny had come to Chessington to recuperate after a bout of inflammation of the lungs.

3. Sarah ("Sally") Harriet Burney (1772–1844), Dr. Burney's second child and only daughter by his second wife, Mrs. Elizabeth Allen, and, accordingly, Fanny's half-sister.

4. Fanny had dedicated *Evelina* to her father; the dedication was in the form of an emotional prefatory ode.

5. Lady Hales was the widow of Sir Thomas Pym Hales, sometime Member of Parliament for Dover. Miss Catherine Coussmaker was her daughter by a previous marriage.

6. Mrs. Mary ("Polly") Cholmondeley (c.1729–1811), sister of Peg Woffington, the famous actress, and wife of the Reverend Robert Cholmondeley. Mrs. Cholmondeley was both socially prominent and an important figure in the Bluestocking Circle. Accordingly, her praise of *Evelina* was important both to the success of the novel and to the social acceptance of Fanny as an author.

7. Streatham Park or Place was the Thrales' principal house since their marriage in 1763. It was then about six miles from London. It was a three-story brick house, surrounded by a 100-acre park. The grounds included greenhouses, stables, an ice house, and farm buildings. The Thrales also owned a house in Southwark, London, near Thrale's brewery, which, as might be expected, was not in a fashionable residential district.

8. Hester Maria ("Queeney") Thrale (1764–1857), Mrs. Thrale's eldest child, who married Viscount Elphinstone in 1808.

9. A character in *Evelina,* originally a waitress at a tavern.

10. Husband.

11. Sir Joshua Reynolds (1723–1792), the celebrated portrait painter and aesthetic theoretician. He was a close friend of the Burneys. His sister, Frances Reynolds (1729–1807), lived with him.

12. *Hamlet,* Act I, scene 5.
13. Characters in *Evelina.*
14. Holborn was the area between the Fleet Prison and Tyburn, where the gallows stood.
15. Reverend Michael Lort (1725–1790), an antiquarian, Greek scholar, and noted book collector. Mrs. Thrale, who knew him since 1767, essentially agreed with Fanny's assessment of him.
16. Thomas Chatterton (1752–1770), a poet who was fascinated by the Middle Ages and wrote forgeries which he attributed to Thomas Rowley, a fifteenth-century poet. He poisoned himself at the age of eighteen after failing to live by his writing.
17. Alexander Pope (1688–1744), the preeminent English poet of the eighteenth century. This allusion is to his *Prologue to the Satires* (1735).
18. A Streatham clergyman, otherwise unidentified.
19. A comedy written by Coleman and Garrick in 1766, in which one of the characters is named Fanny. It was a great favorite of the Burneys.
20. Fanny was, in fact, at this time writing a comedy which she eventually called *The Witlings.*
21. The first of Samuel Johnson's *Lives of the Poets,* published in 1779.
22. Written by the Reverend John Norris (1657–1711), and published in 1688.
23. Miss Gregory was Mrs. Montagu's companion who lived with her from 1773 to 1784. In 1784 she married the Reverend Archibald Alison and quarreled with Mrs. Montagu, who objected to her marriage.
24. S. N. H. Linguet (1736–1794), a political and miscellaneous writer.
25. She was probably afraid of robbers.
26. As a young man, Daddy Crisp had been a man-about-town, a musician, a painter, and one of the circle of wits that included the actors Quinn and Garrick. About 1750 Crisp wrote a tragedy, *Virginia,* which was produced in 1754 and flopped after eleven performances. This failure embittered him and is said to be a major reason for his subsequent retirement from fashionable life to the seclusion of Chessington. His advice to Fanny is thus based on personal experience.
27. Mrs. Sheridan, originally Elizabeth Ann Linley (1754–1792), the daughter of a composer and an accomplished singer in her own right. She married the dramatist Richard Sheridan in 1773.
28. Miss Linley was Mrs. Sheridan's sister.

29. Mrs. Frances Anne Crewe (1748–1818), noted beauty and Bluestocking and the daughter of Fulke Greville, Dr. Burney's old patron and Fanny's godfather. Mrs. Thrale despised her.

30. Gasparo Pacchierotti (1740–1821), a celebrated Italian male soprano singer, much admired by Fanny for his voice.

31. Mrs. Anna Ord (d. 1808), the wealthy widow of William Ord, and a friend of the Bluestockings. She became a good and close friend to Fanny, often chaperoning her to parties.

32. Hannah More (1745–1833), one of the Bluestockings and a friend of the Garricks, the Thrales, and the Burneys. After 1780 she became quite religious and even evangelical. A writer of ability, her works include poetry, plays, several novels, various religious works, and her autobiography.

33. Richard Brinsley Sheridan (1751–1816), the noted and successful playwright (his most famous work, *The School for Scandal,* had been produced in 1777). He became director of the Drury Lane Theater, entered Parliament in 1780 and became Secretary of State, and an important political figure. He was one of those responsible for the attempted impeachment of Warren Hastings in 1787.

34. A character in Sheridan's *The School for Scandal* (1777).

35. *The Witlings.*

36. Mrs. Frances Greville (d. 1789), Fanny's godmother and author of the celebrated poem *Ode to Indifference,* and the wife of Dr. Burney's old patron, Fulke Greville.

37. Lowndes, the publisher of *Evelina,* commissioned John Mortimer to make these drawings for the fourth edition of *Evelina.* They were engraved by Hall, Bartolozzi, and Waler in 1779. Lowndes paid £73 for the plates, £43 more than he had paid Fanny for the novel.

38. Arthur Murphy (1727–1805), an author and actor.

39. Mrs. Thrale was pregnant and suffered a miscarriage in August 1779. She was not in good health at this time, and became oppressed by the fear of dying.

40. A character in *The Witlings.*

41. Brighthelmstone was the old name for Brighton, the seaside resort fifty miles south of London.

42. Mr. Thrale had suffered a stroke about six months before, partly caused by the discovery that the estate of his deceased brother-in-law was in bad financial condition and that he might have to repay its large debts that he had guaranteed.

43. Knowle (or Knole) House in Kent is one of the great Elizabethan year houses (so-called because they have 365 rooms) owned by the Sackville-West family, the then-owner being

the Duke of Dorset. It was the setting for the opening scene in
Virginia Woolf's novel *Orlando* (1928), which was dedicated
to Vita Sackville-West.

44. Tunbridge Wells was a resort town located in Kent, thirty miles
south of London, famous, like its more popular rival, Bath,
for its mineral waters.

45. A character in *The Witlings*.

46. It was literally true that Fanny was required to spend a considerable amount of her time working on her clothes. This may
have been because of her limited funds for such luxuries, the
fact that she had no personal maid, and the complexity of
women's clothing in the late eighteenth century.

47. Fanny was in Bath.

48. Sir Phillip Jennings Clerke (c.1722–1788), created a Baronet in
1774 and a Member of Parliament for twenty years. He was a
close friend of the Thrales and helped them in many difficulties.
In addition to having had an affair with Mrs. Thrale's sister,
Lady Ladd, he made advances to Mrs. Thrale in 1782, after she
was widowed.

49. Anne Jane Cholmley (c.1750–1820), the third wife of Nathaniel
Cholmley. She is not to be confused with Mrs. Cholmondeley,
the Bluestocking.

50. Mrs. Lambart was Sir Phillip Jennings Clerke's sister.

51. William Hoare (c.1707–1792), the fashionable Bath portrait
painter and one of the original members of the Royal Academy.

52. Shakespeare's *Cymbeline*, Act I, scene 1.

53. The reference is to Cecilia, the heroine of Fanny's second novel,
Cecilia, which she had started writing at this time. It was published in 1782.

54. Christopher Anstey (1724–1805), a then popular satiric poet
whose only significant though minor work is the *New Bath
Guide* (1766).

55. Beilby Porteus (1731–1808), bishop of Chester from 1776 to 1787.

56. William Melmoth (1710–1799), translator of Pliny's *Letters*
from the Latin.

57. Lady Ann Miller of Bath Easton, a village two miles from Bath.

58. The laughter arose from the fact that Lady Miller and her
husband fancied themselves as romantic literati, which they
were plainly not. (*See* Edith Sitwell, *Bath* [London, 1948], pp.
209 ff.)

59. Fanny is referring to the anti-Catholic riots (the Gordon Riots)
which paralyzed London for a week in June 1780, during which
a rampaging mob caused 300 deaths and the destruction of
millions in property. Popular anti-Catholic sentiment, which led

to the riots, had been aroused by the eccentric Lord George Gordon (1751–1793), who, as president of the Protestant Association, opposed the broad repeal of anti-Catholic laws which Parliament had enacted in 1778. It was only firm action on the part of the King in calling out the militia that prevented the riots from spreading.

60. Thrale and his property were in danger because he was characterized as a papist for his vote for the Catholic Reform Bill of 1778.

61. Mr. Perkins was the manager of Thrale's brewery.

62. The Borough of Southwark, London, where Thrale's brewery was located.

63. Dr. Burney's servant.

64. Mr. Thrale died suddenly of a stroke on April 4, 1781.

65. Mr. Charles Scrase (1709–1792), a retired attorney who had helped the Thrales during their financial crisis of 1771–1772, and who acted as confidential adviser to Mrs. Thrale on business matters. She respected him for his clear judgment and friendship, unbiased by personal interest.

66. Mr. John Cator (1730–1806), a London timber merchant; Mr. Henry Smith (c.1756–1789), Mr. Thrale's cousin; and Mr. Jeremiah Crutchley (1745–1805), Mr. Thrale's natural son. Crutchley was at best an enigmatic person. At Streatham during the summer of 1781 he paid considerable, if ambivalent, attention to Fanny. But Mrs. Thrale believed that he was using Fanny to mask his attraction to his half sister, Queeney Thrale.

67. As Austin Dobson neatly put it, Mrs. Thrale and her executors "were fast brewing themselves into bankruptcy." Finally Perkins, the manager and one of Thrale's executors, found a buyer for the brewery, to whom it was sold for £135,000. Perkins went into partnership with the new owner. Under her husband's will, Mrs. Thrale received £30,000; the balance was held in trust for her daughters.

68. One of Mr. Thrale's sisters.

69. Fanny seems to have been unaware that Queeney, Mrs. Thrale's daughter, was probably Crutchley's chief attraction to Streatham.

70. An insect also called a "daddy longlegs."

71. Possibly Griselda, legendary for her patience.

72. Fanny's sister Susan had married Lieutenant Molesworth Phillips on January 10, 1782. He was a shipmate of her brother James on Captain Cook's second Pacific voyage and later a gentleman-farmer.

73. Fanny had finished the first draft of her novel *Cecilia*, and was at this time copying it (by hand, of course), for the publisher.

74. *Cecilia, or Memoirs of an Heiress,* was published in five volumes on June 12, 1782, by the firm of Payne and Cadell. Fanny was paid £250 for the copyright. Fanny's brother James was at this time courting Payne's daughter, Sally, and eventually married her in 1785.

75. Fanny is referring to her sister Susan's marriage.

76. Edmund Burke (1729–1797), the famous Parliamentarian and orator and, at a later date, the author of *Reflections on the Revolution in France,* which announced his changed views on monarchy, which he had previously opposed. He was one of the key figures in Parliament behind the attempted impeachment of Warren Hastings.

77. One of Sir Joshua Reynolds's two nieces, Mary Palmer (1750–1820), later Marchioness of Thomonel. The other was Theophilia ("Offy") Palmer (1756–1848), later Mrs. Gwatkin.

78. Edward Gibbon (1737–1794), the historian. By this time he had already published half of his *Decline and Fall of the Roman Empire.*

79. William Weller Pepys (1740–1825) was in 1775 made a judge (Master in Chancery). He was noted for his long nose, his Bluestocking parties, and his Prime Ministership to Mrs. Montagu, the "Queen of the Blues." He is not to be confused with his brother Sir Lucas Pepys, the physician.

80. Cecilia Thrale (1777–1857), Mrs. Thrale's youngest child. She married John Mostyn in 1795.

81. Dr. John Delap (1725–1812), a Sussex clergyman. He had written a play called *Macaria* which was probably produced in 1781 under the name *The Royal Suppliants.* Fanny said he was "a man . . . of deep learning, but totally ignorant of life and manners."

82. Mr. Selwyn was a wealthy and elderly banker. Fanny characterized him as "uncommonly good, full of humanity, generosity, delicacy and benevolence." He admired Miss Burney, but Mrs. Thrale thought him too old as a husband for her.

83. Mr. Henry Cotton was a relative of Mrs. Thrale's (her mother's maiden name was Cotton). Fanny called Cotton and Swinerton "our two young beaus."

84. Elizabeth Woodcock, second wife of Sir John Shelley (died 1783).

85. Mr. (Captain) Wade was Master of Ceremonies at Brighton, an office he filled until 1807.

86. Captain Kaye was a baronet's son and a captain in the Dragoons. Tall, handsome, and agreeable, he was the one, Fanny said, "for whom all the belles here are sighing."

87. Mr. Phillip Metcalf, a friend of Dr. Johnson.

88. Mr. Richard Owen Cambridge (1717–1802), and his son, the Reverend George Owen Cambridge (1756–1841). Fanny fell in love with the son, who paid considerable attention to her, but never actually proposed. Fanny's strong feelings for him persisted well after she entered service at court in 1786. Later in life, he became a good friend to her. Fanny deleted most of her personal references to him from her diary.

89. Susan Burney's husband.

90. Mrs. Mary Delany (1700–1788), wife of Mr. Alexander Pendarves (d. 1724) and then of Jonathan Swift's friend, Dr. Patrick Delany (d. 1768). She was the intimate friend of the Duchess of Portland, was on close terms with Queen Charlotte, and was noted for her kindness and "angelic" quality.

91. Mrs. Hester Chapone (1727–1801), a friend of the novelist Richardson, one of the Bluestockings, and author of *Letters on the Improvement of the Mind* (1773). Mrs. Chapone was a vocal admirer of *Evelina*.

92. Charlotte Walsingham (d. 1790), a woman of high birth, talent, and wit who Fanny said had "the character of being civil to people of birth, fame, or wealth, and extremely insolent to all others." When Fanny had been introduced to Mrs. Walsingham the previous month, Fanny had retreated from her effusive welcome.

93. Margaret Cavendish Holles Harley (1714–1785), the only child of the second Earl of Oxford, and the widow of the Duke of Portland. She was sixty-eight at this time. Although she was prejudiced against women novelists, the Duchess read and approved of *Cecilia* and, in fact, enthusiastically recommended it to her friends.

94. Samuel "Daddy" Crisp's sister.

95. This remarkable collection is now at Harvard University.

96. Mrs. Sarah Siddons (1755–1831), perhaps the best comic and tragic actress of the eighteenth century. In 1794 she acted in *Edwy and Elgiva*, the only of Fanny's plays to have been produced.

97. Samuel Crisp had died in April 1783.

98. Mrs. (or Miss) Anna Williams (d. 1783), the mistress of Dr. Johnson's household after the death of his wife in 1752, and one of a number of destitute or semidestitute pensioners who lived with Johnson. At this time she was totally blind.

99. Elizabeth Vesey (c.1715–1791), one of the Bluestocking Circle and an intimate friend of Mrs. Montagu. Because of her absentminded and impulsive character, she was known among her friends as "The Sylph."

100. Horace Walpole (1717–1797), fourth Earl of Orford and wealthy son of the famous British Prime Minister, Sir Robert Walpole. He was an important collector of art and curiosities, an author, and his personal correspondence is one of the great records of upper-class eighteenth-century life. He was a waspish and somewhat reclusive person, and a friend of many of the Bluestockings, whom he often criticized.

101. The famous club founded by Johnson and Sir Joshua Reynolds in 1764. Its members included Boswell, Burke, Goldsmith, and Hawkins.

102. Possibly her brother Charles Burney.

103. Francesco Sastres (d. 1822), an Italian teacher and translator. Johnson bequeathed him £5 for "books of piety."

104. Mrs. Thrale is referring to the three years following her husband's death in 1781. They had been years of intense emotional conflict for her, principally because she had fallen in love with Gabriel Piozzi (1740–1809), her daughter's music master. Her stated intention of marrying Piozzi horrified both her daughter, Queeney, and Fanny. Finally, in the winter of 1783, after months of vacillation, she succumbed to the pressures and broke off with Piozzi to satisfy Queeny and quiet rumors then rampant in fashionable London circles. But from the despairing tone of this letter, it is obvious that she had not reconciled herself to this decision.

105. Frederica ("Fredy") Locke (1750–1832), Fanny's contemporary. This visit of Mrs. Locke's was the beginning of a lifelong friendship and, in a sense, Mrs. Locke replaced Mrs. Thrale as Fanny's patron and friend. Fanny's sister, Susan Phillips, had about this time settled in Mickleham near the Lockes' country house, Norbury Park.

106. Early in 1784 Mrs. Thrale decided to marry Piozzi and came to London from Bath in May to make the final arrangements. At this time Mrs. Thrale began to suspect that Fanny had encouraged Queeney in her opposition to her marriage, and this led to the rupture in their friendship that was never really healed. Mrs. Thrale married Piozzi on July 23, 1784. Her marriage—that of a rich widow to her daughter's music master—caused outrage and her virtual ostracism in London social circles.

107. Francis Barber, Dr. Johnson's black servant, who had been with him since 1752.

108. Reverend George Strahan (1744–1824), vicar of Islington. He was one of the witnesses to Johnson's will.

109. Richard Warren (1731–1797), one of Johnson's doctors.

110. Dr. Johnson died on December 13, 1784.
111. Mr. Bernard Dewes, one of Mrs. Delany's nephews; Miss Georgiana Port (1771–1850), Mrs. Delany's niece.
112. King George III (1738–1820) had succeeded his grandfather, George II, to the throne in 1761. He was the first of the Hanoverian Kings actually to have been born in England. He married Charlotte Sophia, younger sister of the Duke of Mecklenburg-Strelitz in 1761, after having been persuaded that it was his duty as King to renounce his love for the beautiful Lady Sarah Lennox. His popular image was that of a parsimonious, dull, and stubborn country squire. Despite the partial truth of this characterization, he was a loyal and, to a great extent, an effective monarch in a difficult transitional period for the English monarchy.
113. A collection of satirical poems by various authors published in 1785 on the death of William Whitehead, then poet laureate. One of the poems, satirically attributed to a Major Scott, has the lines "What?-What?-What? Scott!-Scott!-Scott!" to which Fanny is alluding.
114. Queen Charlotte Sophia (1744–1818), wife of King George III, whom she married after George's mother had searched the Protestant courts of Europe for a suitable wife for her son. She met her husband only one day before her wedding, the day she first arrived in England. As Queen she led a purely domestic life, the King rarely discussing affairs of state with her. She had fifteen children—nine sons and six daughters—and as a consequence she was almost constantly pregnant between 1761 and 1780.
115. Where the younger members of the Royal Family lived. The King, Queen, and two eldest Princesses lived in the Upper (or Queen's) Lodge. The lodges had been built as temporary residences while Windsor Castle was being repaired. They were notoriously cold and drafty in the winter.
116. The Lower Lodge.

COURT [1786-1791]

1. The position offered to Fanny was that of Second Keeper of the Robes, an office previously held by Mrs. Haggerdorn, a Hanoverian, who retired from the position for reasons of health. Despite the menial nature of this office, essentially that of

a maid, it was much sought after by persons of fashion and rank. Fanny's father and his friends saw the position, as Dobson put it, as "affording a certain prospect of an honorable and advantageous establishment for life."

2. Leonard Smelt (1717–1800), Deputy-Governor to the Royal Princess.

3. Charlotte Cambridge, George Cambridge's sister.

4. That is, to her sister Susan, to the Lockes, to her family visiting Chessington, to the Cambridges, and to her sister Charlotte. In February 1786, Charlotte married Clement Francis, a surgeon, who practiced in Aylsham in Norfolk. Francis had been secretary to Warren Hastings in India.

5. Miss Port, Mrs. Delany's niece. She later married Benjamin Waddington, who was twenty-three years older than she.

6. Possibly her literary ambitions.

7. Elizabeth Juliana Schwellenberg (c.1728–1797), First Keeper of the Robes to Queen Charlotte and Fanny's immediate superior at court. She was a blustering, peevish, insensitive woman who, as the diary plainly shows, made Fanny's life miserable.

8. Fanny's apartment at Windsor was in the Queen's (or Upper) Lodge.

9. The *Dialogues* was an Italian phrasebook published in 1775 by Joseph Baretti (1719–1789), Queeney Thrale's Italian teacher from 1773 to 1776. *The Tablet of Memory* was a popular chronology of memorable events. It had been given to Fanny by Mrs. Locke.

10. While at Windsor the King and Queen usually strolled on the terrace each evening, often giving informal audiences.

11. The Equerry in Waiting to the King.

12. Margaret Planta (1744–1827), governess to the Princesses and a good friend of Fanny's while at court.

13. Kew, the second of three principal residences of the King and Queen, was located in what was then the outskirts of London. It was small, cramped, and particularly uncomfortable in winter, having been built as a summer house. The third residence, St. James's Palace, was located in London and was used principally for ceremonial occasions.

14. Lady Elizabeth Waldegrave (1725–1823), Lady of the Bedchamber to Princess Charlotte (the Princess Royal). In 1791 she married James Brudenell, fifth earl of Cardigan.

15. The entire Royal Family was an impressive crowd. The nine sons were George, Prince of Wales and later George IV (1762–1830); Frederick, Duke of York (1763–1827); William, Duke of

Clarence and later William IV (1765–1837); Edward, Duke of Kent (1767–1820); Ernest, Duke of Cumberland and later King of Hanover (1771–1851); Augustus, Duke of Sussex (1773–1843); Adolphus, Duke of Cambridge (1774–1850); and two sons, Octavius and Alfred, who died in infancy. The six daughters were Charlotte, the Princess Royal and later Queen of Würtemberg (1766–1828); Augusta (1768–1840); Elizabeth, later Princess of Hesse-Homburg (1770–1840); Mary, Duchess of Gloucester (1776–1857); Sophia (1777–1848); and youngest and darling of the King, Amelia (1783–1810).

16. That is, when you are Mistress of the Robes.

17. The King had been crowned on September 22, 1761.

18. Jean André de Luc (1727–1817), a Swiss geologist and meteorologist, and a reader to Queen Charlotte since 1774. Fanny had met him and his wife sometime before she went to court.

19. Mr. Turbulent, Fanny's pseudonym for the Reverend Charles de Guiffardiere (1740–1810), the Queen's French Reader and a minister of the French Chapel in St. James's Palace. He was married and was a great favorite of Queen Charlotte.

20. Stephanie, Countess de Genlis (1746–1830), a prolific French writer of novels, plays and letters. In 1785 she visited Fanny in England. Fanny was captivated with her, but the friendship lapsed. When Madame de Genlis sought to renew the friendship in 1786, Fanny was reluctant because of Madame de Genlis's not unspotted reputation even though Fanny did not believe the rumors. Much later in France, Fanny continued to avoid Madame de Genlis, although a part of her regretted it and she often defended her.

21. Thomas James Mathias (c.1754–1835), editor, author, and Treasurer's Clerk to the Queen.

22. The official register of servants of the Royal Household.

23. On January 11, Fanny was taken ill with what she calls a "bilious fever, long lurking."

24. Lady Rothes was the wife of Sir Lucas Pepys, the physician.

25. Fanny's servant.

26. Lady Bute (1718–1794), the only daughter of Lady Mary Wortley Montagu, who had introduced the smallpox vaccination into Europe, after having observed the practice in Turkey when her husband was the British ambassador there. She is not to be confused with her cousin by marriage, Elizabeth Montagu, the Bluestocking. Lady Louisa Stuart (1757–1851) was Lady Bute's youngest daughter.

27. One of Fanny's nicknames for Mrs. Schwellenberg.

28. This was an advance copy of Mrs. Thrale's book *Letters to and from the Late Samuel Johnson LL.D.*, which was published on March 8, 1788. This was the second of Mrs. Thrale's published works; the first was *Anecdotes of the Late Samuel Johnson LL.D.*, published in 1786.

29. The trial was the impeachment inquiry in the House of Commons of Warren Hastings (1732–1818), Governor General of Bengal from 1773 until 1785. Hastings had returned to England to face charges that he had committed "high crimes and misdemeanors" in his administration there. The prosecution of Hastings was led by Edmund Burke and other prominent Whigs who, after several years of hearings, obtained a bill of impeachment in 1788. Hastings was then tried on the charges before the House of Lords and was finally acquitted in 1795. The King and Queen were generally sympathetic with Hastings, possibly in part because his detractors were Whigs.

30. Mrs. Delany died on April 15, 1788, at her home in St. James's Place.

31. Mr. Fairly was Fanny's pseudonym for Colonel Stephen Digby (1742–1800), Vice Chamberlain to the Queen since 1783. His first wife had died in 1787, and he was still grieving for her.

32. Cheltenham in Gloucester, ninety miles west of London, known for its mineral springs.

33. Mr. Fairly's.

34. Mrs. Thrale's name on her second marriage.

35. From Canto I of William Falconer's poem, *The Shipwreck* (1762).

36. *Original Love Letters between a Lady of Quality and A person of Inferior Condition*, by William Combe, a parodist of the Pre-Romantics, better known for his *Three Tours of Dr. Syntax* (1812–1821).

37. Colonel Francis Edward Gwynn (d. 1821), an Equerry to the King.

38. Miss Fuzilier was Fanny's pseudonym for Miss Charlotte Grunning (1759–1794), Maid of Honor to the Queen since 1780.

39. Jacob Columb, Fanny's manservant during most of her tenure at Court. He had replaced Groter.

40. An extremely popular poem by Mark Akenside (1721–1770), first published in 1744.

41. Used in the disparaging sense of "intellectuals."

42. Mr. Fairly had decided to leave the excursion before its conclusion, to be with his children on the anniversary of his wife's death.

43. He is alluding to Fanny and Mr. Fairly.

44. The Royal Family was then at Kew. The King's illness referred to is one of the first signs of his later insanity. The traditional diagnosis is that the King was suffering from a manic-depressive psychosis. Recent research has shown that the King was probably not insane at all, but was suffering from a rare hereditary metabolic disease known as porphyria, which attacks the nervous system and disorders the brain with toxins.

45. *Edwy and Elgiva* was the first of a number of tragedies Fanny wrote while at Court, none of which was published. It was produced at Covent Garden in March 1795 and closed after one night.

46. Sir George Baker (1722–1809), appointed Physician to the King in 1776.

47. What actually happened is not clear. The Prince of Wales's version was that the King had a fit at dinner and seizing him by the collar, thrust him violently against the wall. Another version was that the Prince, never remarkable for nerve, almost fainted when the King had the attack.

48. Mrs. Sandys, the Queen's wardrobe woman.

49. Dr. William Heberden (1710–1801), the first of a number of physicians called in to consult on the King's illness. The other person referred to, Sir George Baker, was another of the physicians.

50. The King's prolonged incapacity forced the House of Commons to consider a Regency under the Prince of Wales and led to a rather bitter political struggle between the Prince and the Whigs on one hand, and Queen Charlotte and Prime Minister Pitt on the other. At issue were the custody of the King's person and the breadth of the powers that would be granted the Regent. Overtones of this struggle, of which Fanny must have been aware, remain in the diary. The issues became moot upon the King's recovery.

51. Henry William Majendie (1754–1830), a clergyman and in 1788 serving as a canon at Windsor; General William Harcourt (1743–1830), an aide-de-camp to the King, had fought for the British in America during the War of Independence.

52. The Queen's Lodge at Kew.

53. The official physician's report for November 30 deceptively states, ". . . His Majesty arrived at this place [Kew] from Windsor and bore the journey extremely well." Obviously official reports have not increased in reliability over the past 200 years.

54. Mr. Charles Hawkins, described by Fanny as "the household surgeon."

55. Dr. Francis Willis (1718–1807), a clergyman and physician. He had experience in the treatment of the insane and had a private asylum in Lincolnshire. Dr. Willis had been sent for about the beginning of December. He proved to be the most influential of the physicians called in to help. These included Dr. Richard Warren, Dr. Johnson's physician; Sir Lucas Pepys, an old friend of the Burneys; Dr. H. R. Reynolds; and Dr. Thomas Gisburne. One of Dr. Willis's sons, Dr. John Willis, assisted him in treating the King.

56. *Ode to Wisdom,* by Mrs. Elizabeth Carter (1717–1806), which had been used by Richardson in his novel, *Clarissa* (1747–1748). Mrs. Carter was a close friend of Mrs. Montagu, was extolled as a Greek scholar by Dr. Johnson, and was a musician and occasional writer (contributing to Johnson's *Rambler*). She and Fanny had become friends at Bath in 1780.

57. Dr. Johnson had begun to teach Fanny Latin in May 1779. In 1780 Fanny talked of renewing her Latin exercises with Dr. Johnson. She was clearly ambivalent for, as she put it, "I have more fear of the malignity which will follow it [my knowing Latin] being known than delight in what advantages it may afford."

58. Cerbera, after Cerberus, the mythical vicious dog that guarded the gates of hell, was another of Fanny's nicknames for Mrs. Schwellenberg.

59. The Queen.

60. Lady Charlotte Finch (d. 1813), governess to the children of the King and Queen.

61. *The General History of Music* was Dr. Burney's magnum opus. Fanny had worked as a copyist for her father in preparing the first two volumes, published in 1775 and 1782, respectively. The third and fourth volumes were published in 1789.

62. George Frederick Handel (1685–1759), the great eighteenth-century composer and favorite of King George II, who loved his music and was his patron. As a young man, Dr. Burney had played in Handel's orchestra.

63. Frances Boscawen (1719–1805), the widow of Edward Boscawen. Another of the Bluestocking Circle, she was noted for her politeness and singled out by Mrs. Thrale for her conversational powers.

64. Frederick Montagu (1733–1800), Member of Parliament and former Lord of the Treasury.

65. In May 1786, just before Fanny went to Court, Dr. Burney had applied to the King for the then vacant position of Master of the King's Band. The post was instead given to William Parsons. These sinecures were almost invariably political rewards or for

the benefit of family members, and were rarely awarded on the basis of merit.

66. In January, Parliament had formed a committee to examine the King's doctors to determine whether he would recover or whether it was necessary to declare a Regency. The King's recovery staved off the Regency Bill, hence Fanny's jubilation.

67. Dr. Joseph Warton D.D. (1722–1800), headmaster of the Winchester School and author of *Essay on the Genius and Writings of Pope*. Both he and his brother Thomas (1728–1790), the literary historian, were longtime friends of the Burneys. Fanny's half-brother Richard Burney (1768–1808) had attended the Winchester School.

68. King George's third son, Prince William Henry.

69. Mrs. Piozzi's (Thrale) childhood home.

70. Fanny is referring to the French Revolution. The Bastille had been stormed on July 14, 1789.

71. That is, the Princesses would not have publicly acknowledged Miss Gunning's (Fuzilier) engagement unless it was true. Fairly married her in 1790.

72. The Handel Commemoration had taken place in 1784–1785 to commemorate the one hundredth anniversary of Handel's birth. Probably what is referred to here is a benefit concert by the Royal Society of Musicians, an outgrowth of the Handel Commemoration.

73. Dr. Burney's apartment at Chelsea Hospital, to which he moved in 1787.

74. Apparently numerous strangers had attempted to gain introductions to Fanny through her father in hopes that they might obtain government jobs, pensions, and other preferments from the Royal Family. Madame de Boufflers, accustomed probably to the far different French customs, was amazed that someone in Fanny's position had no such preferments under her control.

75. The first tragedy was *Edwy and Elgiva*, the second probably called *Cerulia*. In all, Fanny wrote four tragedies while at Court.

76. Mlle. Montmollin, French teacher to the Princesses.

77. A draft of her letter of resignation from Court.

78. The war referred to was that with France.

79. Thomas Gisburne (d. 1806), Physician in Ordinary to the King and one of the physicians who attended him during his illness.

80. The Queen was proposing to give Fanny an allowance of £100 per year.

81. Mlle. Jacobi was Fanny's successor as Second Keeper of the Robes. She remained in the post until 1797, when she retired and returned to her home in Hanover.

MARRIAGE [1791-1840]

1. By 1785 all of Dr. Burney's six children of his first marriage, with the exception of Fanny and Charlotte, had married and had left home. Charlotte's marriage in February 1786 left a big void for Fanny who, until she went into court, lived alone with her father and stepmother.
2. Lord Macartney (1737–1806), the British ambassador to China from 1792 to 1794.
3. Fanny, a staunch supporter of the Crown, had been upset with Burke's Whig political views and his role in the impeachment of Warren Hastings. Burke, however, partially reversed himself after the French Revolution, and this restored him to Fanny's good graces.
4. As a result of the political events in France in 1792, England became flooded with noble, but penniless, French emigrants who had fled the Jacobin reign of terror there. In November 1792, a decree of the Girondists confiscated the property of all who had left France in July and had not returned.
5. Her sister Susan's son.
6. The Comte de Narbonne (1755–1813), Minister of War to Louis XVI from December 1791 to March 1792. He fled France in August 1792. He was a close friend of Mr. d'Arblay and became godfather to Fanny's son and only child.
7. The Duc de Montmorency (1766–1826).
8. The execution of King Louis XVI in Paris on January 21, 1793.
9. Alexandre d'Arblay (1754–1818), who married Fanny in 1793, had fled from France to England in 1792, and settled with other emigrant friends at Juniper Hall. He met Fanny for the first time at Mrs. Locke's house, Norbury Park, a few days before this letter was written.
10. A French "man of letters" whom Fanny had met in July 1787.
11. Fanny had spent all her time with Mrs. Locke at Norbury Hall, and had not visited her sister Susan, who lived at Mickleham. Mickleham, Norbury Park, and Juniper Hall were all within a few miles of each other.
12. Susan Burney's husband, Molesworth Phillips, had property in Ireland.
13. This letter is placed correctly according to the events it describes, but was evidently misdated by Fanny.

14. Madame de Staël (1766–1817), one of the most fascinating, brilliant, and politically and personally controversial women of her period. Her father was an important figure at the court of Louis XIV, and her husband, whom she married in 1786, was the Swedish ambassador to France. She published her first work (on Rousseau) at the age of twenty-two.

15. Louis XVI.

16. Fanny was wrong. Madame de Staël had a long liaison with Narbonne as well as, at a later date, with Benjamin Constant, the painter, and John Rocca.

17. Charles Maurice de Talleyrand (1754–1838), former bishop of Autun, the great architect of French foreign policy from 1814 to 1835.

18. These and following explanatory interjections first appeared in the 1904–5 edition of the *Diary and Letters.* They were evidently added by either Charlotte Barrett, Fanny's niece, who edited the material, or by Austin Dobson, who added the Preface and notes.

19. Mr. d'Arblay had visited Fanny at Chessington, where she had gone to decide whether to accept his proposal.

20. A second ceremony in the Roman Catholic Church was performed so that Fanny might have rights under French law should Mr. d'Arblay ever recover any of his property lost in the Revolution.

21. Mrs. Waddington, formerly Miss Port, Mrs. Delany's niece.

22. It was called Phenice Farm.

23. Alexander was born on December 18, 1794.

24. The awful state of public affairs that Fanny refers to were caused by the war with France. Not only did England suffer military and naval reverses in 1794, but the cost of prosecuting the war caused severe dislocations in England's domestic economy.

25. John Merlin (1735–1803), a French piano maker and tuner who had been fashionable in London fifteen years earlier.

26. Abdolomine, an ancient gardener king of Sidon. This was Fanny's nickname for her husband.

27. Fanny was at this time writing her third novel, *Camilla: or, a Picture of Youth,* published in 1796.

28. *Edwy and Elgiva,* which was staged on March 21, 1795, and ran for one night only.

29. Her third novel, *Camilla.*

30. In order to maximize her profit and obtain much-needed money, Fanny, at the urging of her family, decided to publish *Camilla* by subscription. Fanny's friends rallied to her support

and made the subscription very successful. One of the subscribers was the then unknown Jane Austen.

31. Fanny's sister Susan had left for Ireland to live there with her husband, Molesworth Phillips, and their two children.

32. While many of the reviews commended the moral lesson of *Camilla*, there was some serious adverse criticism of Fanny's writing style.

33. In fact the 4,000 copies of the first edition were completely sold, and Fanny received about £2,000 for her efforts.

34. The correct figure is 500.

35. In the fall of 1796 the d'Arblays began building their own house on a plot in Norbury Park which Mr. Locke had leased to them. The profits of *Camilla* were used to pay for its construction; hence its name, Camilla Cottage.

36. Dr. Burney's second wife, Elizabeth Allen, died on October 20, 1796.

37. The husband of Fanny's half sister, Maria Allen.

38. To their new home, Camilla Cottage.

39. The crib of his cousin, John William Phillips.

40. Susan had been seriously ill for some time, but her husband had hidden the seriousness of her illness from the Burneys. When it became apparent to Dr. Burney that she might not live through the winter, he arranged to have her return to London.

41. Her brother Charles was to meet Susan at the port town of Chester and accompany her to London.

42. Susan died on January 6, 1800, before she reached London. Only her brother Charles was with her.

43. Fanny had just returned from Greenwich where she was staying with her brother, Charles. She was extremely distraught at Susan's death and did not recover from her grief for many months. She marked the anniversary of Susan's death for the rest of her life. Curiously enough, Fanny herself died on the same day and month as Susan.

44. Harris had offered Fanny £400 for the play.

45. The preliminary articles of peace (the Peace of Amiens) between Britain and France were signed on October 1, 1801.

46. The purpose of his journey was to obtain his military half-pay (pension) as a recognition of his past service. He failed to obtain it.

47. December 6.

48. Mr. d'Arblay had suggested in his letter of December 6 to Fanny that he attempt to obtain the post of French Commercial Consul in London, or in one of the English ports. This would have meant their leaving Camilla Cottage.

49. General Leclerc (1772–1802), Captain-General of the French Colony of Santo Domingo (Haiti). Toussaint l'Ouverture (1743–1803), a revolutionary leader in Santo Domingo, and the first black revolutionary of modern times.

50. Adrienne de Chavagnac, whose father had asked Fanny to take her back to France.

51. Napoleon Bonaparte. It was not until later that he assumed the title of Emperor.

52. Pierre Augustin, Comte Hulin (1758–1841). He had participated in the siege of the Bastille in 1789.

53. Princess d'Henin (1750–1824), an émigré friend of the residents of Juniper Hall. She was one of the few émigrés who had gotten money out of France and consequently could afford her own house.

54. Joigny, located about seventy-five miles southeast of Paris, was Mr. d'Arblay's birthplace.

55. Despite the Treaty of Amiens, war between England and France broke out again in 1803.

56. Pension.

57. The pension of £100 per year from the Queen. This had been cut off because there was no mail or visitors between the two countries.

58. A position as a clerk in the Ministry of the Interior.

59. Joachim Breton (1760–1819), Secretary of the Liberal Arts section of the National Institute of France.

60. Probably Fanny's niece Maria Bourdois, the daughter of her sister Esther.

61. Mrs. Locke, whose first names were Augusta Frederica. Usually Fanny called her "Fredy."

62. England had been continually at war with France since 1803, and virtually all private communication between the two countries was cut off.

63. Princess Amelia died on November 2, 1810. Her death was said to have been the cause of the King's relapse into insanity, from which he never recovered. A Regency was established in 1811.

64. Mr. Locke died on October 5, 1810, at age seventy-eight.

65. In September 1811, in Paris, Fanny had undergone a mastectomy as a result of a mestatic abscess in her breast that had become cancerous. The operation, which took about twenty minutes, was performed without an anesthetic, and Fanny was fully conscious throughout it.

66. Fanny began work on her fourth and last novel, *The Wanderer; or, Female Difficulties,* before 1800, but most of it was written in France. She hoped this novel would bring her money to

supplement their meager income and to cover the expenses of her son's education.

67. The English lieutenant in charge of the boarding party.
68. Fanny's sister, Charlotte, had married Ralph Broome (1742–1805) in 1798. Her first husband, Clement Francis, died in 1792.
69. Perhaps the Battle of Leipzig.
70. Through Fanny's efforts, Alexander obtained a university scholarship of £120 per year.
71. *The Wanderer*, published in 1814.
72. Fanny in the end received about £2,000, as only one edition of 3,600 copies was printed.
73. Dr. Burney died on April 12, 1814, at age eighty-seven.
74. The reviews were in some instances rightly harsh. The critic William Hazlitt said the novel represented "no decay of talent but a perversion of it."
75. Fanny had considerable difficulty with her son's education. He had a passion for mathematics and chess, to the exclusion of everything else.
76. Charlotte Broome.
77. Clement Francis, Jr., his cousin.
78. Captain James Burney, who by this time had retired from the navy.
79. Amelia Locke (1776–1848), daughter of William Locke, who married John Angerstein in October 1799.
80. In July 1815, while on military duty, Mr. d'Arblay's leg had been severely injured by a kick from a horse.
81. Sarah Holroyd (1739–1820), Lord Sheffield's sister. Mrs. Frances and Harriet Bowdler were the sisters of Thomas Bowdler, the expurgator of Shakespeare. Fanny had first met Frances Bowdler at Teignmouth in 1773.
82. Mrs. Piozzi's husband had died on March 26, 1809.
83. Alexander had lost his Cambridge scholarship late in 1816.
84. Mr. d'Arblay had contracted jaundice.
85. Dr. Alexander Hay, Mr. d'Arblay's physician.
86. Alexander had been disappointed by a young woman, possibly Mrs. Locke's granddaughter.
87. On July 1, 1817, Fanny and her son went to Ilfracombe on the Bristol Channel in Devon, both for a holiday and so that he could study free from the distractions of London.
88. "I don't know whether this will be my last word . . . but this will be my last thought—our reunion!"
89. In this period it was her brother James to whom she turned for comfort and advice.
90. Elizabeth Ramsay was the eldest daughter of Mr. Ramsay, a

shoemaker, whom Fanny met in Ilfracombe and from whom she rented rooms in July 1817. Fanny took to the Ramsays, and Elizabeth came to London as her companion.

91. A painting by Benjamin West.

92. By Mary Wollstonecraft Shelley (1779–1851), daughter of Mary Wollstonecraft, author of *A Vindication of the Rights of Woman* (1792), and wife of the poet Percy Bysshe Shelley. *Frankenstein* was published in 1817.

93. She had been sporadically engaged in editing her father's papers since 1797. Her *Memoirs of Dr. Burney* did not appear until 1832.

94. Her sister Susan.

95. Mrs. Piozzi died on May 2, 1821.

96. Mrs. Locke's house.

97. Mrs. Thrale's daughters.

98. Sir William Pepys, one of her few remaining friends, died on June 2, 1825.

99. George Canning (1770–1827), an important political and literary figure of the time, one of the contributors to the *Anti Jacobin*, an important satirical periodical at the turn of the century, and a contributor to various reviews.

100. Charlotte Barrett (1786–1870), Fanny's niece, the daughter of her younger sister, Charlotte Francis Broome. She became very close to Fanny in Fanny's later years, assisted her in editing the *Memoirs of Dr. Burney* (1832), and was appointed her literary executor and custodian of her voluminous papers. She edited the first edition of Fanny's *Diary and Letters*, published 1842–1846.

SELECTED BIBLIOGRAPHY

d'Arblay, Madame (Frances Burney). *Diary & Letters*. Edited by Charlotte Barrett. Preface and Notes by Austin Dobson. 6 vols. London: Macmillan and Co., Limited, 1904-5.

———. *Early Diary of Frances Burney*. Edited by Annie Raine Ellis. 2 vols. London: George Bell and Sons, 1907.

———. *Evelina*. London: J. M. Dent & Sons Ltd. (Everyman's Library), 1951.

Clifford, James L. *Hester Lynch Piozzi (Mrs. Thrale)*. London: Oxford University Press, 1968.

Dobson, Austin. *Fanny Burney*. London: Macmillan and Co., Limited (English Men of Letters Series), 1903.

Hemlow, Joyce. *The History of Fanny Burney*. London: Oxford University Press, 1958.

Krutch, Joseph Wood. *Samuel Johnson*. New York: Henry Holt and Company, Inc., 1944.

Macaulay, Thomas Babington. "Madame d'Arblay." In *Literary Essays Contributed to the Edinburgh Review*. London: Oxford University Press, 1923.

Scholes, Percy. *The Great Dr. Burney*. 2 vols. Westport, Conn.: Greenwood Press, 1971.

Sitwell, Edith. *Bath*. London: Faber & Faber, Ltd., 1948.

Tuberville, A. S. *English Men and Manners in the Eighteenth Century*. New York: Oxford University Press (Galaxy Book), 1957.

White, R. J. *The Age of George III*. Garden City, New York: Doubleday and Company, Inc. (Anchor Books), 1969.

Woolf, Virginia. "Dr. Burney's Evening Party." In *The Common Reader (Second Series)*. London: The Hogarth Press, 1965.

ABOUT THE EDITORS

Barbara G. Schrank's strong interest in women's issues, especially women's literature, led her to begin work on this collection of Fanny Burney's diaries and letters. Born in Warren, Pennsylvania, she received her Bachelor of Science degree in journalism from Boston University. She has been a newspaper reporter-photographer and, for the past fourteen years, a magazine editor in New York City.

David J. Supino was born in Paris, France, and came to the United States during World War II. He has a Bachelor of Arts degree in English literature from Yale University and a Bachelor of Laws degree from Harvard University. His interest in Fanny Burney and her writings goes back to his years at Yale. He currently is a partner in an international investment banking firm.